Communication in the Age of Suspicion

Also by David Barlow

THE MEDIA IN WALES: Voices of a Small Nation (*with P. Mitchell and T. O'Malley*)

Communication in the Age of Suspicion

Trust and the Media

Edited by

Vian Bakir and David M. Barlow
University of Glamorgan, UK

First published 2007 by
PALGRAVE MACMILLAN
Houndmills, Basingstoke, Hampshire RG21 6XS and
175 Fifth Avenue, New York, N.Y. 10010
Companies and representatives throughout the world

PALGRAVE MACMILLAN is the global academic imprint of the Palgrave
Macmillan division of St. Martin's Press, LLC and of Palgrave Macmillan Ltd.
Macmillan® is a registered trademark in the United States, United Kingdom
and other countries. Palgrave is a registered trademark in the European
Union and other countries.

ISBN-13: 978-0-230-00254-8   hardback
ISBN-10: 0-230-00254-4   hardback

This book is printed on paper suitable for recycling and made from fully
managed and sustained forest sources.

A catalogue record for this book is available from the British Library.

A catalog record for this book is available from the Library of Congress.

10   9   8   7   6   5   4   3   2   1
16   15   14   13   12   11   10   09   08   07

Printed and bound in Great Britain by
Antony Rowe Ltd, Chippenham and Eastbourne

Contents

List of Figures

List of Tables

Acknowledgements

The catalyst for this book was a conference organised by the Centre for Public Communication Research at Bournemouth University in February 2004. It was attended by theorists from a range of communications-related disciplines as well as communications practitioners, together covering the fields of politics, commerce, media, public relations and psychotherapy. Some while after the conference, and with the agreement of the organisers, we began developing plans for this volume. The book's organisation and content evolved over a number of months in the course of discussions between the editors, contributors and the publisher. We would like to extend a heartfelt thanks to all those who have made this book possible, not least, the authors for their contributions as well as their patience and good humour in dealing with our requests for revisions.

Vian Bakir
David M. Barlow

Notes on the Contributors

Gillian Allard lectures in media, culture and communication at the Cardiff School of Creative and Cultural Industries, University of Glamorgan, UK. She has published in the fields of cultural enterprise and cultural policy and is editor of a forthcoming series of books on cinema adaptations for Palgrave Macmillan.

Jeff Archer is Head of the School of Social Science and Associate Professor of Political and International Studies at the University of New England in Armidale, NSW, Australia. He has published widely on Australian politics, comparative politics and political theory and is a frequent media commentator on Australian current affairs.

Vian Bakir lectures in risk communication, media history and research methods at the Cardiff School of Creative and Cultural Industries, University of Glamorgan, UK, where she also convenes two postgraduate courses. She has recently published in the areas of risk communication, policy agenda-setting, news management, dataveillance and ethics, and grounded theory and cultural strategy.

David M. Barlow lectures in media, culture and communication and directs the Centre for Media and Culture in Small Nations at the University of Glamorgan, UK. He is an honorary visiting research fellow in the School of Critical Enquiry at La Trobe University, Melbourne, Australia. He has published widely on community communication and is co-author of *The Media in Wales: Voices of a Small Nation*.

Jeremy Collins lectures in media studies at London Metropolitan University, UK. His research interests include risk communication, political communication, media ethics and news management, and he is course organiser for the postgraduate programme in Communications Management.

Chas Critcher is Professor of Communications at Sheffield Hallam University, UK. He is the author of *Moral Panics and the Media* (2003) and the editor of *Critical Readings in Moral Panics and the Media* (2006).

Susan J. Drucker is Professor in the School of Communication, Hofstra University, USA. She is an attorney and her work examines freedom of expression, media regulation and relationships between media technology and human factors, particularly from a legal perspective. Among her publications is *Real Law @ Virtual Space: The Regulation of Cyberspace*.

Gary Gumpert is Emeritus Professor of Communication at Queens College, City University of New York, USA. He is the co-founder of *Communication Landscapers* and President of *Urban Communication Foundation*. His research focuses on the nexus of communication technology and social relationships. His numerous publications include *Talking Tombstones and Other Tales of the Media Age*.

Janet Jones lectures in screen studies at the University of Wales, Aberystwyth, UK. Previously, she worked for the BBC, primarily as news and current affairs producer. She has recently published on the reception of contemporary global television, critical discourses surrounding television and the Internet, and journalists' role in mediating democracy. She is co-editing a book on *Peacock and Broadcasting Policy*.

Andrew McStay teaches advertising at the London College of Music and Media, Thames Valley University, UK. His research interests and publications include examinations of creativity and liquid modernity, future dynamics of advertising in the light of technological convergence, and dataveillance and ethics.

Amisha Mehta lectures in the School of Advertising, Marketing and Public Relations at Queensland University of Technology in Brisbane, Australia. Her research interests and publications are in trust, organisational legitimacy, public relations campaign trends and higher education assessment strategies. Amisha teaches public relations theory and corporate communication strategy.

Michael Redley is Secretary to the Board for Continuing Education at Oxford University, UK, where he also teaches modern history. He has a doctorate in African history and has researched and published on various aspects of colonial, literary and media history.

Barry Richards is Professor of Public Communication and Head of Research in Bournemouth Media School at Bournemouth University, UK and Director of the Centre for Public Communication Research there. His many publications include the forthcoming *Emotional Governance* and *The Dynamics of Advertising*.

Kaja Tampere is Senior Research Assistant in Public Relations and Organisational Communication at the University of Jyväskylä, Finland. She teaches public relations and organisational communication at the University of Tartu, Estonia. Her research interests include communication management in transition societies, governmental communications and media propaganda, and she has various publications on public relations.

Sherryl Wilson lectures in media theory at the University of Gloucestershire, UK. Her interests include contemporary American culture, reality television, television talk shows, gender and screen representations of older women. She is author of *Oprah, Celebrity and the Formation of Self* and has published on Trisha, commercialism and public service broadcasting.

Part I Communication in the Age of Suspicion

1
The Age of Suspicion

Vian Bakir and David M. Barlow

The generalised mood of modern times is that trust is on the wane and that this is problematic (Misztal, 1996; Duffy, Williams and Hall, 2004). A widespread consciousness has emerged that existing bases for social cooperation, solidarity and consensus have been eroded. When this erosion began is hard to pinpoint. Some suggest the 1980s, with its deregulation, privatisation and reliance on individualistic culture (Galbraith, 1992). Others (for instance, Michael Redley, this volume) suggest much earlier. What is certain is that from the 1950s onwards, polls and surveys proliferate showing the absence of trust in key institutions, while the news regularly proclaims a crisis of trust (in politicians' character and policies; experts' pronouncements; the competence and integrity of private and state institutions, and so on). This decline in trust matters because there are strong links between levels of trust and all sorts of positive social, political and economic outcomes. These matters are discussed further in Chapter 2.

There follows below a brief overview of where trust is present and absent in society's key institutions in countries that reflect the interests of this book – namely the United Kingdom (UK), the United States of America (USA), Australia and Central and Eastern Europe. We start by looking at generalised trust, and then progress to look at trust in institutions, particularly the media. This chapter concludes with an overview of the book's structure.

The decline in trust – An issue of societal concern

The picture we build up in this section is based on a range of poll data. As such, we attach a health warning that these figures are indicative rather than conclusive. Ironically, we cannot always trust people to say what they mean when asked potentially emotive questions like 'who do you trust to tell the truth?' Some say that they trust others because they feel it is a socially desirable response, and others say the opposite to avoid being seen as naïve in the face of fashionable cynicism (Duffy et al., 2004).

Generalised trust (trust in other people)

Polls show that the proportion of people that express generalised trust in others has continuously declined since the 1950s in the UK (Duffy et al., 2004) and the 1960s in the USA (Putnam, 2000), and is on the wane in Australia (Hughes, King and Bellamy, 2004). In the UK, the proportion of people who say others can be trusted declined from around 60 per cent in the 1950s, to around 30 per cent (Hall, 1999) to 44 per cent (British Social Attitudes survey, 2000, cited in Duffy et al., 2004) at the turn of the millennium. Similar levels of generalised trust have been polled in the USA (Rose-Ackerman, 2001; Lichtman, 2006; Scott, 2006)[1] and Australia (Hughes, Bellamy and Black, 2000; Hughes et al., 2004).

While most agree that generalised trust in the USA, the UK and Australia is low and declining, generalised trust in post-socialist countries is not particularly low (Rose-Ackerman, 2001). For example, in 1998, 51 per cent of those surveyed in Central and Eastern Europe by the New Democracies Barometer said that most people can be trusted; in 2000, 66 per cent of Russians agreed that most people can be trusted, up from 34 per cent in 1998 (Rose, 2000a; Uslaner, 2000). However, there is large variation among countries in Central and Eastern Europe. For instance, over two thirds of people in Bulgaria and Bosnia and Herzegovina said that corruption very significantly affects their personal and family life, while less than one quarter of the Russian Federation and Poland agreed (Transparency International, July 2003).

Trust in institutions

If generalised trust is low in the USA, the UK and Australia, trust in specific key institutions is even lower. Numerous surveys over the past decade in the USA and the UK suggest that industry officials, government officials and journalists rank lowest on the trust scale (Worcester, 1995; Taylor and Leitman, 2001; Duffy et al., 2004; Harris Poll, January 2005; MORI, March 2005; Scott, 2006). The most trusted institutions in the USA and the UK include: doctors (these persistently top the lists in the UK), the military (in 2004 and 2005 this was top of the list in the USA) (Saad, 2006), scientists, academics, clergymen and priests, judges, non-profit making voluntary organisations and television (TV) news readers (MORI, March 2000; MORI, March 2005). Recent polls show that the UK and the USA experience appears to be duplicated more widely in the European Union (EU) (Harris Poll, January 2005) and in Australia (Hughes et al., 2004).

Institutions scoring highly on trust tend to be those perceived to be independent, and existing mainly for the good of others rather than for the interests of the organisation itself (Petts, Horlick-Jones and Murdock, 2001; Hughes et al., 2004). Organisations scoring low on trust are those perceived as demonstrating lack of accountability or corporate irresponsibility (Duffy, 2003; Levine, 2003). In general, deference to authority has declined and people are less willing to unquestioningly accept government or expert advice due to a combination of the power of local knowledge, the rise in individualism and distrust in the wake of publicised past mistakes on public safety issues (Duffy, 2003). In terms of distrust of government in particular, people's concerns include campaign finance; corruption among political elites; conflicts of interest (Transparency International, July 2003); government misinformation (Levine, 2003); and pro-active government news management strategies (Government Communication Review Group Interim Report, 2003; Levine, 2003; Duffy et al., 2004). Government spin, in particular, has generated challenging and adversarial media responses, leading the public to expect the worst of politicians, even when evidence supports the government's position (Government Communication Review Group Interim Report, 2003).

While trust in many organisations that are independent of the state is high in the USA, the UK and Australia, in terms of the Central and East European experience of trust in civil institutions, survey findings range from scepticism (rather than positive trust or active distrust) (Mishler and Rose, 1995) to high distrust (Rose, 2000). As trust in government is low in the USA, the UK and Australia, so it is in many post-socialist countries (Rose-Ackerman, 2001; Transparency International, July 2003). Furthermore, even more so than in the USA, the UK and Australia, there appears to be widespread distrust in economic institutions. For example, over 70 per cent of Bulgarians, Croatians and people in Bosnia and Herzegovina saw corruption as very significantly affecting the business environment (Transparency International, July 2003). This scepticism and distrust is likely to be a hangover from the area's Communist past. The Soviet system was complex and full of organisations that were not transparent, predictable or controlled by the rule of law, and thereby were severely discredited among the population while institutions independent of the state were crippled or eliminated (R. Rose, 1998; Rothstein, 2004).

Below, we shall briefly elaborate on trust in the institution central to this book – the media.

Trust in media

There has clearly been some erosion of American public trust in the media since the mid-1970s (Carlson, 2002). For instance, whereas 55 per cent of Americans in 1985 agreed that most of the news they see is accurate and unbiased (Gillespie, 2003), as of May 2006, only 19–25 per cent said so (Scott, 2006). Like US citizens, UK citizens are much less likely than those in other parts of the world to think that the media report all sides of a story, with 64 per cent disagreeing that the media achieves this. Also 43 per cent disagree that the media report news accurately (BBC/Reuters/Media Center Poll, 2006). Similarly, in 2005, 67 per cent of Australians say the media are not objective enough and 58 per cent say that the media is too close to politicians (Morgan Poll, December 2005).

Of course, the media are not a homogenous group, and there are significant differences in trust levels according to medium and country. When asked how much they trust different news sources, Americans give the highest trust ratings to local newspapers (81 per cent say they have a lot or some trust), whereas UK citizens give the highest ratings to national TV (86 per cent say a lot or some trust) (BBC/Reuters/Media Center Poll, 2006). In 2006, the two media least trusted by Americans are international newspapers (52 per cent) and blogs (25 per cent) whereas in the UK the least trusted are news web-sites on the Internet (44 per cent) and blogs (24 per cent) (BBC/Reuters/Media Center Poll, 2006). Only 34 per cent of Australians distrust big international TV chains like the *British Broadcasting Corporation* (BBC), *Cable News Network* (CNN) and *Fox* while the majority do not trust newspaper journalists (63 per cent), talk-back radio hosts (57 per cent) and TV reporters (53 per cent) to tell the truth (Morgan Poll, December 2005).

Polls on trust in media in Central and Eastern Europe are much less prolific than in the USA, the UK and Australia. However, a recent poll indicates that 54 per cent of Russians say they trusted their media (BBC/Reuters/Media Center Poll, 2006). When asked how much they trust different news sources, like UK citizens, Russians give the highest ratings to national TV (84 per cent say a lot or some trust). While like the USA and the UK, Russia also has minimal trust in international newspapers (32 per cent), news web-sites (22 per cent) and blogs (16 per cent), it also has minimal trust in commercial radio (29 per cent).

While the news is perhaps the most scrutinised genre in terms of trust, more attention is being paid to the Internet as it assumes an increasingly significant role both as information broker and in e-commerce. In terms of trusting online information, an organisation's reputation is an important factor: people are more likely to trust web-sites of more established organisations like libraries and archives, than more commercial web-sites such as travel agencies and internet-only retail companies (MORI, 10 February 2005). In terms of e-commerce, consumers' lack of confidence in online security has hindered the expansion of Internet shopping (MORI, August, 2000; United Nations, 2001). Consumer concerns include releasing credit card details online and ignorance about legal rights and redress for consumers when things go wrong (MORI, August, 2000).

Thus, key institutions are distrusted, as are major segments of the media. What role have the media played in bringing about this pattern of distrust – this Age of Suspicion? To answer these questions, the rest of this book interrogates and explores the relationship between media and trust.

Overview of book's structure

This book is divided into four parts. Part I introduces the idea of Communication in the Age of Suspicion. Here, Chapter 1 has outlined the decline of generalised trust and trust in key institutions including the media. Chapter 2 explores the concept of trust more deeply, and outlines the dimensions of the field of Trust Studies to date, so allowing an appreciation of how Media Studies may contribute to this field.

Moving onto our contributory chapters, Part II explores the relationship between a range of media genres and forms and the erosion of trust, and Part III looks at the relationship between the media and the building of trust. That more chapters explore the erosion of trust than trust creation is testimony to the ease with which trust is destroyed and the difficulty of creating trust. We note, however, that these parts are somewhat artificial, and while chapters have been allocated to sections according to their main emphasis, the reader will also find reference to trust-building mechanisms in Part I and trust-destroying mechanisms in Part II. Throughout this book, a range of intersecting themes is explored, in particular, those of the public sphere, economic sphere and identity (concepts unpacked further in Chapter 2). We introduce the following chapters by these themes, rather than by their sequential appearance in this book.

In terms of public sphere issues, many chapters explore the implications for trust of the relationships between the media, the public, the government and civic and commercial institutions. In particular, government–media relationships are examined in four chapters. In Chapter 3, Michael Redley examines what can arguably be called the start of the Age of Suspicion in the modern era, with his focus on the aftermath for trust of state (the USA and the UK) appropriation of civil institutions (including publishing houses) during World War One. In Chapter 4, Jeff Archer explores the media management of Australia's Howard Government (in office for the decade since 1996), in a media environment of infotainment and dumbing-down. In Chapter 6, Barry Richards examines the press's role in generating confidence or doubt in governments (the UK and the USA) to mange the global risk of terrorism. Exploring a range of 'new' media forms in Chapter 16, Gary Gumpert and Susan Drucker explore the implications for the 'Social Contract' of the defining characteristics of new media that allow for manipulation, alteration and changes by artistic and editorial forces.

The relationship between the public, experts, pressure groups, interest groups and different types of news media is scrutinised in three chapters. In Chapter 8, Chas Critcher explores the role played by a key section of the British mid-market national press in undermining trust in those who would normally be regarded as expert authorities on the safety of the vaccine for measles, mumps and rubella. In Chapter 11, Vian Bakir examines the role of trust in TV news-oriented environmental risk communication from two trans-national organisations – environmental pressure group, Greenpeace and oil and gas corporation, Royal-Dutch Shell. In Chapter 13, Amisha Mehta examines the role of the Australian press as a guardian of trust in social systems, drawing on mass-mediated exchanges between the

Australian Federal Minister for Health and the Australian Medical Association President.

The commercialisation of the media and its implications for trust are explored across four chapters. In Chapter 5, David Barlow analyses how the commercialisation of independent local radio in a small nation – Wales, UK – raises issues of trust in the institutional establishment, operation and regulation of a radio sector that was ostensibly provided in the public interest. In Chapter 7, Jeremy Collins examines UK national press coverage of food scares to explore whether consumerist arguments within 'service journalism' provide a space in which a wider, politicised context could develop. Kaja Tampere, in Chapter 12, explores the role of public relations (PR) in forming trust in the transition society of Estonia, given the tensions generated by the liberalisation and marketisation of the Estonian media. In Chapter 15, Janet Jones explores the constraints of technical, commercial and social realities on the potential of new media technologies, such as the Internet and Interactive TV, to change the nature of production towards more equal relationships between users and producers.

Moving away from the public sphere focus and towards the economic sphere, several chapters explore trust and the media in purely commercial environments. Gillian Allard, in Chapter 9, explores the combined distrust in local producer networks and trust in the Internet experienced by an Internet pioneer who was using the Internet to give a platform to minority-interest music at the dawn of the dot.com boom. Following the dot.com crash of the late 1990s and early 2000s, Andrew McStay, in Chapter 10, theorises the negative impact on online user trust of the very security measures designed to build consumers' trust in e-commerce.

Media, identity and trust are explored in Chapter 14 by Sherryl Wilson who analyses how Oprah Winfrey maintains audience trust through building her reputation for ordinariness and authenticity despite fantastic celebrity status, through her talk show, *The Oprah Winfrey Show*.

Part IV, and Chapter 17, of this book conclude by drawing out key themes addressed by the contributory chapters and outlining ways forward. Implications for media communication in this Age of Suspicion are presented, as are future research directions.

Note

1. However, US data are not quite so clear cut, with other polls showing that around three quarters of Americans say that the people they work with and live near are trustworthy (Scott, 2006) and that they would generally trust people to tell the truth (Taylor, 1998).

2
Exploring Relationships between Trust Studies and Media Studies

Vian Bakir and David M. Barlow

As Chapter 1 demonstrated, trust is conspicuously absent in a wide range of political, economic and media institutions. As such, trust is an increasingly studied phenomenon. We have adopted the moniker of 'trust studies', and this chapter will outline the growth of this field, the relative absence of reference to media therein and areas where there has been a recent emergence of interest in trust and the media.

Trust studies – The growth of a field

Georg Simmel (1858–1918) can be seen as a founding father of sociological work on trust (although he did not, in fact, focus his work around this concept), providing a theoretical framework for analysing personal as well as generalised (or social) trust (Misztal, 1996; Möllering, 2001). However, by 1988, Niklas Luhmann (1988) observed that trust had never been a topic of mainstream sociology, with neither classical nor modern sociologists using the term as a theoretical context or conceptually clarifying it.[1] At the same time, Diego Gambetta observed that 'in the social sciences, the importance of trust is often acknowledged but seldom examined' (Gambetta, 1988a).

However, a general consensus has since emerged among contemporary social scientists that social trust is important (Earle and Cvetkovich, 1995; Delhey and Newton, 2003). Scholars like Niklas Luhmann (1988), Diego Gambetta (1988a, 1988b), Anthony Giddens (1990, 1991) and Barbara Misztal (1996) have attempted to refine our theoretical understanding of what trust is. Much current trust research revolves around the functional properties of trust (Luhmann, 1988; Coleman, 1990; Putnam, 1993, 2000; Fukuyama, 1995; Sztompka, 1999). The following two sections outline what trust is and what trust 'does' or 'enables'.

What is trust?

The literature dealing with trust is fragmented with competing definitions, for example, between economic, political, legal and other kinds of trust relations, or between philosophical and psychological perspectives (Seligman, 1997, pp. 17–26), containing sometimes unexamined conflations (Lewis and Weigert, 1985, p. 975). What is certain is that trust is a complex phenomenon, comprising many subtleties centred around a *relationship* between two entities, the trustor (the entity who trusts) and the trustee (the entity being trusted). The following aspects of trust are often described as being its core features: rationality, faith and confidence.

Rationality

The view of trust as rational has a long history, and is expressed in Enlightenment thinking, which suggests that we are trustworthy because we individually and collectively benefit from it (Misztal, 1996; O'Hara, 2004). For instance, Thomas Hobbes's *Leviathan* (1982 [1651]) grounds the political order in fear of others and mutual distrust that can only be overcome by imposition of a new and 'artificial' structure of trust (that is, the state) to ensure the legitimacy of the new regime. More recently, various theorists have focused on the role of rational choice in trust formation (for instance, Dasgupta, 1988; Good, 1988; Coleman, 1990). The language of rational probability is therefore often invoked in attempts to explain what trust is. For instance, Gambetta (1988b) characterises trust as follows:

> Trust (or, symmetrically, distrust) is a particular level of the subjective probability with which an agent assesses that another agent or group of agents will perform a particular action, both *before* he can monitor such action (or independently of his capacity ever to be able to monitor it) *and* in a context in which it affects *his own* actions. (Gambetta, 1988b, p. 217)

However, others argue that trust (or mistrust) exists when one cannot make an assessment of probabilities, when – in a situation of uncertainty – one decides to believe or not to believe in someone or something. People who know everything do not need trust (Misztal, 1996). This is where faith comes in.

Faith

Simmel (1990 [1900], p. 179) notes that trust needs to be 'as strong as, or stronger than, rational proof or personal observation' for social relationships to endure. Simmel argues that trust 'may rest upon particular reasons but is not explained by them' (1990 [1900], p. 179). He argues, for instance, that weak forms of inductive knowledge (like a farmer's belief that his crops will grow) are not proper trust, but that trust contains a 'further element of socio-psychological quasi-religious faith' (Simmel, 1990 [1900], p. 179). This element is 'hard to describe' and concerns 'a state of mind which has nothing to do with knowledge, which is both less and more than knowledge' (1990 [1900], p. 179). Much later, Giddens (1990, pp. 26–7) picked up Simmel's quasi-religious element in trust, noting that trust rests on vague and partial understanding, and differs from weak inductive knowledge in that it 'presumes a leap to commitment, a quality of "faith" which is irreducible' (Giddens, 1991, p. 19).

Möllering (2001) develops Simmel's and Giddens's ideas to form a 'Simmelian model of trust' (p. 407), labelling the mysterious element that Simmel likened to religious faith as 'suspension'. As Möllering (2001, p. 414) notes, we empirically glimpse suspension when people say things like 'everything will be fine' or 'just go ahead'. Thus, suspension can be defined as the mechanism that brackets out uncertainty and ignorance, making interpretative knowledge momentarily certain and enabling leaps to favourable (or unfavourable) expectations (Giddens, 1991).

Confidence

In common parlance, definitions of trust largely merge with the idea of confidence, (Misztal, 1996) – an idea taken forward by various theorists (for citations, see Earle and Cvetkovich, 1995, pp. 61–4). Others distinguish between the two concepts, although in different ways (Hart, 1988; Luhmann, 1988; Giddens, 1991; Tonkiss and Passey, 1999). For instance, Giddens (1991, p. 19) argues that although confidence (based on weak inductive knowledge) may be an element in trust, 'it is not sufficient in itself to define a trust relation'. According to Luhmann (1988), if you do not consider alternatives then you are in a situation of *confidence* and hope rather than trust:

> Trust is only involved when the trusting expectation makes a difference to a decision; otherwise what we have is a simple hope. ... Hence one who trusts takes cognizance of the possibility of excessive harm arising from the selectivity of others' actions and adopts a position towards that possibility. One who hopes simply has confidence despite uncertainty. Trust reflects contingency. Hope ignores contingency. (Luhmann, 1979, p. 24)

What does trust do?

Trust has been conceptualised as the basis for a range of social phenomena, including holding society together and enabling the construction and maintenance of social order (Parsons, 1951; Durkheim, 1964; Simmel, 1990 [1900]); generating social capital necessary for economic and political cooperation (Gambetta, 1988b; Coleman, 1990; Fukuyama, 1995; Putnam, 1995); allowing the operation of social complexity (Luhmann, 1979); acting as a solution to risk (Luhmann, 1988; Giddens, 1990, 1991; Beck, Giddens and Lash, 1994) and nurturing the formulation of self-identity (Giddens, 1990, 1991, 1992). This section will elaborate these functions further.

Acts as social glue

Simmel makes the strongest possible claim for the significance of trust for both society and individuals, suggesting that 'without the general trust that people have in each other, society itself would disintegrate' (1990 [1900], p. 178) and calling it 'one of the most important synthetic forces within society' (1950 [1908], p. 318). For the individual agent, trust acts as 'a hypothesis certain enough to serve as a basis for practical conduct' (Simmel, 1950 [1908], p. 318). Parsons (1951) argues that trust facilitates social integration by helping people accept that they are all working towards a common goal. Durkheim (1964) argues that trust develops from shared commitment to consensual norms of moral behaviour: people trust each other because they come from the same moral community. Hence social solidarity can get off the ground (Misztal, 1996). In general, trust in its cultural context is credited with being the social 'glue' for sustaining bonds between members of cultural groups (Durkheim, 1964; Triandis, 1995).

Generates social capital, so lubricating economic and political cooperation

Social capital refers to the networks of community relationships that facilitate trust and motivate purposeful action (Coleman, 1990) and is characterised by levels of trust, civic engagement and norms of reciprocity (Putnam, 1993). According to Putnam, 'The theory of social capital presumes that, generally speaking, the more we connect with other people, the more we trust them, and vice versa' (Putnam, 1995, p. 665).[2]

Francis Fukuyama (1995, p. 21) provides an exposition of trust as an indispensable ingredient of viable economic systems, as it generates 'social capital'. Drawing on Max Weber (2001 [1904]), Fukuyama contends that while contract and self-interest are important sources of group association, the most effective organisations are based on communities of shared ethical values. 'These communities do not require extensive contract and legal regulation of their relations because prior moral consensus gives members of the group a basis for mutual trust' (Fukuyama, 1995, p. 21). Thus, trust acts as a supplement to, or substitute for, contractual and bureaucratic bonds, and as such, lubricates cooperation (Gambetta, 1988b).

Besides being a central feature of economic life, trust is integral to the functioning of the political system (Putnam, 1993, 2000; Norris, 1999; Sztompka, 1999). Trust, both institutional and interpersonal, is widely hypothesised by cultural theories of democracy as necessary to make new democracies work and to maintain old democracies (Mishler and Rose, 2005). On the macro level, trust is equated with diffuse support and linked to the stability and effective functioning of democratic institutions (Sztompka, 1999; Mishler and Rose, 2005). On the micro level, trust is hypothesised as a primary influence on citizen involvement in political life and a key component of the social capital that contributes to a civil society (Mishler and Rose, 2005).

Thus, as with the economics literature, the concept of social capital and its associated links with trust is important. Putnam (1993, 1995) suggests that we rely on a network of associations to help us develop the social capital that smoothes coordination and cooperation in our society. These various associations build trust and facilitate a 'civil society' – that is, 'the synthesis between collective solidarity and individualism' (Seligman, 1992, p. 169). Putnam (1993, 2000) claims that when social capital is high, citizens express confidence and trust not only in each other but also in public institutions, which in turn encourages citizens to work to improve the state's democratic accountability.[3]

Putnam (1995) warns that as we now 'bowl alone' where once we gathered with others, we are seeing a reduction in our stock of social capital, thereby hindering society's ability to effect social and economic transactions. Similarly, Fukuyama (1999) talks of 'the miniaturisation of community' within the USA, where social networks are more narrowly defined ideologically, religiously and programmatically, destroying generalised trust between people.

Manages social complexity

In 1979, Luhmann related trust to the intensifying complexity, uncertainty and risk characterising contemporary society, trust being the means by which modern society manages complexity.[4]

> Where there is trust there are increased possibilities for experience and action, there is an increase in the complexity of the social system and also in the number of possibilities which can be reconciled with its structure, because trust constitutes a more effective form of complexity reduction. (Luhmann, 1979, p. 8)

With Luhmann's (1979) conceptualisation, for the first time there is a suggestion that trust is not an obsolete resource typical of traditional society, but rather is an indispensable phenomenon of modernity (Sztompka, 1999). Luhmann (1988) points out that social evolution towards increasing complexity and specialisation may increase the benefits of trust in public agents. Trust can facilitate arm's-length activities organised over space and time or indeed an activity in which monitoring is costly.[5]

Following Luhmann's argument of complexity reduction in modern societies, Shapiro (1987, p. 634) analyses the social control of impersonal trust (also known as fiduciary trust – that is, relationships that 'fail to meet the assumptions of personal or contractual control'), providing one of the 'few generalised discussions of trust in systems' (Giddens, 1991, p. 232). Trust in social organisations is invoked when a representative of the organisation (an agent) acts on behalf of others (principals) and where risk is involved (such as an investment of resources or responsibility in another in anticipation of future returns). For instance, in democracies, since elected representatives cannot be perfectly controlled by voters, the electorate must have some level of trust in those it elects. The reliance of principals on agents enables greater exploitation of complexity, as agents provide expert services that people cannot perform for themselves. However, this also produces conditions for abuse as principals cannot directly monitor activity. Shapiro argues that agency relationships are controlled and policed through the social organisation of mistrust – namely, through the establishment of 'guardians of trust', 'a supporting self-control framework of procedural norms, organisational forms, and social control specialists, which institutionalise distrust' (Shapiro, 1987, p. 635). Thus, Shapiro (1987) sees the social organisation of distrust as occupying a functional (rather than dysfunctional) role, integral to the promotion of trust.

Acts as a solution for risk

Following on from his argument that trust manages social complexity, Luhmann later confirmed that 'trust is a solution for specific problems of risk' (Luhmann, 1988, p. 95). Echoing Luhmann's theme that to show trust 'is to behave as though the future were certain' (1979, p. 10), Gambetta posits that trust is indispensable in 'conditions of ignorance or uncertainty with respect to unknown or unknowable actions of others' (1988b, p. 218).

In the first half of the 1990s, the intrinsic links between trust, uncertainty and risk were further elaborated (Giddens, 1990, 1991; Beck, Giddens and Lash, 1994; Earle and Cvetkovich, 1995). Giddens (1990) developed the concept of trust through his elaboration of 'abstract systems' as 'disembedding mechanisms'. In the modern era of globalisation, Giddens observes that social relations have been lifted out from local contexts of interaction and restructured across indefinite spans of time-space (Giddens, 1990, p. 21), in turn generating disembedding mechanisms (or abstract systems) such as 'expert systems'. Expert systems are 'systems of technical accomplishment or professional expertise that organise large areas of the material and social environments in which we live today' (Giddens, 1990, p. 27), such as global financial flows, computer networks, telecommunications, transportation and managerial, governmental or military machineries (Sztompka, 1999).

Giddens (1990, 1991) argues that all disembedding mechanisms (abstract systems) depend upon trust. This is largely because of the necessity of relinquishing local control arising from our dependence on these complex abstract systems, together with the risk that the disembedding mechanism as a whole could falter, affecting everyone who uses it. 'Increasing social and technical complexity elevates the probability that some key portions of the system cannot be safely counted on' (Clarke and Short, 1993, p. 384). As a result, Giddens (1990) suggests that representatives of the abstract systems must work to generate our trust, in what he calls 'facework commitments' – such as the composed cheerfulness of the air steward(ess) and the projected sincerity of the politician.

In Giddens's discussion, trust is inextricably linked to its corollary – risk. Indeed, risk has been increasingly explored over the past two decades, ever since Giddens's (1990) discussion of the *risk profile* of high modernity and the popularisation of Ulrich Beck's (1992) notion of the *risk society*.[6] Beck (1992) argues that in its reflexive phase, society becomes increasingly critical of the conditions of organised irresponsibility of the industrial period that have led to the proliferation of modern hazards (like radioactivity, pollutants and cloning). Society begins to lose trust in the supposed criteria of what is rational and safe, recognising that during its industrial phase, 'risks are industrially produced' (Beck, 1996, p. 183), economically externalised (as companies do not pay for their pollution) and scientifically legitimised. As a result, the issue of trust in the credibility of government, experts, lobbies and pressure groups is repeatedly raised. Giddens (1994b, p. 187) argues that 'wherever there is an awareness of the disputes that divide expert authorities, mechanisms of active trust proliferate' – active trust being trust that must be won and sustained. Active (rather than passive) trust in expert systems emerges when institutions become reflexive and experts' propositions are opened up for contestation from a critical lay public (Lash, 1994).

Correspondingly, a growing risk communication literature has identified the media and trust as key nodes of investigation, in particular, psychological and sociological risk communication theories (for an overview of each, see Earle and Cvetkovich, 1995; Frewer, 2003; Kasperson, Kasperson, Pidgeon and Slovic, 2003). For instance, Frewer (2003, pp. 125–6) notes that two major dimensions emerging from the social psychological literature as important in determining trust are that of communicators' 'competence' (that is, their ability to translate their expertise) and 'honesty' (their truthfulness). Petts, Horlick-Jones and Murdock (2001, p. 89) find a groundswell of demand for greater openness and popular participation in risk debates. They argue that this suggests that public distrust in authorities' risk communication may be generated by seeing audiences simply as 'targets' to be reached at the appropriate time rather than as citizens to be consulted and involved on a continuing basis.

A prerequisite for forming self-identity

Giddens (1991, p. 42) argues that 'basic trust', normally vested by the infant child in its caretakers, is key to the elaboration of self-identity and the development of the child's sense of 'ontological security' (Giddens, 1991, p. 66):

> 'Basic trust' is a screening-off device in relation to risks and dangers in the surrounding settings of action and interaction. It is the main emotional support of a defensive carapace or *protective cocoon* which all normal individuals carry around with them as the means whereby they are able to get on with the affairs of day-to-day life. (Giddens, 1991, p. 40)

Thus, basic trust provides an '*emotional innoculation* against existential anxieties' (Giddens, 1991, p. 39). Violations of basic trust can result in the loss of trust 'not only in other persons but in the coherence of the object-world' (Giddens, 1991, p. 66), with resonances affecting all close social relations formed in adult life.

In addition to basic trust, Giddens explores personal and interpersonal trust as a prerequisite for the formation of self-identity. Giddens (1990) argues that the rise of modernity's abstract systems has renewed the role of interpersonal trust – that is, trust based on the interaction of individuals. The routines that abstract systems structure have more to do with effectiveness than with emotional or moral satisfaction, as they increase impersonalised organised structures and reduce the size of personal life (Giddens, 1990, p. 120; 1991, p. 136). The trust engendered by abstract systems is therefore fragile, left without the external support or psychological satisfaction of kinship ties, local community, tradition or religious authority (Giddens, 1994a). Giddens (1990, p. 121) suggests that, correspondingly, personal trust becomes more valued as a project to be 'worked at' by the parties involved. This entails building up trust mechanisms in intimate situations through reflexive self-construction (Giddens, 1992) and 'demands *the opening out of the individual to the other*. Where it cannot be controlled by fixed normative codes, trust has to be won, and the means of doing this is demonstrable warmth and openness' (Giddens, 1990, p. 121). Here, Giddens enters into the arena of the 'pure relationship' – 'a social relation which can be terminated at will, and is only sustained in so far as it generates sufficient psychic returns for each individual' (1991, p. 187). The emergence of the pure relationship is tied to the rise of therapy, as self-mastery and self-knowledge are the condition of that opening-out process through which trust is generated: 'In so far as a relationship lacks external referents, it is morally mobilised only through "authenticity": the authentic person is one who knows herself and is able to reveal that knowledge' (Giddens, 1991, p. 186).

The emergence of trust studies in media studies?

Having outlined the field of trust studies from a range of academic disciplines, it is notable that the media have not featured prominently (apart from the field of risk). The following section changes the focus from examining literatures centred on trust towards literatures centred on media, to see if these areas have a more developed conceptualisation of the relationship between media and trust.

Within media studies, there is a developing literature that is suggestive of links between trust and the media. At the centre of such debates is the media's power and centrality to everyday life. While public communications systems are part of the cultural industries, and as such, have much in common with other industrial sectors, the informational and entertainment goods that they produce are particularly significant. They 'play a pivotal role in organising the images and discourses through which people make sense of the world' (Golding and Murdock, 2000, p. 70), reworking 'the experiential content of everyday life' (Stevenson, 2002, p. 1) and influencing how we construct our sense of self (Hesmondhalgh, 2002, p. 3). Thus, while the previous section outlined the centrality of trust to everyday life, from the macro level (such as holding society together) to the micro level (such as the formulation of self-identity), we contend that with the mediatisation of society, another layer of complexity in the functions of trust is created, and another level of trust is necessitated. For instance, not only are we asked to trust politicians and their promises, but we must trust that the media through which we learned of those promises presented a complete and accurate rendition, and that the sincerity with which the politicians project their promises has been adequately captured by the media. Not only are we asked to trust that a product that we wish to purchase is not faulty, but increasingly, for example, with e-commerce, we must trust the medium (the Internet) that allows us to look at, order and pay for the product. Thus, the need to understand how the media are imbricated in contemporary trust relationships is essential.

Two broad areas of literature that focus on the media have made inroads into exploring the media's relationship with trust, although as shall become apparent, with different degrees of directness. The first set of literature has a public sphere focus, and is firmly grounded within media studies. The second set of literature focuses on the economic sphere, and comes from the fields of advertising, marketing and new media.

Media, trust and the public sphere

The concept of the public sphere is a useful way of exploring the varied relationships that exist between the media, the state, the people and business (Boyd-Barrett, 1995, p. 235). Inevitably, as in the case of all relationships, this involves the issue of trust. The idea, or ideal, of the public sphere has been developed by Jurgen Habermas (1989), and while his account has been variously criticised, detractors and advocates alike agree that its ideals retain relevance in any study of contemporary communications and culture, particularly regarding the principles it invokes as a model, vision or yardstick of the media's role in democratic societies (see, for example, Golding and Murdock, 2000, p. 77; Stevenson, 2002, p. 48).

Habermas (1974, 1989, 1992) traced the evolution of what he called the 'bourgeois public sphere' in Britain, France and Germany from its origins in the 17th century, to its peak in the 18th century, and through to its subsequent decline in the late 19th and early 20th centuries. It was through the creation of this public sphere that the 'middling classes wrested power from absolute rulers and the feudal aristocracy' (McGuigan, 1996, p. 25). The early public sphere's core physical and cultural institutions were the coffee houses, newspapers and literary journals of 18th-century London; the *salons* in France and *Tischgesellschaften* (table societies) in Germany (Poole, 1989, p. 48; Calhoun, 1992, p. 12). While these institutions differed in terms of their publics, size, style and topics of discussion, they demonstrated a central characteristic of the public sphere in that they were neither controlled by the state, nor were they part of the private world of the home or business (Habermas, 1989, p. 238). In these institutions, the normal inhibitions of social status, political influence and political power were set aside in order to prioritise the importance of argument over that of social hierarchy. Discussion centred on – and problematised – those areas of common concern that had previously been the preserve of the church and state authorities. With access open to all, the very act of private citizens joining together as a public body to discuss matters of general interest constituted a public sphere – 'a realm of our social life in which something approaching public opinion can be formed' (Habermas, 1964, p. 49). In this context, public opinion is to be distinguished from the views of isolated individuals – mere opinion – and can only emerge from those who have participated in rational-critical debate on a particular matter (Calhoun, 1992, p. 17). Thus, the public sphere acted as a 'mouthpiece for the public', enabling citizens to engage in critical discussion of the state (Stevenson, 2002, p. 49).

Poole (1989, p. 14) identifies civility as a principal virtue of the Habermasian public sphere, as participants had the right to engage in debate but were expected to listen and respond critically to the points being discussed, on the basis that this would eventually lead to agreement or a position approaching consensus. The rationale underpinning this approach to communication, or communicative action – which aims to bring about trust through mutual understanding and sharing knowledge – can be contrasted with that of its polar opposite, strategic action and instrumental rationality, where communication is goal-oriented and manipulative (Dahlgren, 2001, p. 40). The former corresponds to Habermas's 'ideal speech situation', which posits that in any communication the speaker is making four validity claims: that what is being said is comprehensible, true, appropriate and sincere (Garnham, 1986, p. 30). The utility of this idea becomes evident when examining certain forms of 'distorted' communication, such as political propaganda and advertising campaigns. Here, while attempting to deceive and manipulate in order to bring about acceptance or closure, the communicators make the same four validity claims, 'using the language of reason even as they abuse it' (Poole, 1989, p. 19). While undistorted, or unconstrained, communication may be unrealisable (Eagleton, 1991, p. 130), Habermas believes that it is essential to retain a belief in the theoretic possibility that people both have the will and capacity to communicate in this way (Dahlgren, 2001, p. 41).

In contemporary society, the media are the core institutions of the public sphere (Habermas, 1964, p. 49). As a result, citizens must rely on, and trust, the media to maintain an independent forum for public debate, thereby enabling the formation of public opinion to keep the state in check, and also to provide the necessary information to enable the achievement of full citizenship (Curran, 1991, p. 29). Thus, our increasingly media-saturated environment prompts two key debates, both of which involve the issue of trust. One centres on the role of the media in relation to the process and practice of citizenship, while the other focuses on the extent to which the media enable the public to 'talk back' to power, thus making the state accountable. Essentially, the key elements of citizenship are 'freedom of assembly and freedom to impart and receive information' (Garnham, 1992, p. 364). To enable the achievement of 'full citizenship' – which spans both consumer and citizen identities – communications systems are expected to make available information not only about people's rights and how they can be exercised, but also to provide the widest possible range of analysis and opinions so that citizens can make informed political choices on matters of personal and societal interest (Golding and Murdock, 2000, p. 77). On the second and related role of the media, that of 'talking back', it is only when citizens become empowered through the debates and deliberations enabled by a 'free' media that they can make the state accountable (Rose-Ackerman, 2001, p. 542).

However, as the poll data in Chapter 1 indicated, trust in much (although not all) of the media is in short supply, as is trust in politicians and government. Yet, while this suggests that the public sphere is not working, it does not deliver detailed reasons for these low trust levels. For an explanation, it is instructive to return to Habermas's rendition of the decline of the public sphere. This decline, from the mid-19th century onwards, is attributed to a number of factors, including the development of the popular press (Dahlgren, 1991, p. 4). For Habermas, the world of business invaded the public sphere: as the press became more commercialised it no longer provided the same kind of free access to the public for rational debate. The growth of the modern state, with its accompanying institutions of pressure groups, political parties and a centralised electronic media, began to order, regulate and control the flow of debate and public opinion, leading to what Habermas famously describes as a 'refeudalisation of the public sphere' (1964, p. 54). State and private control over the flow of information became a matter of the manipulation of public opinion, rather than the promotion of rational public debate to formulate public opinion. Capturing this process, Peters (1993, p. 543) refers to 'representative publicity' – which is similar to the context and pomp of the theatre where a scripted display takes place before a passive audience. Representative publicity, as practiced by the feudal lords of pre-modern Europe, involves display rather than critical discussion, spectacle rather than debate, 'appearance *before* the people' rather than *for* the people and is linked to individuals rather than principles (Peters, 1993, p. 545). This process of refeudalisation not only excludes or marginalises oppositional voices (media theorists use concepts such as primary definition [Hall, Critcher, Jefferson, Clarke and Roberts, 1978], framing [Hallahan, 1999] and the propaganda model [Herman, 2001; Herman and Chomsky, 1994] to capture this process), it ensures that the battles over political ideas are won not by rational debate but 'through the exercise of power, concealment and subterfuge' (Poole, 1989, p. 16).

While polls show public concern about bias, inaccuracies and distortion in the news media, all of which damage trust (Lichtman, 2006), the media's agenda-setting role (McCombs and Shaw, 1972) (that is, its ability to tell the public what to think about, if not what to think), its ability to define and elaborate issues for the public and the perception that the media embody public opinion for policy-makers (Herbst, 1998; Bakir, 2006) suggest that its role as institutional informer remains crucial. Indeed, critics of Habermas's thesis of refeudalisation argue that Habermas failed to take account of the very real progress that has occurred in extending people's democratic rights (Hjarvard, 1993, p. 88), and overlooked the benefits that have resulted from the spread of commercially and publicly funded mass media, both of which have on occasions made power accountable through various programming genres (Curran, 2000, pp. 125–7).[7] The operation of the public sphere is far from ideal, but in today's complex society, we cannot do without the media in this role. To understand the imperfect functioning of the public sphere, we would do well to pay closer attention to the myriad trust relationships sustained between publics, the media and political and economic power-holders.

Media, trust and the economic sphere

As the public sphere has become mediatised (and commercialised), so also has the economic sphere, perhaps most notably, the field of advertising. The branding of products and services is, by definition, an abstract benchmark of trust in the quality of the product or service. As Lau and Sook (1999) note, brands are the interface between company and consumer and this relationship is predicated upon trust. The usage of trademarks and logos as arbiters of trust marks, and the rise of advertising and wider marketing communication programmes in the promotion of these, find their expression in the shift of public sphere power away from the populace to a scenario where reality is mediated in favour of economic interests back to citizens. This has found wider expression in what is today described as "relationship marketing" (Morgan and Hunt, 1994).

Relationship marketing's core rationale is that it makes sense to foster a continuous relationship between marketers and consumers, since it is more expensive to replace an existing customer with a new one (Schiffman, Sherman and Kirpalani, 2002). The philosophy of relationship marketing, coupled with rapidly advancing computer and software technologies, has focused attention even further on trust, as it has made it possible to use database marketing methodologies to dramatically alter marketers' precision in identifying, researching and catering to particular customers' unique needs – a process of customer relationship management (Shaw and Stone, 1990; Holtz, 1992; Pickton and Broderick, 2001). Such Internet marketing techniques have generated a range of privacy concerns relating to consumers' trust of business and what is done with transactional information (Caudill and Murphy, 2000; McStay and Bakir, 2006). Furthermore, the anonymity and the physical distance between consumer and product, typical of e-commerce, generate tangibility issues, making it more difficult to establish trust and raising security concerns, including misuse of credit cards and Internet fraud (Fam, Foscht and Collins, 2004). Thus, the development of trust across a range of dimensions is seen as the fundamental solution to increasing the percentage of purchase transactions and information exchange online (Cheskin, 1999; Koufaris and Hampton-Sosa, 2004).

Conclusion

This chapter has shown that while trust has been explored within a range of academic disciplines (in particular, sociology, politics and economics), the media have not featured prominently within these.[8] This is so, even where direct links would seem hard to avoid. For instance, there are links to be made between Giddens's analysis of trust as a prerequisite for the formation of self-identity (1990, 1991, 1992, 1994a, 1994b), with its centrality of therapy and authenticity, and the many forms of therapeutic media genres, including talk shows and reality TV. Yet the role of trust in mass-mediated pure relationships remains relatively unexplored. More significantly within trust studies, specific inroads into the relationship between media and trust have begun in the risk communication literature. That risk issues, above all other issues, have been explored in this way is to be expected, given the close relationship between risk and trust (outlined earlier in this chapter). However the focus on trust within risk communication is relatively undeveloped with little textual or discursive analysis of trust relationships within media texts or practices (although, see Bakir, 2006). While audience trust is more frequently researched within risk communication, particularly from a psychological perspective, there is conceptual confusion due to the conflation of interpersonal and social trust (Earle and Cvetkovich, 1995) and many questions surround the interpretation of trust and its effects (Cvetkovich and Lofstedt, 1999; Kasperson et al., 2003).

In moving from literatures centred on trust towards literatures centred on media, an uneven pattern of attention towards media and trust is uncovered. Whereas the public sphere literature has implicit links to trust in its exploration of the relationships between publics, media and power-holders, and in its assessment of the media's capacity to generate mutual understanding and share knowledge, it does not directly address trust and the media as a central issue. The economic sphere literature more specifically addresses trust and the media – for instance, in relation to e-commerce. However, while much is written about trust in the advertising and marketing literature, the writing does not have the discursive reach of sociological theory, for instance, tending to quantitatively use trust as an analytical category in establishing the barriers to trust in e-commerce and marketing (Morrison and Firmstone, 2000).

By bringing these two spheres of media-focused literature together through the lens of trust, this book opens up a new field of media studies within trust studies. We hope that this book, through a range of empirical case studies, widens and deepens understanding of how different media forms and genres (including, but not limited to the Internet and advertising) interact with, and perhaps modulate, trust across a range of social phenomena (including, but not limited to, risk issues).

Notes

1. Earlier sociological works on trust include Blau's (1964) writings on trust, influenced by Simmel's non-trust-based work rather than by his thoughts on trust (Möllering, 2001). While phenomenologists have long noted the importance of trust (for instance, Garfinkel [1963] illustrated the importance of trusting other persons' claims regarding the nature of social reality in his now infamous rule-breaching studies), the loss of trust in those experiments was understood as an individual ontological problem, rather than a collective one (Carolan and Bell, 2003).
2. The concept of social capital encompasses various types of social relationships such as informal, generalised, civic and institutional (Stone, 2001; Stone and Hughes, 2002). For further distinctions made in social capital theory, see Narayan (1999) and Woolcock (1998).
3. Notably, there is disagreement on the direction of causality between the nodes of social capital, trust and civil society (Uslaner, 2000; Rose-Ackerman, 2001; Duffy, Williams and Hall, 2004; Rothstein, 2004). As Rothstein (2004) argues, the most important causal force may not go from the sociological level (civil society networks) to the political (the state and its institutions); rather it may be that a

particular type of state institution produces individuals and organisations with high (or low) social trust. Rothstein (2004) goes on to suggest that social capital can be affected by how the state organises the public institutions intended to implement public policy. People care not only about the final result of personal interaction with public institutions (such as receiving a benefit), but often also with whether the procedure that led to the final result is fair – procedural justice (Mishler and Rose, 1998).

4. For more on trust as a functional alternative to rational prediction for the reduction of complexity, see Lewis and Weigert (1985).
5. Also see Earle and Cvetkovich (1995) for a discussion of social trust as a strategy for the reduction of cognitive complexity.
6. For a full account of risk in modernity, see Luhmann (1988), Giddens, (1990), Beck (1992), Beck, Giddens, and Lash (1994) and Beck (2000). Deborah Lupton (1999) offers a good overview.
7. For other criticisms of the public sphere, see, for example, Stevenson (2002, pp. 56–62) and Thompson (1994, p. 42) and for Habermas's defence of the public sphere, see Habermas (1992).
8. Tentative statements on media and trust were made by some trust theorists in the 1980s and 1990s. For instance, Luhmann (1988, p. 103) notes that the development of trust depends on local milieu and personal experience but also suggests that these 'conditions may be extended by television culture, for instance in the case of political leaders'. Later on, Luhmann argues that the selection principles used by TV editors to determine what news is, for example the news values of novelty and 'conflict', 'constantly stress discontinuity' and so tend to undermine confidence (1990, p. 96).

Part II Media and Erosion of Trust

3
Origins of the Problem of Trust: Propaganda during the First World War

Michael Redley

War is famously the pretext for encroachment by the lawless state upon civil society. The right superseding law to resort to arms in self-defence – Cicero's 'Silent enim leges inter arma' ('Laws are put aside when arms are raised') (Cicero, Pro Milone, IV. 11, cited in Clarke, 1895, p. 10) – set out in the first century BC the basic justification that applies to this day. The state may formally withdraw when peace returns. However, appropriation of civil institutions outside the framework of law may well have changed irrevocably the way they are regarded.

Something very like this happened when the media establishment was harnessed to the war effort on both sides of the Atlantic during the First World War. As familiar landmarks of civil society reappeared with the return of peace, it became apparent that a profound but subtle change had occurred. As the tendentious nature of much wartime propaganda masquerading as factual information emerged after the war, a crisis of trust quickly developed. In a book widely read on both sides of the Atlantic which documented the way during the war governments had manipulated public information, a British Labour MP, Arthur Ponsonby, put it thus:

> There is not a living soul in any country who does not deeply resent having his passions roused, his indignation inflamed, his patriotism exploited, and his highest ideals desecrated by concealment, subterfuge, fraud, falsehood, trickery and deliberate lying on the part of those in whom he is taught to repose confidence and to whom he is enjoined to pay respect. (Ponsonby, 1928, p. 29)

Trust in the media, which before the war had shaped and guided political opinion, had diminished, and was replaced by what one post-war commentator called 'vigilant scepticism' (Montague, 1968, p. 70). The media had also adjusted to the change in their circumstances. One of the principal symptoms was impatience among young and old alike with the rhetoric of pre-war Liberalism – what the same commentator called 'the strident enunciation of venerable political principles' – which had also been the dominant tone of national propaganda during the war (Messinger, 1992, pp. 44–5). The time when bets were settled by reference to what the papers said (Montague, 1968, p. 77), and – as John Buchan,[1] the popular novelist and publisher who led Britain's propaganda effort and influenced propaganda in the USA during the war, put it – 'a man was as loyal to his paper as to his club and his particular brand of cigar',[2] was at an end. This chapter explores the origins and nature of the emerging problem of trust at the start of the era of modern mass media.

Propaganda during the First World War

Professor Niall Ferguson has pointed out that the First World War was the first media war (Ferguson, 1998, p. 212). Whereas the conduct of previous wars had been influenced by press comment, and efforts had been made to keep the press on side, the case during the 1914–18 War was entirely different. There occurred a convulsive upturning of a consensus that had built up over a century and determined thinking about the distance which should properly exist between media and state. Vibrant media industries that had grown rapidly across the western world in the years immediately before the war constituted a highly capable mechanism with global reach for influencing opinion. The talent base and industrial organisation of the 'free' press, publishing and film industries of the belligerent powers were co-opted by their governments, often by informal and personal means rather than through acts of nationalisation, to be systematically reapplied as instruments of war under public influence rather than simply answering to demand in the market place. Trust vested in them by publics was precisely what made them of value to the belligerent powers (Sanders and Taylor, 1981, pp. 1–12).

To begin with, propaganda was used to ensure that the government's case gained a proper airing. The shorthand for this in Britain was 'placing the truth before reasonable people'.[3] The Committee for Public Information (CPI), the propaganda agency created by Woodrow Wilson's administration when the USA entered the war in April 1917 adopted the same doctrine. Its director, George Creel, with characteristic bravura, called the CPI 'The House of Truth' (Ewen, 1996). However as the prospect of victory on the battlefield receded, emphasis shifted towards what its proponents called 'penetrative propaganda'.[4] This relied heavily on censorship, which cleared away contradictions to the central message, as well as placing the state's conduct of propaganda beyond the scope of public debate. Freed from traditional constraints, propaganda began to focus on influencing the mood of the mass of ordinary people rather than simply addressing opinion formers. This was associated with a shift of its target from the populations of allied and neutral powers, who by 1917 had largely made up their minds, to public opinion in the belligerent countries, both civilians and men under arms, where public morale as weariness with the war grew on all sides became vital to the outcome. The appeal of penetrative propaganda was that it held out the prospect of victory far more quickly and cheaply in terms of resources (including, of course, human life) than military combat (Sanders and Taylor, 1982, pp. 55–97; Gebele, 1987, pp. 20–8; Taylor, 1999, pp. 17–29 and pp. 49–60).

Public trust was invoked in Britain under the wartime slogan, 'business as usual'. Bookshops continued to be stocked with the works of well-loved authors writing on patriotic themes under familiar imprints. The press retained the physical appearance it had before the war, until paper shortages from 1916 caused some reduction in size. Newspapers and magazines continued to trumpet their political independence through their editorial columns, so much so that their proprietors, particularly Lords Northcliffe and Beaverbrook, were considered by many far too independent of government for the good of the war effort (Koss, 1990, pp. 712–44). Films and popular exhibitions reflected the concerns of a population at war. Particularly among soldiers, there was deep cynicism about the truth of official pronouncements. Fighting men read with disbelief newspaper accounts claiming victory for the chaotic military engagements in which they had been involved. A catchphrase – 'you can't believe a word you read' – became commonplace in the trenches (Montague, 1968, p. 75). However the content of the media was regarded in general as the product of well meaning private enterprise doing its best to serve consumers in trying times. As Buchan put it in a report to Ministers: 'Camouflage of the right kind is a vital necessity...[Propaganda] can advertise its wares, but it dare not advertise the vendor' (Sanders and Taylor, 1982, p. 120). The British public was certainly never aware how far production of the printed word across the whole field of public information had been infiltrated and suborned.

Few people knew, for example, that dozens of Britain's best-loved authors had been sponsored to write for the national interest (Sander and Taylor, 1982, pp. 48–53; Buitenhuis, 1987, pp. 5–20).[5] A London-based organisation known as 'Wellington House' commissioned books and pamphlets and brokered arrangements with publishers under which they paid no royalties but diverted surpluses into extra promotion to improve the reach of the material. By the middle of 1915, Wellington House was already operating as 'a very large publishing establishment', although notice of its involvement never appeared in the many books and pamphlets with which it was associated. At the end of 1917, four million copies of its publications were being produced each month, including 700,000 of a magazine called *War Pictures*, which appeared in eight different foreign language editions, including Arabic. As well as to the British Empire and the Dominions, Wellington House supplied significant amounts of material, never identified as official propaganda, to the USA. By the end of the war, a single Boston publisher had over a hundred Wellington House titles in its list. The longest running title – a collection of war poetry sponsored by Wellington House – was still in print in the USA at the start of the Second World War (Redley, 2000, p. 24). This was part of a much wider informal management of the media that had emerged by 1916. When conduct of propaganda operations was criticised inside Government, Buchan hit back by claiming that '...often people refer to publications, exhibitions etc with the comment that it is shameful that such matters are left to private enterprise. In nearly every case, the things referred to have been the work of the Department'.[6]

The effective government takeover in 1916 of news agency operations based in Britain, feeding news by telegram to hundreds of newspapers around the world, was known only to a handful of press owners and their senior managers. The Treasury's logic when the idea was first mooted at the end of 1915 could not be faulted. Funding was refused on the grounds that unless news agencies preserved their standing as entirely financially independent of government, they would in any case be without value for official propaganda purposes. When the secret deal was finally done, using blocking shareholdings, the War Cabinet was kept officially unaware for fear of 'blabbers'. At the end of 1917, news agency staff were producing to order over a million words of material a month from temporary buildings in the Lord Chancellor's Court in the House of Lords which were despatched through normal agency channels (Read, 1992, pp. 111–31; Sanders and Taylor, 1982, pp. 37–8).[7]

In the USA, until war was declared on Germany and its allies in April 1917, the case was a different one. Desperate efforts by the European belligerents to influence America's politics in breach of its neutrality, in part by spoiling each other's operations, led to sensational revelations about the extent of covert propaganda activities on American soil. Each characterised the work of the other as the cynical abuse of neutral hospitality. In 1916, the British obtained through a secret service operation the contents of a German diplomat's briefcase that revealed the objectives and methods of their propaganda operation in North America. Its contents were systematically leaked to the press in New York (Sanders and Taylor, 1982, pp. 182–3). The British were also occasionally caught out. Nevertheless, aspects of their own covert operation in the USA in 1915–6 found their way into the propaganda operation created by Woodrow Wilson's government after the USA entered the war. Run entirely by American nationals, the British operation used as its spokesmen tens of thousands of American citizens influential in their own communities who had no idea that the arguments on which they relied in discussion with their fellow citizens had been supplied by official propaganda agencies in London.[8] Trustworthy people lending their authority to messages that the public might otherwise be inclined to disbelieve became the basic stock-in-trade of wartime propaganda on both sides of the Atlantic.

Once trust in the source of information was achieved, those in charge of propaganda were able to concentrate on content. A senior intelligence officer at British General Headquarters in France wrote to the Foreign Office in the middle of 1916: 'The question of propaganda appears to me to be chiefly one of how the news is dished up more than what the news actually is'.[9] But those who wrote propaganda knew that its effectiveness also depended on tuning the substance, '... abbreviated or amplified to suit the requirements of the immediate situation'.[10] The Foreign Office went to great lengths to try to wrest from the military control of the production of news and information. Writers were employed who knew their readership, imparting the particular 'spin' required to reach readers at home and abroad, adding verisimilitude by the use of first hand description, and diminishing the significance of a setback by the flat words chosen to present it. John Buchan, chief 'spin doctor' at the Foreign Office in 1916, was ordered to General Sir Douglas Haig's army headquarters during the Somme offensive to help draft his military despatches (Adam Smith, 1965, pp. 197–8). German newspapers were allowed to carry enemy army reports, provided that they were published in full (Welsh, 2005, p. 35). It was therefore more important that they were constructed of compelling language.

Personal links across the Atlantic helped to get the USA's official propaganda operation started. But as a crusading journalist, George Creel took an approach to propaganda in the USA tailored to local circumstances. Unlike its counterparts in Europe, the CPI had the declared purpose of mobilising the American public for war. Public trust was to be earned, as it had been in the Progressive era of American politics during which Creel and the generation of journalists and publicists he recruited to the war effort had made their names, through moral fervour and the espousal of 'Americanism' (Vaughn, 1980, pp. 23–38; Ewen, 1996, pp. 102–26). The cooperation of the media was obtained largely through a public mood encouraging conformity rather than by means of covert operations. The CPI addressed the American public directly through its network of 75, 000 public speakers, the 'Four Minute Men', who were briefed to insert topics at specified times into public discourse by addressing local gatherings throughout the country. 'Junior Four Minute Men' also operated in the school system. This attempt at micromanaging the political thought-processes and discourse of a nation, coupled with encouragement to the populace to inform on neighbours who expressed dissenting opinions and with censorship of the media, helped to engender a tide in public opinion that effectively removed the possibility of meaningful debate about the conduct of the war. The CPI found itself the subject of criticism for not being zealous enough. But its own propaganda methods undoubtedly stoked the public pressure to conform, which in the USA took the place of secrecy as a way of enhancing the reach and effectiveness of official propaganda.

It would be wrong to suggest – the CPI excepted – that governments brought to the manipulation of public opinion a sustained plan of campaign. Private initiatives were important, and only gradually did government begin to take an overarching role. To give a concrete example, Buchan, in October 1914, already an established author as well as director in the Edinburgh publishing firm of Thomas Nelson and Sons, embarked in his own name on a contemporary chronicle of the conflict, a new volume every three months or so to bring the story up-to-date. It was to be called *Nelson's History of the War*, in order to distinguish it from any other proprietary enterprise of a similar kind, but also to underline its independence from government. It is plausible that, to begin with, Buchan's account of the war was put together, albeit under a degree of self-censorship, solely on the basis of private conversations and publicly available information. But there is no doubt that by the end of 1915, the history had come under official control. Buchan had in the meanwhile joined the Foreign Office to write official propaganda for consumption abroad. On Volume X dealing with the occupation of the Gallipoli Peninsular and the Battle of Loos in Flanders which appeared in December that year, he wrote to a friend: 'A few things had to be put in for political purposes, and a great deal left out. So much of Loos was a hanging business that it will be quite a long time before the full story can be told' (Adam Smith, 1965, pp. 193–4).[11]

When Buchan joined Haig's staff at the start of the Somme offensive in 1916, the Army made it a condition that he severs all connection with *Nelson's History*. The Director of Intelligence at General Headquarters (GHQ) in France said: 'Critical words should not come from anyone who has access to such papers as we propose to show Buchan'.[12] They pointed out that a public role for Buchan would in any case blow his cover. But the Foreign Office refused to let Buchan give up *Nelson's History*. The Minister responsible wrote 'It is certainly very popular and widely read both at home and in foreign countries, and from the latter point of view is good propaganda for us'.[13] The matter had finally to be settled between Haig and the Foreign Secretary, Sir Edward Grey. Buchan continued to write the history on the basis that his role at GHQ remained a secret, publication would be held up for at least five months after the events described, and he submitted all chapters dealing with the Western Front to censorship by GHQ. He personally undertook to '... avoid anything in the way of criticism or comment and to be content with a chronicle of events'.[14] Although control over the content of the book had shifted fundamentally, its inherent trustworthiness was preserved. Buchan claimed with good reason after the war that *Nelson's History*, '... by its sanity of view and reasoned optimism did much to balance and inform the public mind, and had, notably in America, a far-reaching influence'.[15]

In Britain, the ambitions of propagandists increased substantially towards the end of the war as newspaper proprietors, known to civil servants in

Whitehall as 'the Press Gang', took charge. They saw their role as creating the 'atmosphere' in which the public mood became more susceptible to influence. Lord Beaverbrook, Minister of Information in Britain during the last year of the war, explained to the Secretary to the Cabinet, Sir Maurice Hankey, how propaganda worked

> [The] real object is to work in close accord with the Press, and to create an atmosphere around an event, such as a meeting of the Imperial War Cabinet. For the purpose we have to pour out a continual stream of cables, wireless articles, press notices – or inspirations .... The information we give to the Press is in fact not an official Departmental communiqué, but a series of hints to the press. (Beaverbrook Papers, 1918)[16]

In the USA, George Creel said 'I do not believe that public opinion has its rise in the emotions, [but] ... in the minds of the people, ... and that it expresses slow forming convictions rather than any temporary excitement or any passion of the moment' (Ewen, 1996, pp. 121–2). However the way the CPI deployed propaganda to influence the public mood suggested otherwise.

During the war, on both sides of the Atlantic the state had encroached, both in providing information and shaping opinion, on areas which before the war had been the preserve of the private sector; but it had also done this through alliances with the owners of the media, who placed their organisations, talent and skills at the disposal of the state. Here was a powerful incubator of mistrust – a new and powerful instrument of political communication in the hands of power brokers, civil servants and media moguls as well as politicians, who had developed the skills and the appetite to use it. Whether they did so to their own benefit or to the advantage of the state, and whether there existed any meaningful line between the two was by no means clear. What was the public in the post-war world to make of this?

Implications for trust

The unexpectedly rapid collapse of Germany and Austro-Hungary temporarily silenced concerns about the implications of wartime propaganda for the post-war world. Buchan claimed that his department had matched the Germans blow for blow, with the result that '... eighteen [neutral countries] have declared war on her, and nine more have severed relations with her, while in most of the others the Germans bewail the fact that public opinion has definitely turned against them .... This is not a result of which any propaganda department need be ashamed' (Sanders and Taylor, 1982, pp. 74–5). Lord Northcliffe, who managed propaganda to enemy countries during the last year of the war, suggested modestly that his efforts had 'to some extent hastened the end' (Pound and Harmsworth, 1959, p. 670).

In the USA, George Creel suggested in the introduction to his history of the CPI that it had for the first time articulated 'the gospel of Americanism' and carried it throughout the world.[17] Liberal opinion that had been split by the debate over wartime conscription was similarly divided over the state's propaganda activities. The Liberal elder statesman, Lord Rosebery, told Buchan on his appointment as Director of Information in February 1917: '.... [It] is a department of which I have always had a dubious opinion'.[18] But Rosebery's Liberal idealism belonged to a world that had ceased to exist by the end of the war.

In the circumstances of war it could be argued that the end had justified the propaganda means. But even before the war ended, hidden costs began to be identified. During a debate on propaganda in the House of Commons in August 1918, it was suggested by Liberal members that anti-Labour propaganda agents, redeployed from war work, were already operating inside the Labour Movement.[19] This quickly became incorporated into the Marxist syndicalist critique of political progress by parliamentary means that was espoused by many on the Left in Britain at the end of the war. Lloyd George's coalition government did indeed use covert propaganda methods to undermine public support for strikes and to weaken the Trade Union movement from within. Newspapers were 'nobbled' on a substantial scale. Public funding found its way into anti-Leftist 'front' organisations controlled by dubious individuals who had gained skills and experience from official wartime propaganda work (Middlemas, 1979, pp. 131–2). The Liberal Chief Whip expressed the concern many felt about these operations: 'There are grave objections to the employment of taxpayer's money for this purpose, as many members of the Labour Party could justly claim that their own money was being used to overcome their political creed' (Middlemas, 1979, p. 132, note).

Although Lloyd George enhanced his public reputation as the tough man who could master the Unions, class conflict sharpened as trust in the fairness of the political process was further undermined. When the Lloyd George coalition government fell after the Conservative Party withdrew its support in October 1922, this was in part because of '... a more general objection to press and public opinion manipulation and a sense that old decencies and conventions were being overridden' (Middlemas, 1979, p. 169). Stanley Baldwin, who became Prime Minister in the middle of the following year, told the House of Commons: 'We realise that when men have their backs against the wall they will adopt any means of self preservation ... we have all of us slipped down in our view of what constitutes civilisation'. The war had shown the whole world 'how thin is the crust of civilisation on which this generation is walking'.[20] Under Baldwin's premiership, the political parties were to make ruthless and effective use of propaganda techniques within the parliamentary system, but the twilight world of private 'fronts' for official policy was by and large disavowed. But in the inter-war years, trustworthiness was an attribute to which politicians had to prove their claim rather than attaching automatically to politicians as a class (Williamson, 1999, p. 37).

The press also found itself in a new world. Lord Northcliffe initially tried to perpetuate into the peace the power he had gained over policy-making in wartime. The *Daily Mail* ran a calculated campaign in the run up to the General Election of 1918 against leniency in the peace terms accorded to Germany by the victorious allies. The pressure politicians found themselves under at the hustings may have resulted in some toughening of Britain's negotiating stance at the Versailles peace conference (Haste, 1977). But Northcliffe had also overplayed his hand, and his papers never regained the influence they had previously enjoyed. Even a sympathetic commentator concluded that they had undermined trust by 'affecting a foolish omniscience, when their ignorance was palpable, and a foolish air of impartiality when their bias was glaring' (Koss, 1990, p. 796).[21] The press owners deliberately cut loose from their pre-war party allegiances and moved to a position of studied impartiality, the better to barter their editorial support for inside information and political influence. But this was not the end of the matter. When Stanley Baldwin in 1930 faced a challenge from Lord Beaverbrook's United Empire Party, supported by both Beaverbrook and Rothermere newspapers, he hit back by accusing their proprietors of 'aiming at ... power, and power without responsibility – the prerogative of the harlot throughout the ages' (Taylor, 1996, pp. 273–4; Williamson, 1999, pp. 231–5). Baldwin had drawn successfully on a residue of public anxiety about press power that resulted from their propaganda activities during the war.

Comprehension of the horror and inhumanity of war on the Western Front, which had to some extent been blocked by censorship and propaganda during the war, flooded in when the war ended. Younger adults who had survived the war reacted by abandoning pre-war cultural heroes who they deemed to have abused the trust vested in them by contributing to propaganda that had wilfully concealed the truth. The historical and literary Modernist, exemplified by the essayist and historian, Lytton Strachey, the poet, T.S. Eliot and the novelist, Virginia Woolf, attracted interest through the simple fact of being unencumbered by the baggage of this past. The prestige that had clung to the names of literary figures generally before the war was diminished after it (Buitenhuis, 1987, p. 180). Satire became one of the most successful literary genres of the 1920s. Worthy works in pre-war formats often received good reviews but sold no more than a handful of copies. In reaction to the inflated rhetoric and high-flown sentiments of propaganda masquerading as literature, written language was stripped back to its bare essentials, and obscenity in modern literature became in the 1920s almost an established convention (Buchan, 1940, pp. 183–7; Hynes, 1992, pp. 395–404).

The opportunity in the 1920s to start an entirely new medium, radio, was addressed in Britain against the background of the issue of trust arising out of the war. The idea that radio should be required to provide information and education as well as entertainment was eagerly seized by the political class in Britain. The scheme of a cultural mission to the newly enfranchised working classes quickly took hold (LeMahieu, 1988, pp. 141–54). Ironically it was the experience of providing propaganda during the war – delivering information from a trusted source – which in post-war circumstances led to the idea of a monopoly over the new medium being given to a public corporation, in public ownership but not under political control. The phrase 'to do good by stealth' which came to characterise Sir John Reith's British Broadcasting Corporation (BBC), had been used earlier in wartime Cabinet debates on propaganda (Sanders and Taylor, 1982, p. 174).

The abuse of trust and its consequences also came sharply into focus in the USA as the war ended. The British Foreign Office had consistently argued during the war that propaganda was such a dangerous commodity that it could be handled safely only by its own experts. Lord Robert Cecil, whose ministerial portfolio included responsibility for propaganda, told his Cabinet colleagues in 1916: 'It is much easier to do harm than good with propaganda. A tactless interview will sweep away the results of months of patient work'.[22] Yet the Foreign Office was caught unawares by the backlash against British wartime propaganda in the USA that occurred at the end of the war. Local employees of the British campaign in boastful mood gave their stories to the press, revealing for the first time in public just how wide and deep the deception aimed at enticing the USA into the war on the side of the Allies had been (Taylor, 1999, pp. 43–4). The anti-British Hearst newspapers gleefully took up the tale. Trust had been brutally and systematically betrayed, and Republican America had once again been duped by its old imperial foe. The isolationist impulse ran deep, and was perhaps no more than reinforced by the revelations. But they helped to put British diplomats and politicians on the defensive in the USA throughout the inter-war years, aware that any public statement they made on American soil would be scrutinised for hostile attempts to take undue advantage of an overly trusting American public (Taylor, 1981, pp. 68–77). Wartime propaganda that had aimed to break down American isolationism ended up by reinforcing it.

The CPI's legacy was also a dubious one. Historians have argued that the refusal by the USA to sign the Treaty of Versailles and to join the League of Nations, which President Wilson had done so much to promote, owed something to its activities. In its zeal to identify objectives for the war that would appeal to the American public, the CPI had neglected to situate American involvement in its international context (Vaughn, 1980, p. 349). The crisis of trust extended in the USA to academic enquiry as to whether the belief of America's Founding Fathers in informed discourse, a rational public and the eventual triumph of truth and good government had been undermined by the experience of mass manipulation during the war. Walter

Lippmann's work on the way public opinion was formed, arising out of his experience at the CPI, influenced a generation of liberal intellectuals (Gary, 1999, pp. 15–53). The Chicago sociologist, Harold Lasswell, in an influential book on wartime propaganda published in 1927, expressed the prevailing cynicism about democracy: 'The public has not led with benignity and restraint. The good life is not the mighty rushing wind of public sentiment. It is no organic secretion of the horde, but the tedious achievement of the few .... Thus argues the despondent democrat' (Lasswell, 1927, pp. 4–5). Lasswell's work did little to dispel the gloom. It was feared that 'invisible rulers' using techniques developed during the war for 'regimenting the public mind' would take control of politics away from the people (Gary, 1999, pp. 55–84). It took another world war to show that this was not necessarily the case. Intensive exposure to a further round of official propaganda, together with the defeat of Hitler's Germany, a state constructed around the premise of the power of propaganda, helped societies to learn to come to terms with it, gaining in the process some understanding of its limitations.

However, if the circumstances out of which problems of trust had arisen had not deliberately been obscured by governments, things might well have turned out differently. It was unfortunate that the propaganda machinery of the belligerent powers was so thoroughly and rapidly dismembered at the end of the First World War, because subsequent generations were denied the chance to know how effective (or otherwise) it had been. In Britain, something approaching panic set in with the departure from office in November 1918 of Lord Robert Cecil, on whose informal say-so many of the secret arrangements had been established. To a man like Sir Henry Newbolt, the patriotic poet who was closely involved with wartime propaganda, there seemed no doubt that in 'the Ten Year debating society which will be the World-After-The-War' the capability to project the national viewpoint would remain vital. But the judgement that trust would ebb away from a political process which continued to embrace propaganda reflected the stronger and more immediate concern (Redley, 2003, p. 31). There ensued, in the words of a circular in the Ministry of Information, '... a liberal destruction of obsolete documents', including apparently all policy papers, and the whole contents of the Ministry's Record Department library in which had been carefully stored the documentary evidence of propaganda and counter propaganda on both sides throughout the conflict with analysis of its effectiveness.[23] Official histories of the war omitted the propaganda campaign altogether.

A similar process unfolded in the USA. The CPI's funding was stopped immediately after the war. Its official history written largely by Creel was suppressed, although he eventually published it in 1920 under his own name (Creel, 1920). Mass destruction of wartime documents also took place, although a significant proportion turned up in a basement in the Department of Defence twenty years later (Vaughn, 1980, p. 339). The way governments reacted against their own involvement in propaganda, destroying the evidence in the process, meant that the ghosts from the First World War were never confronted, or properly laid to rest. It is perhaps an aspect of the problem of trust, and a feature of the Age of Suspicion, that they haunt us still.

Notes

1. The author acknowledges permission given by A.P. Watt Ltd on behalf of The Lord Tweedsmuir and Jean, Lady Tweedsmuir to quote from the papers of John Buchan in the National Library of Scotland.
2. Montague, p. 77; Buchan to Oxford Luncheon Club, 25 February 1927: Mss 321/18, National Library of Scotland.
3. Buchan to Professor Gilbert Murray, 17 December 1918: Mss 126/28. Bodleian Library, Oxford University.
4. Donald to Carson, 6 January 1918: FO395/235, National Archives.
5. The writers included Sir James Barrie, Arnold Bennett, Robert Bridges, G.K. Chesterton, Anthony Hope, John Masefield, A.E.W. Mason, Sir Henry Newbolt, Gilbert Murray, George Trevelyan and H.G. Wells.
6. Report on the Department of Information, 1 December 1917: FO395/235, National Archives.
7. Memorandum 'Department of Information', 1 December 1917: National Archives, FO 395/235.
8. Second Report on the work conducted for the Government at Wellington House, 1 February 1916: Inf4/5, National Archives.
9. Charteris to Montgomery, 23 June 1916: FO 395/51, National Archives.
10. Charteris to Newton, 23 June 1919; Newton to Charteris, 5 July 1916: FO 395/51, National Archives.
11. John Buchan to Frederick Britten Austin, 24 February 1916: Acc. 7151/2, National Library of Scotland.
12. Charteris to Newton, 15 July 1916: FO 395/51, National Archives.
13. Newton to Charteris, 13 July 1916: FO 395/51, National Archives.
14. Buchan to Charteris, 20 September 1916: FO 395/51, National Archives.
15. Buchan to Beaverbrook, 13 May 1922: Acc. 7006, National Library of Scotland.
16. Beaverbrook to Hankey, 15 June 1918: BBK/E/3/36/83, Beaverbrook Papers, House of Lords Record Office.
17. Memorandum 'Department of Information', 1 December 1917: National Archives, FO 395/235.
18. Rosebery to Buchan, 10 February 1917: Acc. 6975 13/28, National Library of Scotland.
19. Hansard 5th Series, Vol. 109, 29 July 1918, cols 962 and 966.
20. Hansard 5th Series, Vol. 167, 23 July 1923, col. 176–7.
21. Buchan to Oxford Luncheon Club, 25 February 1927: Mss 321/18, National Library of Scotland.
22. 'British propaganda in Allied and Neutral Countries', paragraph 2, 29 December 1916: CAB24/3, National Archives.
23. John Buchan to Dr Seaton, n.d.; and Office Memorandum: FO 395/235/242835, National Archives.

4
The Erosion of Trust in Australian Public Life

Jeff Archer

In common with much of the western media, and indeed like many other western institutions, such as universities and political parties, the Australian media is relatively less concerned with issues of public interest than was the case two or three decades ago. For example, it is generally true that newspapers and television networks now devote fewer resources to long-term investigative reporting and are more concerned with 'infotainment', or merely with entertainment. This is most evident in the arena of commercial television, but the phenomenon of dumbing-down is widespread, even with the national Australian Broadcasting Corporation (ABC) and the broadsheet newspapers. This retreat of the fourth estate has been accompanied by a massive increase in the resources devoted to government media management and control. These twin trends pose major challenges to the public good. The democratic polity is under threat if the power of governments and commercial interests are not put under the spotlight of a strong independent media. Public scrutiny is essential for democratic and responsible government, but the symbiotic interests of government and media now tend to reduce scrutiny. They both wish to provide the public (especially the politically uninterested floating voter) with quick and relatively inexpensive information that is often pre-packaged and produced by government and corporations – with all the spin that involves. And they both have an interest in promoting public perceptions of sensational dangers and threats that will excite public interest while simultaneously presenting a reassuring image of the government as the solution to the perceived danger. Perceptions of rampant crime, terrorism and economic ruin sell copy, and they also present an opportunity to governments and oppositions to present populist remedies. This response is more likely to achieve electoral success than can be achieved by addressing the less inflammatory but more prosaic questions of social, economic, environmental and political analysis, and by the subsequent development of detailed, thoughtful policy. In this chapter, I shall concentrate on one aspect of this phenomenon in the Australian political context: the media management of government.

The media control by the Howard Government (in office for the decade since 1996), particularly by Prime Minister John Howard himself, has been exceptionally successful. In almost all respects, the government has been able to dominate the political agenda (Craig, 2004, p. 79), deflect unwelcome public criticism, and present itself as strong, united and in tune with public opinion. In 2004–5, there was some dissent within the coalition parliamentary ranks, but this was itself used to present an image of openness and attachment to democratic debate, and the continuing use of media has been very professional and successful. As the Howard Government moves into its second decade in office, and particularly since it secured a majority in both chambers of the Parliament in the session starting in August 2005, there are new arenas of dissent from within the coalition parties that will test Howard's media management skills. As former Coalition Prime Minister, Malcolm Fraser, found in the early 1980s, the majority control of the upper house can make management of government business harder. The need for tight party discipline is reduced when majorities are taken for granted.

Why has the Howard government received such a good press, and maintained such a high approval rating for so long? There are many reasons why this is the case. For example, these years were marked by some strong economic indicators at the national and international level, and whereas the responsibility of the government for these factors may not convince all economists, it has been an easy message of success to sell to the electorate. Also, for example, security and international threats have dominated the non-economic agenda, making it easy to present critiques of the government (however reasoned) as motivated by lack of patriotism, or even to view them as seditious. Another reason is that the moguls of print and electronic media have been broadly supportive of the government, and one has campaigned vigorously to give favourable treatment to the contentious war in Iraq in 2003, to give one example. Also, the so-called shock jocks of radio talkback have presented divisive and often highly prejudiced material that has been legitimised and merged with the Government's attack on political correctness and its uptake of the harsh policies on the treatment of asylum seekers put forward by a new minor political party, the One Nation Party, in 1996 (Archer, 1997). Another compelling reason for this media success is that the parliamentary opposition, particularly the Labor Party, has been inadequate, tactically outmanoeuvred and divided.

In this chapter, however, I wish to discuss some of the other reasons for the media success of the Howard Government. These reasons include its use of governmental media rhetoric and practice, the rise of political public relations and the advantages of political incumbency. These categories are illustrated later in this chapter in a short case study of the Palmer Report of 2005. It will be argued that these devices work at the level of political populism, but that they threaten traditional notions of trust in public life. This argument is not aimed exclusively at the Howard Government. In many respects these Howard Government practices follow the techniques of earlier governments, the Hawke (1983–91) and Keating (1991–6) Labor Governments at the federal level, and a host of Australian state governments, as well as closely following the practices of governments in other states such as the UK and the USA.[1]

Media rhetoric and practice

First, however, let me establish some elements of Howard's success in maintaining high levels of popularity over many years in government. While there is some evidence for a general decline in public trust in political institutions, the public's view of politicians individually is often more positive than how they are viewed collectively (Papadakis, 1999; Bean, 2001). Sydney Morning Herald journalist Geoff Kitney reported that after his first eight years in office, Howard's rating of trustworthiness was almost the same as when he first became Australian Prime Minister. Approximately 60 per cent of those polled considered him trustworthy. This is in spite of a number of issues where his truthfulness was seriously questioned. Examples are the ditching of various election promises as non-core promises; the 2001 misleading statements made prior to a national election about the alleged reckless actions of asylum seekers arriving in Australian waters in a leaky boat (the Children Overboard Affair) and the associated order to the Australian military in the same year to board and repulse a Norwegian commercial ship carrying shipwrecked asylum seekers towards Australia (the Tampa Affair) and the false arguments for war in Iraq (Kitney, 2004).[2] It is obvious here that Howard has remained popular despite antagonising significant sections of the population, especially those who are tertiary educated or well informed about current affairs. One explanation for this is that the general public tends to be more critical of lapses in personal integrity and honesty than it is for apparent dishonesty about abstract and complex public issues (Lumby, 2002).[3] However, Howard has been more successful in his populism and use of spin to promote his position than other leaders of the so-called Coalition of the Willing in the 2003 war in Iraq. George W. Bush in the USA and Tony Blair in the UK have attracted much more robust criticism from leading politicians in their own countries.

Howard is the second most electorally successful politician in Australian federal politics. While he has an unprepossessing appearance, and very little charisma, he is a dogged, determined politician, with great experience of both policy formulation and media management (Archer, 2005). As the twice-deposed Leader of the Opposition during the Hawke and Keating Governments, he is painfully aware of political risks, and has learnt how to avoid the repeat of such pitfalls. In opposition, he experienced personal career setbacks and low opinion poll satisfaction ratings, but in his third period of party leadership he has exhibited determination to manage the media. More than any of his predecessors as Prime Minister, with the possible exception of Bob Hawke, he treats each day as a contest to win the approval of carefully defined sections of Australian public opinion. As long as he delivers electoral success he has guaranteed party support, and is therefore able to keep a reputation for strong leadership. His style is an odd blend of public belligerence and affability. In Parliament he is able to deflect criticism with relative ease.

Howard's use of media rhetoric is by no means confined to set speeches. Rather, he conducts an almost daily commentary on radio and television, concentrating on short radio interviews with sympathetic talk back hosts, in which he continually introduces new fronts of distraction from any difficult issues, and re-emphasises simple messages using strong and emphatic language. This battle for control of the daily news agenda amounts to playing quasi-electoral politics every day of every year. This level of prime-ministerial media intensity was not known in Australian politics before 1996, and may have risked over-exposure if played by a less experienced hand. It went far beyond the soundbite and the favourable media image, to draw on an extensive range of media expertise. Media control, or spin as it is increasingly described, became almost the highest priority of government. Of course, there were still a number of set speeches, and electoral broadcasts and debates, as well as very formal speeches to the nation in ways that reflected the style of monarchical messages. The opening of the Sydney Olympic Games in 2000 was an illustration of this last point.

In the more formal set-speeches, and especially in televised electoral debates with Labor Party leaders Kim Beazley and Mark Latham, it was not easy to present Howard in such a favourable light. Lacking control of the format and the detailed agenda, the Prime Minister sometimes looked quite uncomfortable. In contrast, in a short, live radio or television interview, especially with a close ally such as the Sydney commercial radio presenter, Alan Jones, or with less experienced interviewers, Howard was able to control the message with great skill. His carefully chosen words, and the carefully constructed answers, gave sharp messages, often simultaneously to very different audiences, while allowing for possible repudiation of the position in the future if one unpacked the complex nuances contained within the message. These techniques mirrored the media successes of Tony Blair in the UK. It created a wedge-effect, where his opponents had lost political ground from which to respond. This is not to argue that the agenda-setting was either random or pragmatic, although Howard has always been prepared to negotiate pragmatic outcomes, with either minority senators before 2004, or with his own coalition backbenchers after gaining control over the upper house in 2005.

Howard's weaving of his messages within his political rhetoric set out to build coalitions of support for an ideological transformation from the previous Labor and Coalition governments since 1975. Howard's use of populist patriotism, especially as represented by a jingoistic appeal to the honour of the Australian military, reinforced his constant message of economic prosperity and a valorisation of individual choice that privileged the private over the public spheres. Howard's messages very often emerged using the same language phrases and the same spin techniques as those of Tony Blair in the UK and George W. Bush in the USA. But there were some unique aspects to the pattern of the ideological amalgam.

Political public relations and the advantages of political incumbency

In the case of the Clinton (1993–2001) and the Bush (2001 to present) Administrations in the USA, and in the case of the Blair Government (1997 to present) in the UK, there has been much debate about the extent political spin has overtaken issues of substantive policy. Media minders and strategists, such as Karl Rove in the USA and Alastair Campbell in the UK, have taken on a level of authority that eclipses that of almost all senior politicians. Arguably, their audience is not the politically informed, but rather the most impressionable part of the population, especially those who can be persuaded by media management to influence the outcomes of keenly contested marginal elections. In Australia, successful electoral strategists, such as Lytton Crosby, have not had quite such a central role as either Rove or Campbell. Indeed, Crosby's attempt to emulate his Australian success as advisor to Conservative leader Michael Howard in the 2005 UK election indicates that spin is insufficient for victory, as the UK Labour party won a third term.

As Sally Young makes clear throughout her 2004 study of Australian political advertising, Australian governments, both state and federal, have allocated millions of dollars to public relations staff, media liaison officers, and public relations. Incumbent governments have the financial and logistical support of an expanding and well-resourced private office (Stewart, 2002, p. 75) as well as the grand resource of the public service. They are able to fund the generation of good news, the monitoring of all media, and intense sectional and geographical polling, including the specialised use of focus groups. They are able to devote huge resources to detailed local issue campaigning, especially in marginal seats, and massive advertising for policy implementation as well as for expensive election campaigns. This trend, together with the politicisation of the senior public service (a large topic that is not discussed in this chapter), has, as I shall discuss below, reduced accountability in government. Ministerial advisers have filled a role in Australian government that has escaped the accountability of either politicians or public servants.

Incumbent parties devote massive resources to both national and local issue campaigning. In marginal seats, a massive saturation of targeted advertising is the norm. Sally Young (2004) has documented the extent of this impost on the public purse, as well as showing how little control on truth in advertising exists in Australian politics. Incumbent governments, at federal and state levels, are able to use public funds, especially in the lead up to elections, in ways that give them a partisan advantage over their political opponents. Although the Howard Government is following a well-worn path in this regard, Young documents new, much higher levels of spending from the public purse under the Howard Government. Public funds are also paid directly to incumbent politicians that can be used for publicity and electoral matters, and massive public funds are provided for party use according to the electoral success of the parties. All these funds taken together greatly favour incumbent governments, and actively discriminate against new or minor parties. This raises important questions about the ways that the major parties have achieved high success despite rapidly declining membership and less direct fundraising from their own supporters.

Political public relations and media advice, also funded by the public purse for the most part, are now a major industry. Its practitioners include private consultants and members of a new political elite operating in the private offices of senior politicians (and ministers in particular). The industry delivers another great advantage to incumbent governments. In 2002 there were over four hundred ministerial advisers in Canberra acting as bridges between the public service and politicians in high office (Stewart, 2002, p. 75). At the state level there are sometimes more senior media advisors than there are ministers. As with the politicisation of the senior public service, this trend has had the effect of reducing accountability in government. Ministerial advisers or staffers have a role that insulates ministers from the public service. If they are responsible for sensitive briefing and for dealing directly with the senior members of the public service, they effectively insulate the minister from the chain of communication that can be questioned by Parliament. Of course, with sufficient political will and agreement between major parties, there is nothing to stop staffers from becoming politically accountable (Hindess, 2004), but as yet both major parties prefer to insulate staffers from parliamentary (specifically Senate committee) questioning. This political expediency is understandable from the perspectives of the short-term gain to incumbents and the possible longer-term gain of aspirant ministers now in opposition, but there are constitutional dangers here. For example, in the Children Overboard Affair, the role of advisers in insulating Ministers and the Prime Minister from written advice that could prove politically costly meant that senior politicians could in public plausibly deny being informed of facts that were common knowledge in the bureaucracy (Jupp, 2002; Marr and Wilkinson, 2003; Uhr, 2004; Archer, 2005; Maddox, 2005).

The Palmer Report

In July 2005, the Palmer Report was made public (Palmer, 2005). It contained possibly the most critical and damaging account of policy implementation ever instanced in such an official report in Australia. Two Australian citizens, Cornelia Rau and Vivian Alverez, were punished because they were unable to immediately prove their identity to officials. Both were female, from non-British migrant backgrounds, with serious health concerns. There is no doubt that these actions by public officials were indefensible, and that the credibility of the Government's detention policy was liable to be subjected to intense media scrutiny. Incidentally, the Opposition failed to subject the government to very much scrutiny in this case.

Cornelia Rau was held in custody in a Queensland jail for six months, and in the Baxter Immigration Detention Centre in rural South Australia for four months, enduring long periods of punishment and solitary confinement in both institutions. Her mental illness was not diagnosed or properly treated in this time. When detained in March 2004 she was confused about her real identity and had claimed she was a German tourist. Vivian Alvarez was deported to the Philippines in a wheelchair in 2001. She was detained following an unexplained accident or possibly an attack, a few months earlier in northern New South Wales. Like Rau, she appeared to have mental health problems. There was some evidence that immigration staff during 2003 and 2004 may have realised that they had mistakenly deported an Australian citizen, but nevertheless Alvarez stayed for these years in a hospice run by nuns in the Philippines, with no communication to the outside world, and at the time of writing she remains in the Philippines while her case is investigated further. In both cases family members had no knowledge of the situation, and regarded their relative as a missing person. Two Australian citizens had been caught up in a policy of preventive detention aimed at illegal migrants or uninvited asylum seekers. A further 200 cases with some similar problems to those of Rau and Alverez were referred to Palmer's successor for subsequent report (Palmer, 2005, p. 193).

It is worth noting that the Palmer Report (Palmer, 2005, p. 195) condemned the use of the term 'reasonable suspicion' by immigration department officials in two ways: first as an unqualified trigger for mandatory detention under Section 189 of the Migration Act (Palmer, 2005, p. 168); and secondly in the context of failing to realise that review of decisions and supervision of staff were essential to any processes leading to either detention or deportation. Further, the report argued that a culture of denial and defensiveness pervaded the immigration department (Palmer, 2005, p. 194), where outcomes were sacrificed to a preoccupation with process. Whereas the report criticised this culture only up to the level of senior executive management (Palmer, 2005, p. 169), it is clear from the Minister's media interviews that the problem went much higher, right up to the level of the Secretary and the responsible ministers. Indeed, the report implies that Government contributed to the problems that faced an unreflective and untrained immigration department staff: 'The speed of change in the immigration detention environment since 2000 has led to policy, procedures and enabling structure being developed on the run' (Palmer, 2005, p. viii).

The release of the Palmer Report posed media management and damage limitation issues for the Howard Government. It is instructive to consider how the Government managed the media in order to minimise damage to its reputation. One tactic was certainly to limit the terms of reference and the powers of the inquiry. The Palmer terms of reference changed twice in the months leading up to the report appearing, and many related issues are still awaiting report. However, it is clear that the terms of reference never included the wider policy settings, or the responsibility of the relevant ministers. Further, the inquiry lacked judicial authority or the capacity to compel witnesses to give evidence. The report expressly refused to seek out individual blame for the abuses of power, preferring instead to reflect on processes that could be improved. With such terms of reference, authority to investigate, and approach to accountability, most of the potential difficulties for the Government were defused. It could then be plausible, in the manner of the response of the British (and also the Australian) Government to the Hutton Report (2004)[4] about alleged spin in intelligence reports in the UK, to claim that as there were no adverse findings about the Government, the policy and the Ministers, this amounted to a vote of support.

In the months before the release of the Palmer Report, all public criticisms (including many demands for increasing the terms of reference of the inquiry to include wider policy issues, and demands for extended judicial powers of investigation) were deflected by the Minister, Senator Amanda Vanstone, by her calling for the inquiry to report before any comment could be made. In the days before the report was tabled in the Federal Parliament (a draft had already been tabled in the Queensland Parliament), three tactics for media risk minimisation were adopted. First, the Prime Minister announced on the *Sunday* Channel 9 television program (discussed in more detail below) that the senior management of the immigration department was about to be changed. Second, the previous minister, and the one in office when the initial mistakes were made, Attorney General Phillip Ruddock, made a public statement that the two women concerned had failed to cooperate with officials, thus implying that the mistakes made were the fault of the victims. Ruddock also defended the Secretary of the Department, Bill Farmer, calling him, 'a very senior foreign affairs official who has served Australia well' (ABC Newsonline, 2005).[5]

Thirdly, the decisions of Cabinet just prior to the release of the report were reported, implying a selective leak to say the least (*Sydney Morning Herald*, 2005).[6] The Government agreed to improve procedures and training in the immigration department, to improve mental health services at detention centres, to strive to improve information systems for checking the identities of missing persons, to re-examine the detention services contract with the private provider and to change the senior staff at the department. Interestingly, the Government also ruled out either forming a Royal Commission to con-tinue the inquiries, or removing the responsible minister. These actions served to take attention away from the report itself, and the decision to remove the Secretary of the immigration department effectively pre-empted some later criticism and drew a bureaucratic line to prevent, or at least hinder, any fur-ther investigation. It did not escape attention that the fallen departmental head had recently been awarded an Order of Australia and was now to be sent to a senior, highly sensitive overseas posting. It could hardly be seen as a demotion or a punishment.

On the day the report was released, a joint press conference was held with Minister Vanstone and the Prime Minister. Critical questions were met with the response that nothing useful could be discussed unless the questioners had read the whole report of over 200 pages that had only just been released. Any detailed criticism as cited in the report was met with the reply that the report also said that the department made good decisions in the great majority of cases. By apologising in general terms to the two women involved, the Prime Minister and the Minister appeared to take some responsibility, but as soon as the questions became specific it was clear that all direct responsibility was placed on officials. No concession was made that the ministers concerned, or the Cabinet or the Prime Minister, had any part in the chain of events. The draconian detention policy was defended. The unintentional outcome in maintaining a draconian departmental culture that was insensitive to the rights of Australian citizens was presented as a lapse by unidentified junior officials that would be put right by a new departmental management team. A new culture in the department was promised under the new head.

Two interviews relating to the Palmer Report, both by veteran commen-tator Laurie Oakes on the Channel 9 television program, *Sunday*, are worth reporting in more detail. On 10 July 2005, before the report was announced, the Prime Minister further defused the newsworthiness of the report. Howard announced that the Secretary, Bill Farmer, was leaving the Department to let others drive the required changes, but he made it clear that he had done a good job in immigration. Further he announced that Andrew Metcalfe, formerly of the immigration department, and a Deputy Secretary in the Department of Prime Minister and Cabinet was to replace Farmer. Howard went on to say that 'We cannot as a nation have it both ways. We expect the immigration department to be there to implement a firm and strong policy tied up with the protection of our borders. But on the other hand, some suggest that we be totally unforgiving if there are errors'.

On 17 July, after the Palmer Report was released, Oakes interviewed Minister Vanstone. The introduction to the interview referred to the wrong-ful detentions of the two women. Vanstone's first comment was to make a correction, saying, 'Mr Palmer actually found that Ms Rau was lawfully detained. What he's critical of – and very critical of – is that the reasonable suspicion which was properly made at the time wasn't sufficiently revisited.' This answer implied that the questioner's reference to wrongful detention was unfair because at least initially it could be justified. It further suggested that critics of the process were uninformed about the correct legal and bureaucratic meaning of the term reasonable suspicion.

At the joint press conference when the report was released, Howard was quoted as defending the *status quo*, saying

> I would not want the opportunity to go by without saying something positive about the department's performance ... It's salutary to note that despite the obvious errors and mistakes that have been made here, public confidence overall in the administration of the Government's migration program remains strong. (cited in *Sydney Morning Herald*, 2005, p. 28)[7]

During the week after the delivery of the Palmer Report, the Prime Minister raised the question of introducing national identity cards, which always produces furious (and distracting) argument, and as he moved on to visit Washington, bombs exploded in London, and the Palmer Report was no longer newsworthy. This short Palmer Report case study shows successful government media management and damage limitation in action. But it is also possible to see the narrative of detention policy, and many other policy areas, as exercises in media management and agenda setting rather than as good policy for its own sake.

The policy of preventive mandatory detention had not been introduced by the Howard government, but it gained much public support by making the policy much tougher, and by encouraging minimal tolerance of border incursions. Former Minister of Immigration, Ruddock, was lauded in the Liberal Party for the part played by his draconian policy in securing electoral victory in 2001. Now it appeared that this same lack of compassion had contributed to a culture in his department that resulted in the illegal deportation of one Australian citizen and the illegal long-term incarceration of another.

Clearly the reforms that led to a harsh and inflexible approach to suspected 'unlawful non-citizens' (the Orwellian description used by the department to describe a migrant unable to present a valid visa) were politically highly successful for Minister Ruddock and the Howard Government, but led directly to the departmental culture depicted in the Palmer Report. However, the wider question of how media control can become too high a priority in government, and how public trust is weakened, deserves a little more discussion.

Accountability and responsibility

Parliamentary democracy is a comparatively rare and highly valued institution. Australia is among a mere handful of states with a relatively successful record of working within a version of this institution for over a century. A long-term, if disputed, aspect of Australian parliamentary democracy is a version of the Westminster system of responsible government, including the old political chestnut of individual ministerial responsibility (Archer, 1980). One can discuss at great length the essential items of this procedure and principle, including how they have been transformed by time and cultural context (Patapan, Wanna and Weller, 2005). However, there would surely be agreement that the institution of parliamentary democracy is weakened if ministers do not tell the truth to Parliament, or if they do not take some personal responsibility for major problems in their own department which they personally caused or that they should have been able to prevent.

There is evidence that the principle of telling the truth to Parliament or resigning has been weakened. Witness the politics of spin over the war in Iraq, the Children Overboard Affair in October 2001, which scapegoated refugees as a divisive but highly successful electoral strategy, and the further evidence of a senior public servant, Mike Scrafton to a Senate Inquiry in 2004 about the extent of the Prime Minister's knowledge about the falsity of the Children Overboard claims at the time of the 2001 election (Maddox, 2005, p. 472). Opening the 2004 electoral campaign, Howard took his critics head on, arguing that the election would be about trust, but at the same time redefining trust as the confidence of the electorate in the capacity of the government to maintain a healthy economy. The ethical basis of trust and legitimacy is swept away by this rhetoric and spin (Uhr, 2004; Archer, 2005). Trust is therefore redefined as an asset for the Government, but this is done at a possible cost to the institutional health of Australian parliamentary democracy.

As argued above, the institution of parliamentary democracy is also weakened if ministers avoid taking some personal responsibility for personally caused or foreseeable and preventable significant problems within their own department. There are many examples that could be cited as breach of this principle in recent years, despite the attempts of the first Howard Government to adhere to this in the Ministerial Code of Conduct (Uhr, 2004, p. 142). The example of the Palmer Report, however, demonstrates a very considerable narrowing in Howard's use of the principle and practice of ministerial responsibility in this context. Howard's use of responsibility is not concerned with constitutional principles or with political ethics. Rather, it is concerned with political realism within a corporate discourse. For Howard, resignation is now required only when a Minister becomes an electoral liability to the Government, and of course this can be countered by successful spin. Blaming minor officials for the failures of political leaders in a carefully orchestrated media management exercise is one part of this spin. This scapegoating is an easier proposition to put within a hierarchical discourse of corporate accountability, rather than in a constitutional, parliamentary democratic discourse where leaders are held accountable to the wider public through the medium of parliament. Political spin, wedge politics and media rhetoric are the stuff of Howard's political populism. The Howard Government has been very successful in media control, and partly as a result of this it has not lost public support. But, as I have argued, this has been at the expense of a diminution of trust in Australian public life. Much of the Australian media is either negligent or complicit in this diminution of trust. At the very least, newspapers and television and radio stations have generally failed to provide a critical and informed check on executive government. The failure of this fourth estate function thus contributes to a wider lack of trust in public life.

Notes

1. For example, it was possibly Karl Rove who coined the phrases 'stay the course' and 'we're not going to cut and run', which have been used by recent governments in the USA, the UK and Australia to deflect criticism of their Iraq occupation policy.
2. G. Kitney, 'Trust Honest John – he's a politician', *Sydney Morning Herald*, 16 January (2004) p. 13.
3. C. Lumby, 'Lies, dammed lies and politics', *The Bulletin with Newsweek*, 26 February (2002), pp. 33–4.
4. Hutton Report, 'Summary of Findings', *Guardian*, 28 January 2004. Retrieved 28 January 2004 from the World Wide Web: http://media.guardian.co.uk/huttoninquiry/story/0,13812,1133168,00.html.
5. ABC, Newsonline, (Sydney, ABC), 7 July 2005. Retrieved 7 July 2005 from the World Wide Web: http://www.abc.net.au/newsitems/s1411571.htm.
6. *Sydney Morning Herald*, 15 July (2005) p. 6.
7. *Sydney Morning Herald*, News Review, 16–7 July (2005) p. 28.

5
Manufacturing Authenticity in a Small Nation: The Case of Independent Local Radio in Wales

David M. Barlow

Unlike in the USA and Australia where commercial radio began in the 1920s, it was not until the early 1970s that it was introduced in Britain (Baron, 1975; Johnson, 1988; Briggs and Burke, 2002). Rather than simply describing the new sector as commercial radio, it became known as Independent Local Radio (ILR). ILR ended a BBC radio monopoly only previously interrupted by offshore pirate stations during the 1960s and intermittent incursions over a number of years from mainland Europe by *Radio Luxembourg* and *Radio Normandie* (Crisell, 1986). With spectrum space for radio in short supply the decision to introduce ILR curtailed the expansion of BBC local radio services that began in Leicester in 1967 (Crisell, 1997),[1] and further delayed the introduction of a specific community radio sector.[2] However, the *quid pro quo* for allocating scarce and publicly owned spectrum space to the new sector required ILR services to broadcast in the 'public interest' (Hooper, 2001a, p. 2). As a result, after nearly 50 years of public service radio defined and delivered by the BBC to predominantly national and regional listeners, communities throughout Britain – rural and urban, small and large – would now have access to an *independent* and *local* radio service. Or would they?

This chapter draws on a variety of sources, including empirical material from a study of local radio in Wales,[3] to examine the rhetoric and reality of ILR. Essentially, the central argument of the chapter is that the ILR era, a period spanning approximately 30 years from the early 1970s to the early 2000s,[4] can be portrayed as one in which radio industry players, regulators and governments contrived – unwittingly or otherwise – to hoodwink an unsuspecting public. Claims that the ILR sector was independent are palpably wrong. Moreover, almost from its inception, leading players in the radio industry agitated to reduce what were, in effect, minimal local responsibilities, while simultaneously seeking to retain the 'local' epithet solely for purposes of public relations (PR). Inevitably, this raises issues of trust in the people, processes and structures associated with the establishment, operation and regulation of a radio sector that was ostensibly provided in the public interest.[5]

This chapter comprises four main sections. Firstly it examines the wider historical context in which ILR was conceived. Secondly it charts the unravelling of behavioural controls relating to programme content. Thirdly it illustrates how these changes impacted on the 'localness' of broadcast output. Fourthly it turns to the broader political, economic – and increasingly global – context to explain how structural changes to ILR were instrumental in removing any remaining vestiges of localism, leading, in effect, to a sector of radio that was independent and local in name only.

False promises

After coming to power at the 1970 general election, Edward Heath's Conservative administration introduced the Sound Broadcasting Act 1972, paving the way for the introduction of ILR (Baron, 1975). As a result, the Independent Broadcasting Authority (IBA) replaced the Independent Television Authority (ITA) and assumed responsibility for the regulation of both radio and television. Sustained lobbying by business groups, such as the Local Radio Association, was instrumental in helping persuade the Conservative administration to introduce ILR. The Conservatives were also encouraged by a belief that commercial radio would provide an economic stimulus similar to that generated by the launch of commercial TV in 1955 (Barnard, 1989). Although 60 ILR services were envisaged in the first instance, the eventual aim was to provide coverage throughout the whole of Britain (Barnard, 1989).

'Local', though, would prove to be illusory. Even before the first ILR licenses were issued there were serious debates about whether the licensing areas should be described as regional rather than local (Gorst, 1971; Local Radio Workshop, 1983). While commercial operators argued for the retention of the latter to describe the service being offered, they also wanted licenses that spanned large population centres in order to ensure the viability of ILR and to maximise its profitability (Baron, 1975; Lewis and Booth, 1989). ILR's adoption of 'independent' also came under scrutiny as the sector was entirely dependent on advertising and would later also be allowed to use commercial sponsorship (Baron, 1975; Barnard, 1989). Not surprisingly, it soon became evident that the struggle to balance public and private interest had failed. Even Carter (1998, p. 10), an enthusiastic advocate of the sector, acknowledges that while the original mission of ILR was to 'provide a service to the public', the sector quickly began to prioritise the needs of advertisers and investors.

In adopting *local* and *independent* as key descriptors of the sector, those championing ILR outmanoeuvred their detractors and competitors. Such worthy discourse enabled an obvious contrast with the BBC, whose claims about being independent of government have always been an easy target for critics and whose localness has only ever been partial (see, for example, Crisell, 1997, p. 143). Furthermore, a new form of radio broadcasting that claimed to be both local and independent would be an obvious attraction for listeners and, with advertising permitted on local radio in Britain for the first time, would be welcomed by business as a new medium for selling goods. However, as the Conservative administration was intent on using ILR to demonstrate how business could work in the public interest, the sector was subject to a range of controls that reflected the traditions of public service broadcasting in Britain (Barnard, 1989). As a result, the IBA encouraged local ownership of stations and public access to them (Independent Broadcasting Authority, 1976). The IBA also established a Local Advisory Committee (LAC) in each licence area in order to convey local views about how a radio service was operating (Baron, 1975; Local Radio Workshop, 1983). While some considered these bodies 'toothless' (Lewis, 1978, p. 71), they did at least provide some degree of local accountability. An early assessment of *Swansea Sound*, Wales's first ILR service which began operations in 1974, refers to a LAC of eight men and two women – three nominated by the Local Authority – all of whom were residents of Swansea and environs (Watkin, 1976, pp. 23–4). Programming schedules were also pre-vetted (Carter, 1998), thereby enabling the IBA to draw up a contract with *Swansea Sound* requiring 10 per cent of its output to be broadcast in Welsh (Baron, 1975). To ensure diversity of ownership, no individuals or companies were allowed to have a majority interest in more than one station (Baron, 1975; Carter, 1998).

By 1977, there were 19 ILR services and by 1983 this had expanded to 43 (Crisell, 1997, p. 187). However, the expectation that ILR would emulate the earlier financial success of commercial TV proved to be incorrect. A number of stations experienced financial difficulties that were due, at least in part, to miscalculations over both expenditure and income (Barnard, 1989). In a later reflection on the sector, Crisell (1997, p. 187) suggests three reasons for the financial problems experienced by ILR: it was launched during a severe economic recession in Britain, there was increasing competition from other media and the sector was over-regulated by the IBA. The economic fragility of ILR led to criticism of the IBA, and a perceived connection between the lack of bumper profits and over-regulation prompted calls for deregulation (Local Radio Workshop, 1983; Philips, 1982, 1983). Those trumpeting such calls included some of the industry's key players and its representative body, the Association of Independent Radio Contractors (AIRC). In essence, AIRC argued that the sector's financial health would only improve if the regulations were amended to allow investment in other radio services, the use of commercial sponsorship and the networking, or syndication, of programming (Barnard, 1989).

In what became a period of intense pressure exerted by AIRC, the IBA's resolve to hold firm varied according to which government was in power.

Barnard (1989) characterises the IBA's response during the 1974–9 period of the Labour government as one in which ILR stations would attract critical attention if they appeared to prioritise commercial motives over community interests. However, a distinctly different approach was adopted from 1979 onwards when a Conservative government under Margaret Thatcher was returned to power. Hereon, the IBA responded to a climate in which 'the political will to safeguard the "community" aspects of ILR were no longer there' (Barnard, 1989, p. 82). Inevitably, a number of demands made by the industry were met. For example, foreign interests were allowed to invest in ILR stations; solely local financial control over ILR stations was waved; licensing areas were expanded to incorporate adjoining centres of population; the use of sponsorship was allowed and the networking of programmes was permitted (Barnard, 1989).

These changes were implemented without any public consultation or discussion in parliament, and the overall impact was to render as unrecognisable the original conception of ILR, transforming it from a 'locally based, locally *dictated* service to a more commercially viable regional system' (Barnard, 1989, p. 84). While Lord Thomson, Chair of the IBA, enthusiastically characterised the authority's new approach to regulation as 'a lighter touch', not all in the ILR sector were celebrating, with one senior executive at *Radio Clyde* predicting that it would result in 'page three broadcasting' – a reference, of course, to the British tabloid *Sun* newspaper (Barnard, 1989, p. 85, 89).

Slippery regulation

AIRC set out its case for deregulation in a *Plan for Radio*, submitted to the Home Office in 1986. The reward was a Green Paper, *Radio: Choices and Opportunities*, published by Margaret Thatcher's Conservative administration in 1987, which the Chair of AIRC described as exceeding his 'wildest hopes' (Barnard, 1989, p. 180). The Green Paper signalled a direction of travel already adopted by the Federal Communications Commission (FCC) in the USA, where behavioural controls relating to programming content had been removed (Fairchild, 1999). The Green Paper paved the way for the Broadcasting Act 1990, which dispensed with the IBA and established a Radio Authority (RA) solely responsible for radio. This both confirmed and accelerated the 'light touch' regime began earlier by the IBA and led to a further dismantling of regulation, a process that continued with passage of the Broadcasting Act 1996 (Carter, 1998).

By 1999, the number of ILR services had increased to 246, with radio proving to be the fastest growing medium for advertisers throughout most of the 1990s (Crisell, 1997; Hendy, 2000). The ILR boom led to an expansion of services in Wales, with the earlier and now established operators (*Swansea Sound*, 1974; *Cardiff Broadcasting Company*, 1980 – later re-badged as *Red Dragon; Marcher Gold/FM*, 1989) being augmented by new services in Aberystwyth (*Radio Ceredigion*), Newtown (*Radio Maldwyn*), Colwyn Bay (*Coast FM*), Ebbw Vale (*Valleys Radio*), Caernarfon (*Champion FM*), Bridgend (*Bridge FM*), Narberth (*Radio Pembrokeshire*) and Carmarthen (*Radio Carmarthenshire*) (Ellis, 2000; Barlow, Mitchell and O'Malley, 2005)[6] (see Figure 5.1).[7]

While the Broadcasting Act 1990 was the catalyst for an expansion in ILR services, the RA helped the sector's profitability by tweaking regulation in favour of operators. With radio spectrum a scarce resource, access came with public obligations. In this context, 'public interest' was deemed by the RA to constitute 'localness' and 'quality' (Hooper, 2001b, p. 4). Both characteristics and their interpretation by the RA warrant some scrutiny. In the

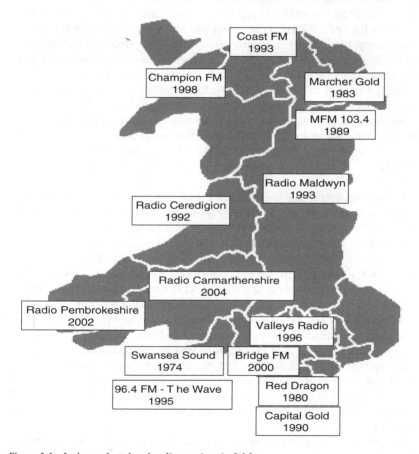

Figure 5.1 Independent local radio services in Wales.

case of localness, guidelines were produced to help determine licence allocations:

> 'Localness' may be reflected in the programming proposals and the impression they convey of the applicants' 'feel' for the local audience. Evidence of 'localness' can take various forms: the make-up and history of the applicant group; its understanding of the local community and market, and its needs; the place of local investors, and local advertisers, in the business plan; and involvement in local life. (Radio Authority, 1999a, p. 5)

Not only were these guidelines extremely vague, they were unlikely to be policed once a licence was allocated. With a staff of 40, the RA were in no position to monitor the output of over 250 ILR stations, and neither was such an approach considered appropriate in a 'light-touch' regulatory environment (Hooper, 2001b, p. 3). There was also little interest on the part of radio companies and the regulator to involve local publics in the licensing and re-licensing process. Locals only became involved in the process if there was more than one applicant for a licence. In such cases licence applications would be lodged in the local library for a limited period of time during which time local people could respond in writing to the RA. However, if no other applicants emerged, the current licensee was automatically re-licensed for another eight years. The licensing period was subsequently extended to 12 years as a result of lobbying by the Commercial Radio Companies Association (CRCA) and active support from the RA (Radio Authority, 2000).[8]

Perhaps not surprisingly, the RA prioritised economic criteria over community, or cultural, concerns when delineating local licence areas (Gorst, 1971; Baron, 1975; Lewis and Booth, 1989). The consequences of this were twofold. Firstly, there were implications for a potential loss of individuality and/or local identity. For example, *Valleys Radio*, based in Ebbw Vale, spans three south Wales valleys with a total population of 445,000. As Davies (1991, p. 110) points out, the licence area – described by the RA as 'Heads of the Valleys' – does 'not comprise a community, whereas the separate valleys do'.

A second and related consequence was the loss of opportunity experienced by population centres that suddenly found themselves incorporated into another's licence area and thereby unable to acquire their own local radio service. For example, *Red Dragon*, based in Cardiff, broadcasts to a swathe of south Wales with a potential population reach of 887,000. Among the population centres 'locked' within *Red Dragon*'s broadcast reach is Newport, Wales's third largest city and a lucrative element in the overall catchment area (Barlow, 2006).

To fulfil the second characteristic of public interest, that of quality, the RA listed a number of requirements. First and foremost, a 'high quality' ILR service was deemed to be one that 'serves its community with commitment, being alive and responsive to events and audience' (Hooper, 2001a, p. 3). Being 'alive and responsive' in Wales was interpreted very differently. Most of Wales' ILR stations rely on syndicated programming to maintain a 24/7/365 schedule. For example, at certain times of the day motorists on the A55 in north Wales can pass through the broadcast reach of three different ILR services (*Champion FM*, *Coast FM* and *MFM 103.4*) and hear the same programme. Similarly, in south Wales, *Red Dragon*, *Capital Gold* and *Valleys Radio* all rely to varying degrees on their respective networks to provide a *local* service. Moreover, a snapshot of services in 2001 indicated that local production/presentation varied from a minimum of four hours (in 24) at two services, to a maximum of 20 hours at another, with an overall average of approximately 13 hours (out of 24) across all Wales' ILR services (Barlow, 2001). However, these figures disguise – or fail to distinguish between – what is live and what is pre-recorded production/presentation, an issue recognised but not actively tackled by the RA, even though its Chair, Richard Hooper, acknowledged that any form of automation 'can hurt the "contract with the listener"' (Hooper, 2000b, p. 4).

Tuning for consumption

A 'Promise of Performance' regime, established by the IBA to specify the types of programmes to be offered by ILR stations, was replaced by the RA with 'Formats' (Radio Authority, 1999b), a much less rigorous and opaque mechanism which simply outlines the broad characteristics of an ILR service. As a result, most services in Wales simply adopted the same moniker, 'music and information stations', providing minimal explanation both about the type of music to be offered and the nature of the material that would constitute information. Irrespective of the genre, music emerges from a pre-determined playlist, leaving the presenter to simply adjust the nature and pace of the patter according to the time of day. This finely tuned format is interrupted intermittently by advertisements, hourly or half-hourly news and weather breaks, and traffic and travel announcements – with some stations sourcing the latter from a central service in Bristol that caters for much of west and south west England and south Wales.[9] News appears in two forms. The first is a pre-packaged format purchased from the Independent Radio News service that targets a UK market but rarely addresses events or issues relating specifically to Wales. This is likely to be coupled with a local news bulletin which, in terms of news values, comprises mostly 'spot news' such as reports of crime, accidents, fires and flooding, but rarely addresses issues relating to local authorities, institutions and other locally constituted groupings (see Hargreaves and Thomas, 2002).[10] Information – whether in the form of news, weather, phone-ins, interviews, discussions, sports reports or community information – features only minimally in a music-dominated format.

While most of the ILR services in Wales list some programming in Welsh, the published schedules of *Red Dragon* and *Capital Gold* (operating in the nation's capital and commanding the largest potential audience reach in Wales) and the south Wales regional service, *Real Radio*, show no such programming. The three most consistent and significant contributors of programming in Welsh have been *Swansea Sound* (Swansea), *Radio Ceredigion* (Aberystwyth) and *Champion FM* (Caernarfon/Bangor). However, the majority of ILR services are reluctant to provide more than a minimal amount of programming in Welsh and even then it is consigned to the least popular times of the broadcast schedule – the 'ghetto slots'. The willingness of the regulator to overlook such a key indicator of localness is evident in the remarks of a chief executive at one ILR station:

> I would suspect that our Welsh output has gone down by over 50 per cent .... But we had a long conversation with [a named person at the RA] and we said to him ... very few people in our area speak Welsh [and] more to the point .... I can't find anyone ... to do the news in Welsh. (Interview, 2002)[11]

Inevitably, the demands of advertisers and investors lead to the marginalisation, or exclusion, of certain segments of a local population. With most ILR services in Wales targeting listeners between the ages of 20 and 50 years, elderly and younger people are barely represented in the schedules, and ethnic minority communities are also unlikely to listen for similar reasons. Furthermore, the increasingly sophisticated market research that informs programme planning is evident in the fact that the larger radio companies now identify a '29 year old woman' as their prime target due to her key role in family decision-making, particularly regarding disposable income. As one presenter commented, 'get her and you get the family'. The music diet is geared to meet *her* needs and it is *she* that presenters must 'imagine' when addressing listeners. One male presenter, reflecting on the station's recent take-over by a large UK radio company, provided some insight into the training being made available, 'this new boss ... has taught us to tap into women's minds' (Interview, 2002).[12] No surprise, then, that most presenters are still men. But where men and women operate jointly as co-presenters, generally at 'breakfast' or at 'drive-time', the latter's responsibility is to retain the interest of male listeners.[13] The planning of communication has also become much more calculated, with the Disc Jockey (DJ) now superseded by the Authentic Radio Personality (ARP). ARPs are expected to make 'links'– about everyday events as well as personal matters – with listeners at certain points during every hour.

Whatever the desired target audience, ILR seeks to create an environment in which consumerism is to the fore. Listeners are imagined and addressed as consumers, and programming is geared to support this goal. Hence, it is 'musical wallpaper' that is preferred, rather than a mix of, for instance, issue-based, speech programming and a variety of musical genres, which genuinely reflect the needs, interests and diversity of a local area. The latter content is rejected because it threatens the prime goal of audience maximisation by detracting from a 'safe' and predictable format designed for selling rather than debating. Such a perspective is reflected in the promotional material generated by ILR services. For example, the mission statement of what was one of the UK's largest multi-service radio groups reads: 'To be the number one provider of local entertainment wherever we are ... by providing compelling radio, for listeners and advertisers alike. Our brand philosophy revolves around the "love of life around here"' (GWR, 2002, p. 4). This prompts recall of Berland's (1993) research on heavily formatted commercial radio in Canada, which she describes as paradoxical because while it appears to be 'omnisciently "local"' it neither emerges from, nor contributes to, local cultures (pp. 111–2).

Local no more

Having persuaded government and regulator to relax some of the behavioural controls related to programming, the next major target for the radio companies was to loosen the structural controls associated with ownership (Hendy, 2004). In particular, this involved lifting the restrictions on the number of radio stations that a single company could own in one area, or market, and relaxing the rules on cross-media ownership. However, while the Broadcasting Acts of 1990 and 1996 did accommodate some demands made by the radio industry, neither piece of legislation fully met the aspirations of its leaders who, yet again, looked to the USA for direction. Here, the Telecommunications Act 1996 removed almost all structural controls over the ownership of local radio services, resulting in a rapid consolidation of ownership (Fairchild, 1999). This has enabled one company, *Clear Channel*, to amass almost 1200 local services in the USA (McChesney, 2002).

Without the opportunity of a similar buying and selling frenzy in the UK – but in readiness for further deregulation which eventually occurred by way of the Communications Act 2003 – the UK radio industry invested in overseas radio markets and in other related media businesses at home, while publishing groups such as the *Guardian Media Group, Associated Media* and *emap*[14] began investing in UK radio (Hendy, 2004). Foreign investment in UK radio, which was initially sanctioned by the IBA, continued throughout the 1990s (Barnard, 1989), indicating an emerging pattern of trans-national ownership (Hendy, 2004). Inevitably, with deregulation firmly established by government, regulator and the radio industry as the preferred direction of travel, the localness of ILR in Wales (and elsewhere) became even more tenuous as ownership consolidated and relocated beyond the immediate locality.

As the buying and selling of local radio stations rarely merits news headlines locally or nationally and because local publics have no formal role in such processes, these transactions tend to occur out of the public gaze.[15]

As a result, the genealogy of local services is not always apparent, and own-ers may be reluctant to provide such information. *Radio Ceredigion* (Aberystwyth) and *Radio Maldwyn* (Newtown) were launched as communi-ty initiatives after much effort and fund-raising by local people. They were also the beneficiaries of significant amounts of public money, but the own-ership of both services has long since passed into private hands. It is prac-tices such as these, along with the 'mopping up' of local stations by large conglomerates that, yet again, exposes the RA's reluctance to intervene on behalf of the public. For example, when issuing ILR licences the RA stressed its intention to ensure that 'external expertise is not merely taking over a local group, and marginalising its members to the extent that "localness" benefits might not be sustained' (Radio Authority, 1999a, p. 5). However, this is precisely what has occurred.

The absence of a local radio service in Newport, a population centre of some 130,000, has its genesis in an earlier decision by the IBA. Under pres-sure from the radio industry as a result of ILR's financial problems, and needing to respond to the market zeal of a new conservative administration, the IBA allowed a fledgling ILR service in Newport, *Gwent Broadcasting*, and the Cardiff-based *Cardiff Broadcasting Company*,[16] to be acquired by *Red Rose Radio* from Preston, who then re-launched the service as *Red Dragon* (Barnard, 1989; Lewis and Booth, 1989).[17] Since that decision more subtle transformations have occurred. For example, at *Bridge FM*, in Bridgend, south Wales, media groups such as *Chrysalis* and *Tindle Radio* were investors from the start, assuming the role of 'stalking horses'. After approximately fifteen months, Tindle gained a controlling influence, prompting the resig-nation of local directors, a turnover in personnel and, according to a num-ber of respondents, a loss of local flavour in the programming. This process has occurred throughout Wales, with large media groups ensuring an invest-ment in all fledgling services with predictable consequences. A review of ILR ownership in Wales illustrates that most of the groups that launched local radio services – whether motivated by profit or community concerns – have been displaced. Moreover, the majority of Wales' ILR services are owned and operated by large media companies, all of which are located beyond its boundaries. The only locally owned services in Wales are *Radio Pembrokeshire* and *Radio Carmarthenshire/Scarlet FM*, both currently operated by the *Radio Pembrokeshire Group* (see Table 5.1).

While multiple ownership of ILR is clearly an attractive option for media companies, consolidated and distant ownership has significant ramifica-tions for a local area. While the syndication of programmes has been a long-standing practice within the radio industry, technological develop-ments facilitate an almost seamless façade of localness whereby local adver-tisements and other soundbites can be inserted with listeners none the wiser (Fairchild, 1999). Consolidated ownership also results in standardised practices across a media group. This was the experience at *Champion FM*

Table 5.1 Ownership of ILR services in Wales

Gcap Media	Ulster TV	Tindle Radio	Murfin Media	Guardian Media Group	Radio Pembrokeshire Group
Marcher Gold	Swansea Sound	Bridge FM	Radio Maldwyn	Real Radio	Radio Pembrokeshire
MFM 103.4	96.4 The Wave	Radio Ceredigion			Radio Carmarthen-shire/Scarlet FM
Coast FM	Valleys Radio				
Champion FM					
Red Dragon					
Capital Gold					

and *Coast FM* after their acquisition by *GWR*. 'Breakfast' was expected to replicate the format established by *GWR* at all its services. When decisions such as these emanate from a distant centre it undermines local autonomy and dissipates a sense of accountability at the local community level. It also becomes less easy for local people to locate and access key decision-makers. Distant owners are also more likely to perceive radio services simply as commodities to be bought and sold as commercial imperatives require, rather than conceiving them as key components of community information infrastructure. Consequently, responses to a local 'sense of place' will be driven by an assessment of the potential financial gains and PR benefits. An obvious example is the sector's enthusiasm for 'good deeds'. Most ILR services are involved in fund-raising for charity or in other 'feel good' projects within their broadcast area. These 'off-air' activities have long been criticised as a substitute for investment in making programmes with and about local communities (Local Radio Workshop, 1983).

Conclusion

The emergence of ILR saw publicly owned radio spectrum allocated to private companies on the basis that broadcast output would respond to and reflect the information needs and musical tastes of local communities throughout Britain. This valuable public resource was hijacked for purposes of profit, leading to listeners being constructed primarily as consumers and subjected to programming that, while presenting as authentically local, was imposed from 'above' rather than emerging organically from a local area. Well away from the public gaze this was enabled by a regulator 'captured' by the industry it was charged with regulating and, as a result, always acquiescent when pressured to ensure that pubic interest remained subservient to private interest. This situation came about as a result of government policies driven by neo-liberal ideology – evident on both sides of the Atlantic – which favoured 'small' government and the delivery of services via market-place mechanisms (Goodwin, 1998; O'Malley, 1994). Consequently, ILR was manufactured to serve economic ends but presented to the public as a radio service that would facilitate local democratic and cultural expression in ways not previously experienced in Britain. The trust necessarily invested by local publics in government, regulator, radio industry and their employees was certainly misplaced – even abused.[18] The implications of this abuse of trust for local publics are that it exposes the failure of regulation to respond to their needs as citizens and consumers, and confirms their lack of power in respect of policy development and implementation.

Notes

1. The Sound Broadcasting Act 1972 outlawed the setting up of BBC local radio stations in any of the 'national regions', of which Wales was one (Davies, 1994, p. 308).
2. It was some 30 years later that a distinct community radio sector – initially known as Access Radio (Stoller, 2001) – was introduced by the Communications Act 2003 (see www.ofcom.org.uk for details).
3. With its own distinct culture and language, Wales is the smallest of the three countries that comprise Britain. It has a population of approximately 3 million people of which around a fifth speak Welsh.
4. In 2004, Ofcom, the regulatory body that superseded the Radio Authority, refers to ILR as 'the former name for local commercial radio in the UK' (Ofcom, 2004, p. 162).
5. Although not within its purview, this chapter also prompts questions about the degree to which the wider public are involved in the formulation and interpretation of communications policy.
6. In November 2005, a 'local commercial radio licence' was awarded for an additional service in the Swansea area. The service is required to begin broadcasting within two years of the licence award (Ofcom, 2005, p. 1).
7. *Real Radio*, based in Radyr, south Wales, is not included here as it is a regional rather than local service.
8. The CRCA replaced AIRC as the body representing the radio industry.
9. When undertaking interviews at one service in south west Wales we were informed that personnel at the 'traffic and travel' service near Bristol needed to be coached on how to pronounce local place names before they went 'to air'.
10. One journalist confirmed that the framing of local news was shaped by the station's 'ideal' target audience, adding that 'if you want current affairs, if you want political stories, you go to *Radio Cymru'* (Interview, 2002). This chimes with Barnard's (1989, p. 78) reference to Piccadilly Radio in Manchester where news bulletins were restricted to two minutes in order to discourage listeners switching stations.

11. This chapter draws on a study of local radio in Wales funded by the Economic and Social Research Council (ESRC: Ref. R000223668) that was jointly conducted by the author and colleagues Dr Philip Mitchell, University of Glamorgan, and Professor Tom O'Malley, University of Wales, Aberystwyth.

12. In order to accomplish the 'tapping in', this interviewee acknowledged being an avid reader of women's magazines. Interviews within stations were conducted with presenters, journalists, marketing/PR staff and, where possible, managers. Group interviews were also conducted with local community organisations.

13. One young woman presenter operating jointly with a male on a breakfast show explained this aspect of her role as 'keep[ing] the white-van guys tuned in' (Interview, 2002).

14. The original name of the company was *East Midlands Allied Press*. This was abbreviated to *emap* in the late 1990s.

15. For example, the merger of the *GWR Group* and *Capital Radio* to form *GCap Media* resulted in 6 of Wales's radio services being under the same ownership. No formal process existed to seek out the views of local publics and neither the Ofcom National Office in Wales nor the Advisory Committee for Wales made any public statements on the merger.

16. Lewis and Booth (1989, pp. 108–14) deal in some detail with the emergence and demise of what was essentially a community radio service.

17. Newport is still without a local radio service.

18. The National Assembly for Wales (NAfW) reach a similar conclusion in its cultural strategy for Wales. After railing at less than satisfactory coverage in rural areas and a limited range of local radio services, generally, the NAfW conclude that Wales has been 'low on the priority list of entrepreneurs and regulators in the broadcasting industry' (National Assembly for Wales, 2002, p. 50).

6
Terrorism and the Microdynamics of Trust

Barry Richards

Fear and protection

Whatever view one takes of the 'terrorist threat' and the 'war on terrorism', it is clear that references to these issues have become central to everyday political discourse (Biernatzki, 2001), where they are the focus of vital questions about trust in fellow citizens, and trust in government to make public space safe. In this chapter, we will be focussing on this second dimension of trust, trust in a government to protect its citizens from deadly attack.

In the relatively stable and secure democracies of the developed world, this kind of trust has not traditionally been at the focus of our conscious attention. We have been more likely to be concerned with how the government is managing the economy and public services, with whether we can trust it with the material and cultural fabric of our society, rather than with whether it will be able to prevent our public space being shattered by bomb blasts. Usually it is only through our fear of crime that we approach an experience of government as directly and physically protective, or have the wish that it should be so, mainly in relation to street crimes and disorders, burglaries and car crime. However in recent years, and, of course, especially since 9/11, we have become more aware of the possibilities of catastrophic terrorist attack. To a degree, there may be more fatalism about this than about mundane crime. While there are certain areas such as airport security where authorities may be held to account, and found to be deficient, there is widespread belief that terrorists are very hard to stop.

Still, one feature of the contemporary world is the tendency to see all problems as preventable or remediable, and all risks as manageable, and to take government to be the ultimate authority responsible for prevention. If, as seems likely, anxieties about terrorist threats intensify, we are likely to see an awareness of the protective responsibilities of government coming increasingly into the public mind, and expectations and demands for protection to be stepped up. This more primordial component of national government might then feature as a dominant issue in electoral politics, in the way that handling of the economy or of welfare and education typically does now. The extent to which citizens can *realistically* expect government to protect them against terrorist attack is largely beyond the scope of this chapter, which will focus on more psychological dimensions of trust in citizen–government–media relationships, beginning with the fact of public anxiety about terrorism.

In both the UK and the USA, terrorism is now well established on the inventory of things people are worried about. It goes up and down the rank order, depending on fluctuations in perceived levels of terrorist threat, and on variations in the urgency of other issues. But it has for some years usually been in the top five of public concerns on both sides of the Atlantic. In MORI's long-running series of polls on what people see as the most important issues facing Britain today, defence/foreign affairs/international terrorism has since 9/11 been near the top of the ratings. In the most recent data (MORI, 2006), it is placed third (named by 29 per cent of respondents), after the National Health Service (37 per cent) and race/immigration/asylum issues (30 per cent). Also, the last of these topics draws some of its salience from fears about terrorists. Crime and education typically complete the top five of this list, with frequent changes of rank order among them. Usually all other issues are some way behind. At the time of writing in February 2006, terrorism stands fourth in the USA list of 'the most important problems facing the country today'. With 9 per cent of nominations it stands behind Iraq (22 per cent), poor leadership and the economy in general, both on 10 per cent (Gallup, 2006a). A different poll in January 2006 had also put it fourth, behind Iraq, the economy and health care (Roper Center, 2006a). In January 2005, it had topped a poll of issues for the President to put at the top of his agenda (Roper Center, 2005).

There are behavioural changes, actual and potential, associated with this anxiety. For example, while very few people have actually cancelled holiday plans, 39 per cent of Londoners reported that they had stopped bringing their children into Central London some months after the 7/7 attacks in 2005,[1] and over half were prepared to pay more than £100 per annum in increased taxes to resource the police better in their fight against terrorism (MORI, 2005b). In February 2003, 60 per cent of Americans had stockpiled food and water, while 46 per cent had designated 'safe rooms' in their homes to use in the event of an attack. These numbers had declined a year later, to 41 per cent and 38 per cent, respectively, but early 2004 was when peoples' worries about themselves or a family member being direct victims of terrorism had declined in the USA to their lowest level since 9/11. By January 2006, however they had risen again such that 43 per cent were reporting significant worry, as high a number as in October 2001 (Gallup, 2006b).

One very important behavioural correlate of this high anxiety is that people are willing to give support to a wide range of counter-terrorism measures.

Strong majorities have been recorded in the UK (though not admittedly among its Muslim communities) in support of prioritising anti-terrorism over civil liberties, and of measures such as deporting radicals to countries that may use torture, detaining terror suspects for up to three months, a provision the government has been unable to secure Parliamentary approval for (ICM, 2005), increasing stop and search powers, and introducing Identity (ID) Cards (Populus, 2005). Americans are more cautious about stop and search, but would similarly welcome national ID cards, and put up with intensive security on all mass transit systems (Gallup, 2006b). En masse, publics in both the UK and the USA would support far more stringent and intrusive domestic counter-terrorism measures than their governments have so far committed to.

Nonetheless American citizens have substantial confidence in their government to protect them from future attacks, and optimism about the war on terrorism remains high. In April 2004, 78 per cent had a 'great deal' or a 'fair amount' of such confidence, while in January 2006, 64 per cent still reported that they had some such confidence in the Bush administration (Gallup, 2006b). The deepening crisis in Iraq[2] probably accounts for the drop between these two dates, but had clearly not eroded the majority base of trust in government to protect against and to vanquish terror. Oddly, however, in March 2004, a majority (53 per cent) also thought that the government was covering up intelligence failures before 9/11, and as many as 42 per cent (and rising) apportioned blame to the Bush administration for the disaster (Gallup, 2006b). Moreover in a survey conducted in January 2006, 80 per cent of respondents were of the view that another large-scale terrorist attack on the USA producing heavy casualties was likely in the near future (Roper Center, 2006b), so the confidence in government does not, paradoxically, extend to a belief in its capacity to protect.

The British public is also more satisfied than not with its government's handling of the terror threat (ICM/News of the World, March 2004; MORI, 2005b). Yet 87 per cent think another attack is likely to happen (MORI, 2005a), and there is a strong feeling that the government's prosecution of war in Iraq has increased the chances of terrorist attacks on the UK (72 per cent think there is a contribution from the UK's Iraq involvement – MORI, 2005c). It is especially difficult in the UK at present to discuss confidence in the government's anti-terrorist strategy – or indeed confidence in any aspect of government – without taking the Iraq War into account. Although Tony Blair's government has since won another election victory, and the increasing unpopularity of the war has therefore not dominated the political landscape, it seems likely that a deep fault line has been created between on the one side those who fundamentally believed the military action to be foolhardy or criminal, and on the other those with pro-invasion or more complex or mixed positions, and that British political discourse will be fractured around that line for some time to come. A clear retrospective view of how the 2003 Iraq action and events associated with it (the Gilligan and Kelly affairs especially[3]) impacted on trust and suspicion in UK politics is not yet available, and may be hard to achieve now that additional issues to do with Islamist jihadism in the UK have since July 2005 become prominent.

We can however draw one strong conclusion from the profiles of public opinion illustrated above (and it should be noted that the few examples which have been given are drawn from and are typical of a large body of polling data). This is that substantial confidence in governments to deal with terrorism, and a wish to give them much stronger powers to do so, coexist with high levels of suspicion and blame in relation to their competence and at times their integrity as protectors of their peoples. There is a high degree of ambivalence, of trust and suspicion in contradictory co-existence.

In order to trust a government to protect its people against attack, we must trust its capacity to perceive and understand the source of the attack. This is often a matter of trust in the competence of the government, rather than trust in its moral integrity, although the two cannot always be cleanly separated, and there is always a moral dimension. In relation to the Iraq War, for example, the competence of the intelligence arm of government has been a major issue for inquiry and debate. This debate, however, overlaps with debates about the morality of government, not least in relation to its use of the intelligence it received. So there are interlinked debates about competence and probity, and this is also the case in relation to terrorism.

To put it more simply, using the analogy of government as parent: the child will feel better protected by its parent if it can believe that the parent understands the world and the nature of the threats it poses. The child will also more readily develop the capacity to manage and contain its anxieties if it can absorb from its parent a trustworthy picture of the world, one that is realistic, and that does not over- or under-estimate the nature of the threats in it. Likewise as citizens we learn not to trust someone whose understanding we sense to be limited or flawed, and we can trust our own responses more if we are guided in our understanding of the world by a government whose perceptions we can trust.

When viewed in this light, what the government tells us about al-Qaida and other terrorist threats becomes an important matter. In the analysis that follows, we will explore what we are told about such threats, not so much in terms of what facts we might be given about them but in terms of how we are encouraged to conceptualise the nature of these threats, to understand the motives that lie behind them and therefore to understand what kind of response they should best meet. Although not something which can be simply judged against a clear body of evidence, this is a question of truthfulness, in that it involves an honesty and open-mindedness about a very complex problem, so once again competence and integrity are blended.

The media discourse of terrorism

The rest of this chapter will examine the media discourse of terrorism, with a focus on the understandings of terrorism propagated by political leaders – and also, inevitably, by the mass media – and the extent to which these are *competent* analyses of the nature of the threat. While we will be unable to demonstrate direct causal links between the content of the media discourse and the ambivalence towards government which polling data demonstrate, we know that media content plays a crucial role in the dynamics of public opinion, giving shape, focus and confirmatory expression to powerful forces of public feeling.

We will be asking what models are on offer in the media of the nature of the terrorist threat, and whether they give an adequate basis for understanding it. We will look at those models offered by politicians, at least as reported in the media, and those offered by the media themselves, in editorials, opinion columns and so on. The credibility of these models among the public, and the extent to which they are taken up, would require another study of public attitudes. Here we will get as far as drawing some conclusions from an analysis of media content. These are conclusions about the nature and adequacy of models of terrorism on offer, and about what these imply for the capacity of the government to inspire public trust in its ability to deal as effectively as possible with terrorism.

This small study began with the hypothesis that two models of contemporary terrorism (with partly different effects on the public's readiness to trust) are predominant in media references to terrorism. One is of an absolute and largely incomprehensible force (the Absolute Model), the other is of a reactive and comprehensible phenomenon (the Reactive Model). In the first, terrorism is seen as something requiring little or no explanation. It is an absolute force for destruction, which brooks no compromise, to which the only adequate response is its eradication. It is well illustrated in many statements by President Bush and others in the US administration, as well as by Prime Minister Blair and other UK politicians. In the second, terrorism is a rational response to overwhelming oppression and hopelessness. It is an understandable if tragic choice by people who have few or no better alternatives. This model is typified by a statement in 2004 by the then UK Liberal Democrat Member of Parliament (MP), Jenny Tonge, who said that she could imagine herself becoming a suicide bomber if she were a Palestinian (Happold, 2004).[4]

Everyday observation of British news reporting, and then some pilot work with a UK newspaper database, led to the hypothesis that these were the dominant models of terrorism. Two previous studies also pointed in a similar direction. One of the first systematic studies of the media discourse of terrorism was by Schlesinger, Murdock and Elliott (1983). In their analysis of UK television news in 1981–2, they identified an 'official' way of talking about terrorism, which tended to essentialise it as illegitimate and criminal. The 'alternative' way saw the term 'terrorism' itself as propaganda; it recoded 'international terrorism' as explicable frustration and legitimate aspiration. These are close to the Absolute and Reactive models, respectively. Schlesinger et al. also described an 'oppositional' perspective, fully supportive of terrorism, and a 'populist' one, demanding a no-holds-barred war on terrorists. Much more recently Norris, Kern and Just (2003) have described the 'War on Terror' frame, which can be equated with our Absolute Model, as the dominant media treatment of the terrorism issue in the USA.

The results of the small-scale but systematic UK study conducted here offer considerable support for the two-models hypothesis, although with an important modification. The study was of references to terrorism and terrorists in the British national press in two sampling periods in 2003. The databases used were *Infotrac* and *News UK*, covering all national daily and Sunday titles (except those titles carrying relatively little 'news' – the *Daily* and *Sunday Star*, the *Sunday Sport*). The sample therefore included titles from across the mainstream spectrum of political and proprietary affiliations, and from all three major 'levels' ('tabloid', 'mid-market' and 'quality') of the UK newspaper market. The search terms were terror, terrorism, terrorist, terrorists, al-Qaeda and al-Qaida. We could also have included bin Laden, and references to other terrorist groups, Islamic and non-Islamic, but decided to focus on global Islamic terror as the leading contemporary issue, and judged that the list of terms used would be sufficient to capture a majority of references to it in these sampling periods. Two 1-week periods were chosen, February 12–18 and November 20–6. The first of these began with the alert that led to troops and tanks being deployed at Heathrow Airport; the second with the bombing of the British consulate and the HSBC bank in Istanbul. They were therefore both periods of high anxiety in which debate about terrorism and how to respond to it was at peak levels, although there are important differences in that, in February, there was some threat to targets in Britain but no attack, while in November there had just been bloody attacks on British targets overseas.

These sampling periods produced several hundred examples of items (such as reports, articles and leaders) in which there was at least one use of one of the search terms. This amounted in total to over a thousand appearances of individual terms. Recording and coding were undertaken of any sentence containing such an appearance where there was some reference to the nature, origins or causes of terrorism.

Such statements are usually either quotes from or are attributed directly to a politician or other public figure, or are expressions of opinion by journalist, columnist or editor or contributor to the Letters page. The statements which comprise the corpus of selected cases are usually brief; one rarely finds extended analyses of the terrorism phenomenon even in the 'broadsheet' press. They are often taken from political speeches or interviews, and so typically have a 'soundbite' quality, in the sense that they have been crafted to convey a key message in a very condensed and powerful way. The statements of media professionals too have been subjected to rigorous editing procedures designed to strip them down to the most economical and succinct form. The sample is therefore largely composed of very compressed messages (Richards, 2000), which in an age of information overload and clutter are of increasing importance. We can call them 'micromessages', and see them as condensations of meaning into small information spaces. They may sometimes seem simplistic or uninformative, but individually and cumulatively they can have major impact. Like the headline and the advertising slogan, they are targeted to colonise key locations in our mental maps of the world.

The description of this study as being one of the 'microdynamics' of trust is intended to convey that trust is continually maintained, or eroded, through the communication and reception of such micromessages. While there may be particularly momentous public events which have substantial impact on levels of trust, these occur in the context of a continuous flow of small, compressed messages. The data collected confirm that in this process in the UK at present there are two models of terrorism which predominate. We can therefore talk about these models as the major ones in the contemporary media discourse of terrorism.

The first of these is that referred to previously as the Absolute Model. This offers an understanding of terrorism as an *absolute* force, which need not be analysed but which must be met with an equally absolute determination and force to defeat it – which means basically eradicating it by force, the 'war on terror' scenario. It sometimes has explicit links to notions of disease, or of evil (Alford, 1997). Its deployment is often linked to affirmations of determination to fight and to overcome the threat (Sparks, 2003). An example is from Tony Blair at a press conference in November 2003: 'to meet their will to inflict terror with a greater will to defeat it ... to rid our world of this evil once and for all' (Guardian Unlimited, 2003).[5] Another is George Bush's statement at the same press conference: 'We see their utter contempt for innocent life. They hate freedom, they hate free nations.'

The second model of the hypothesis, the Jenny Tonge, 'I'd do it myself' or Reactive Model, has not been found in the media discourse with the same frequency as the Absolute Model. Although passionately stated in a few places – for instance, 'I know the depth of pain in me that can seek revenge' (Berry, 2003)[6] – it has so far been rarely encountered as such. What is present with highest overall frequency is what can be called the Retaliation Model, in which terrorism is seen as largely if not entirely *reactive*, but in the specific sense of occurring in *retaliatory* response to perceived attacks on the Islamic world. Examples include 'Yet if we do [invade Iraq], we will be exposed to the most deadly assault we have faced for 60 years' (Voice of the Daily Mirror, 2003)[7] and 'If you make war on a Muslim country you expect a response' (Tony Benn, cited in Prince, 2003).[8] In the sample periods here, this always refers to the pending or recent invasion of Iraq, although of course the Israel–Palestine situation is widely believed to be the most important underlying provocation. The Retaliation Model is commonly deployed in connection with opposition to the Iraq war, and can be seen as a variant of the Reactive Model, while the Absolute Model tends to be linked to support for the war.

Also, there is a substantial occurrence of another model that can be called the Inevitability Model. This is not intrinsically about the causes of terrorism but is a comment on its nature: it sees it as an unstoppable force, and destructive attacks are therefore *inevitable*, at least until it is eradicated or its causes removed. For example, 'Blair tells MPs it is "inevitable" that al Qaeda will try to attack Britain' (Hughes, 2003).[9] This is not really a 'model' in the sense that the Absolute and Reactive models are, and it does not offer a full 'theory' of terrorism. In fact it is compatible with both the Absolute and Reactive models. Finally there are a few other models or part-models, which occur infrequently, for example, one which links terrorism to migration and asylum, and sees the increasing number of asylum seekers as a cause of terrorism (because terrorists are in their number).

The data are summarised in Table 6.1, where the rows represent different sources of statements and the columns are the different 'models' expressed in the statements. The basic unit of analysis was the sentence, and the figures therefore show the row percentages, that is, the percentage of sentences from each source giving expression to each type of model. The two sampling periods are combined as there were no significant differences between them. Different models were rarely co-present in the same news items, and never in the same sentence.

There are complex relationships between these models. They are not logically exclusive; for example, the Inevitability Model may, as noted, be linked with any of the others, though it is most frequently and clearly associated with the Absolute Model. The original hypothesis about the importance of the Reactive Model can be seen to be supported, in that the Retaliation

Table 6.1   Percentage frequencies of different models of terrorism[10]

	Absolute Model	Reactive Model	Retaliation Model	Inevitability Model	Other models
Government politician	72	0	4	24	0
Other politician	40	10	40	0	10
Media comment	33	0	49	10	8
Other (expert, public, ...)	3	16	56	3	22

Source: Various UK newspapers, 2003.

Model is a variant on this. While it does not necessarily represent the terrorist as a 'reasonable' actor taking the only remaining option for political protest, it does basically locate the terrorist act in a rationally comprehensible cause-and-effect sequence, implying that if the proximate cause were removed the threat would disappear. The typical expressions of this model are however not couched in a language of empathy with the terrorist, nor one of calm analysis of the global politics of Islam, but are uttered in a spirit of foreboding, of often angry, helpless fear. This both matches and complements the quality of angry resolution, righteous and unreflective, which is found in the Absolute Model. It is as if this model says 'We are going to get them', while the Retaliation Model says 'They are going to get us', which makes it powerful raw material for what is called a 'politics of fear' (for instance, see Altheide, 2003).

Trust and discourses of terrorism

What has all this got to do with trust? It was argued earlier that trust in government to defend us against terrorist attack must depend on those in power appearing to understand the nature of the threat, and being able to convey to us an understanding of it which we can trust. Do any of these models represent competent and trustworthy analyses of the nature of the threat? It is necessary here to move beyond the strictly academic exercise of identifying the dominant features of the discourse, and to suggest that they do not. On the contrary, each microencounter with one of them – a line read in a newspaper – adds to the microdynamics of the process whereby we find ourselves disabled in thinking about terrorism. Why are these models inadequate? It is because they are high on rhetoric, low (often zero) on analysis and evidence. Terrorism is neither the expression of an absolute inhuman evil (Absolute Model), nor the expression of an ordinary frustration with which we can all identify (Reactive Model), nor is it the embodiment of an explosive force which at all costs must not be provoked (Retaliation Model). It may at times involve elements of phenomena akin to any or all of these, but cannot be reduced to any one of them.

The Absolute Model (and its Inevitability corollary) denies the functionality, the history and the politics which underpin terrorism, and the dynamic of global inequalities and confrontations from which it issues. Its reiterations of resolution to prevail are derived from domestic propaganda in conventional warfare, and may be ill designed to restore morale in the long, invisible and obscure 'war on terror'. It posits us in the West as ultimately triumphant, although at the same time some of its proclaimers insist that we must inevitably suffer further death and destruction from terrorists. Moreover it gives us no reason to understand why we will triumph, other than to see it as the victory of good over evil, of the sanctified might and determination of our leaders, soldiers and spies.

The Reactive Model (which is probably more common in influential left-liberal circles than in the data here) denies the depth and intractability of the hatred, and the murderous quality to the anger. It ignores the fundamentalist outlook which rationalises and sustains the terror, not least now increasingly through the belief in martyrdom.

The Retaliation Model also, albeit in a different way, blocks out the historical depth and psychic complexity of the problem. It does this not so much by denial but simply by ignoring these dimensions: it is fixed solely on the consequences to Britain of doing something which provokes a terrorist attack. It offers a counsel of fear, implying if not stating that if a course of action would do this, then it should be avoided, irrespective of any other moral or political considerations, and so is open to the obvious charge of cowardice.

All models are at best one-dimensional, and are unable to contribute helpfully to the realistic management of fear and the building of trust among the domestic public. While each model has its passionate adherents, none is sufficiently realistic and rounded to inspire the long-term trust of the public at large.

The overall discourse on terror constituted in the media, in this case by these two predominant models, will have effects internationally on the perpetrators of terror and their direct supporters as well as on the national publics who are the primary consumers of the discourse (Nossek, 1985). The argument that it may have an influence in provoking further attacks is being developed elsewhere (Richards, 2007). Here, it is notable that the ambivalence towards government to be found in public opinion (the juxtaposition there of confidence and suspicion) is matched by an ambivalence towards terrorism in the media discourse. It seems that in both the UK and the USA the overall national conversation about terrorism, for which media content is necessarily the major vehicle and of which public opinion is a major, if simplified, expression, is incapable of generating complex accounts of the nature of terrorism and of how we should respond to it. We are either unthinkingly trusting our governments to deal with this incomprehensible threat, or we are simplistically blaming them for having produced the threat by complicity in geopolitical iniquities.

There are predictable differences between the four groups of contributors to media discourse distinguished here. Government politicians stick narrowly to the Absolute Model. Despite the cross-party consensus on terrorism in the UK, opposition politicians are freer to give expression to other models, especially the Retaliation one, alongside the Absolute one. Media commentators also tread that path, while among the contributions members of the public whose voices are chosen to be heard in mediaspace, the Absolute Model is almost absent while the Reactive, Others and especially Retaliation are favoured.

Overall, however, the clearest feature of the media content sampled here is the absence of much curiosity and complexity of thought, and of much evidence, about the nature and origins of terrorism. There are perhaps some signs, since these sampling periods, that the 2005 London bombings have deepened reflection and inquiry in the UK into the roots of jihadism. It is likely though that the major impact of mass-mediated micromessaging on the dynamics of trust and suspicion around terrorism is still either to reproduce a necessarily brittle confidence, or to feed suspicion of leaders (and leader-writers) whose views of the world seem disconcertingly simple and one-dimensional.

Notes

1. On 7 July 2005 four suicide bombers caused explosions on public transport in Central London; over 50 people were killed and hundreds injured.
2. By early 2006 it was becoming common for the post-invasion situation in Iraq to be described as approaching civil war; hopes that the security situation might improve were fading and USA casualty figures were still rising.
3. Andrew Gilligan is a journalist who in May 2003 claimed on BBC radio that the government had 'sexed up' its dossier on Iraq's alleged Weapons of Mass Destruction; his stated source, government scientist Dr David Kelly, committed suicide later that year after his identity was revealed. While an official report published in January 2004 (Department for Constitutional Affairs, 2004) exonerated the government of blame in relation to both the dossier contents and Kelly's suicide, assumptions that the government, and especially the Prime Minister, were culpable in various ways have become axiomatic in much media commentary (see Lloyd, 2004).
4. T. Happold and agencies, 'Tonge Sacked over Bombing Comments', (2004). Retrieved 26 May 2006 from the World Wide Web: http://politics.guardian.co.uk/libdems/story/0,9061,1129744,00.html.
5. Guardian Unlimited, 'Transcript: The Bush-Blair Press Conference', (2003). Retrieved 26 May 2006 from the World Wide Web: http://politics.guardian.co.uk/iraq/story/0,12956,1089630,00.html.
6. J. Berry, Letter: 'Why I Shall be Marching', *The Guardian*, 14 February, (2003) p. 23.
7. Voice of the Daily Mirror, 'Why we're the target of terrorists', *Daily Mirror*, 12 February (2003) p. 6.
8. R. Prince, 'Benn Blasts Blair "Hype"', *Daily Mirror*, 14 February (2003) p. 6.
9. D. Hughes, 'Battle over Bin Laden tape', *Daily Mail*, 13 February (2003) p. 4.
10. The numbers in each cell are the percentages of the total in each row, that is, the percentages within each source category (of the total number of recorded cases) expressing each model.

7
Risk, Advice and Trust: How Service Journalism Fails Its Audience

Jeremy Collins

This chapter examines a particular aspect of British news coverage of two 'food scares' – BSE/vCJD[1] (also known as 'mad cow disease') and salmonella infection in eggs. It focuses on the sub-section of news that can be described as 'service journalism' in order to examine the possibility that such coverage might provide progressive alternative perspectives to those which are part of a dominant 'official' discourse. In terms of the themes of this collection, the question is whether audiences are justified in putting their trust in service journalism; does it address the 'problems of everyday life' (in this case, food scares) as (sub-) political issues demanding collective, and therefore political forms of response, or as individualised problems requiring only consumption-based responses; does it address audiences primarily as citizens, or as consumers? In particular, I want to examine the arguments of Eide and Knight (1999) who suggest that despite the tendency of service journalism to 'individualize problems', it is 'amenable to politicisation' due to its focus on the same kinds of issues that are dealt with by the social movements and pressure groups which drive 'subpolitics' (1999, p. 525; see also Beck, 1994, pp. 22–3). They theorise their arguments via Habermasian notions of the public sphere (Habermas, 1989) and Ulrich Beck's risk society thesis (1992b; 2000) and suggest a hybrid social identity in which citizen, consumer and client roles interact. I would also like to compare this conception (of a particular subcategory of journalistic practice) with the 'public journalism' movement in the USA, where a wider reconstruction of journalistic activity has been advocated. While both of these understandings of journalism are intended to make connections between the news (and news production organisations) and their audiences (and thereby foster a renewed sense of trust in the media), neither, I would argue, fully engages with the interests of their audience(s).

Food scares and social rationality

My research into British news coverage of BSE and salmonella in eggs (Collins, 1999) suggests that, albeit in a limited way, alternative perspectives on these topics emerged due to the efforts of various non-official source organisations, and the divisions within dominant source groups (specifically, the various government departments) involved.

The food scare news coverage provides evidence that news stories can to some extent escape the definitional constraints that the 'official' sources of government and industry attempt to impose. Thus, the exhortations during the early part of the BSE scare in the UK, that beef was no threat to human health failed in many respects to suppress what might be regarded as 'scare stories' (in the most negative, 'irrational' sense).[2] Of course, it might also be argued that while such stories are antagonistic towards specific government policies or announcements, or towards particular industrial practices, they do not represent a challenge to the wider hegemony-reinforcing definitional perspectives surrounding state authority and the relative importance of the food industry. The establishment of the Food Standards Agency in 2000, with a mandate to protect public health and with a separate regulatory role (which the Ministry of Agriculture Food and Fisheries [MAFF] had previously exercised alongside its promotional function) with regard to food production, may be seen as a more concrete example of the effects of (among other things) alternative perspectives in the news media concerning food scares, and thus may illustrate the counter-hegemonic potential of such oppositional strategies. This bureaucratic reorganisation may nevertheless still be seen as *containing* rather than acceding to the oppositional view.[3]

From a Habermasian perspective, the ubiquitous distorting effects of instrumental-purposive rationality (Habermas, 1971) represent a broad, cultural problem affecting modern industrial societies; in terms of the news coverage of food scares, these effects find expression in news accounts which accept as valid only that knowledge produced through the application of scientific principles (generally presented by accredited, official sources), and dismiss or minimise those understandings which are based on lay, contextualised or social knowledges, and which are considered to be 'irrational' (Frankel, Davison and Smith, 1991; Brown, 1992; Wynne, 1996, pp. 66–7).

It is perhaps worth making a further point concerning the extent to which counter-hegemonic tendencies can be ascribed to certain elements within news coverage of food scares, which relates to the notion of consumerism. Much criticism of modern political discourse concerns the way in which members of the public are addressed as consumers rather than as citizens via the communicative techniques of advertising and public relations, and the effects this might have with regards to the 'quality' of political debate and its further effects on the democratic process more generally (for instance,

Davis, 2002; Franklin, 2004). I do not intend to address the issues surrounding the 'politics of consumerism' (Garnham, 1995, p. 247) directly here; nevertheless it could be argued that the notion of consumerist discourse can be employed in relation to the counter-hegemonic force of social rationality. It is quite possible that the coverage of food scares can in some sense be understood as illustrating the negative aspects of this consumerism, in that it arguably emphasises a single issue to which the response is assumed to be a simple 'yes' or 'no', 'dangerous' or 'safe', with little discussion of the complexities of balancing various priorities. Thus the audience is addressed not as a public within a social context, but as a group of private individuals. However, the ways in which such arguments can be framed hint at a particular position that Habermas and Beck in particular might reject. In discussing the politics of consumerism for instance, Garnham argues that 'Politicians relate to potential voters not as rational beings concerned for the public good, but [...] as creatures of passing and largely irrational appetite' (Garnham, 1995, p. 247). By appealing to rationality, such positions arguably imply that consumerism is necessarily a 'dead-end' of irrationality and narrow individualism. In contrast to this, the risk society thesis suggests that the consumerist arguments surrounding food scares provided a space in which, *potentially* at least, a wider context that included a form of social rationality could develop (Beck, 1992b, pp. 29–30; 1996, p. 33). In this way media audiences were offered a more complex and socially situated understanding of an issue that was otherwise portrayed in a narrow, scientifically 'rational' way. I would therefore argue that news concerning issues such as food scares can offer perspectives which can be characterised as 'consumerist' without necessarily engendering the negative aspects of the 'politics of consumerism'.

The potentially positive aspects of what might be called 'consumer perspectives' are also discussed by Eide and Knight (1999) in their analysis of what they characterise as 'service journalism'.

Service journalism

The coverage of food scares can be analysed in a number of ways, but one potentially productive distinction is between 'conventional' news forms which highlight the arenas of classical political debate and those articles which offer advice, help and background information as a service to readers. Eide and Knight (1999) have theorised service journalism via the theory of the public sphere and reflexive modernity, and also place it in the context of Beck's risk society thesis (1992b). They suggest that the way in which newspapers and other media respond to, comment on, and offer advice regarding 'the everyday concerns of their audiences' represents a 'growing role' of modern journalism (Eide and Knight, 1999, p. 526). This growth is due, in part, to the apparent lack of trust in, and resistance towards, 'established forms of professional expertise' (Eide and Knight, 1999, p. 526) which are often represented in news coverage of food scares and other kinds of health risk. They also posit for service journalism in particular the potential, at least, for it to engage in and promote progressive forms of discourse:

> Service journalism, we argue, represents a hybrid social identity – part citizen, part consumer, part client – that is oriented to resolving the problems of everyday life in a way that can combine individualistic and collective, political forms of response (Eide and Knight, 1999, p. 525).

Eide and Knight's focus on service journalism (which they also link directly with popular and 'tabloid' journalistic forms) is, I would argue, only of value if 'normal' or 'traditional' journalism is somehow failing to provide a valid analysis of political problems because it is 'colonised' by systems thinking.[4] If this is the case, then service journalism may at least provide some respite from this in its treatment of the 'problems of everyday life'. Such problems occur in the immediate sphere of individual social action – that is, in the realm of the lifeworld; if service journalism addresses these issues by offering a politicised, collectivised analysis leading to progressive solutions, then it would indeed be a valuable counter to the systems based approach found in 'traditional' news forms.

Food scares as service journalism

In order to provide some empirical data, and to test Eide and Knight's contention about the progressive potential of service journalism, the coverage of two examples of food scares in Britain (newspaper coverage of the emergence of BSE/vCJD from the mid-1980s onwards, and of the infection of eggs with salmonella bacteria in 1988–9) was examined for items which could be argued to represent different examples of service journalism. These service journalism articles were selected from three sources: a comprehensive collection of news articles on BSE/vCJD derived from an online news article database (FT Profile) covering the period 1988–96; a comprehensive database of detailed notes on the salmonella-in-eggs newspaper coverage from 1988–9; and an additional (and unsystematic) collection of cuttings from later periods on both topics. A total of 30 articles were selected as representing the different kinds of news articles that could nevertheless be understood as representing a form of service journalism. These range from those that are close to the traditional news forms and emphasise system issues (usually focused on the political 'fallout' from the topics concerned) but which also offer some hint of advice to the reader, to those that are explicitly addressing their audiences with advice about how to avoid the particular risk involved. The articles break down into a set of six categories (A–F) along this continuum; the following discussion provides examples for each category.

A – Implicit advice

News items in this category are very similar to those food scare articles which cannot be considered to be 'service journalism', as they take as their main theme the dealings of politicians, the economic problems of the food industries concerned, and the general scientific debates which accompany food scares. The difference is that in some sense an implicit warning or advisory element can be discerned in these articles that may be missing in the general news coverage. An illustrative extract follows below:

Gummer fights Mad cow boycott on British beef

FARMS Minister John Gummer is today poised to take the Germans to court if they do not lift their beef blockade. He flew into Brussels last night promising a 'bit of a battle' over the boycott of British meat because of 'mad cow' disease. But his tough stand was undermined by his own chief vet who said the risk to humans could not be ruled out. (Wilenius, 1990)[5]

This article is ostensibly set primarily in the world of international political diplomacy, and much of the rest of its 200 words concerns the legal and diplomatic relationships between Britain, Germany and the European Commission. The final two sentences return to a quote from the UK's Chief Veterinary Officer who suggests that the long incubation period of BSE makes it difficult to predict the risk to humans:

However, Keith Meldrum, head of the Agriculture Ministry's veterinary service, said: 'I cannot say that there is no risk to man from BSE. It is too early.'

'We have only had this disease in this country for three years, and the incubation period in man in these cases is very long indeed.' (Wilenius, 1990)[6]

It is in this element that we might suggest an implicit warning is being presented to readers; and it is this that allows the article to be categorised as a form of service journalism. By suggesting the possibility of a risk to humans, the article implies the need for some kind of preventive action by its readers in order to avoid this potential hazard. Of course, much of the coverage of food scares carries such an implication, and as such this category of service journalism is rather loosely defined and delineated. However, it is also, for our purposes, the least interesting of the categories because it is closest to the traditional forms of news which Eide and Knight have already implicitly dismissed, and which others have criticised as reflecting the degradation of the public sphere (for instance, Meyer, 2002; Franklin, 2004).

B – The domestic sphere

Some of the coverage impinged a little more directly on the lifeworld due to the context of the stories involved:

'Mad cat disease' found by scientists

A CONDITION closely resembling 'mad cow' disease, the brain disorder that has killed more than 13 000 British cattle, has been diagnosed for the first time in a domestic cat, the Ministry of Agriculture, Fisheries and Food disclosed yesterday. (Hornsby, 1990)[7]

The possibility of BSE 'crossing the species barrier' to infect cats prompted a significant number of articles in May 1990. While the possibility of a link to humans was at this time considered to be speculative (and categorically ruled out by the government), the official confirmation of the emergence of *feline* spongiform encephalopathy represents an incursion into the domestic sphere (of cat owners) of a disease previously confined to industrially farmed cattle. This can be understood as a lifeworld problem, as pet owners are presented with the need to ensure the safety of their own cats; the risk is 'imported' into the domestic sphere. Similarly, generalised concerns around salmonella in eggs were provided with a specific domestic 'hook': 'Egg peril in mum's cake at Christmas' (Kemp, 1988);[8] 'Throw away cake if it's iced' (Grant-Evans, 1988);[9] 'Don't use raw eggs if you ice the cake' (Greig, 1988).[10] These stories all reported concerns that Christmas cakes made with raw eggs might contain salmonella bacteria; again, these articles convert a generalised problem (salmonella poisoning via eggs) into one which has a specific everyday context, and which therefore moves towards the lifeworld as a 'problem of everyday life'.[11]

As with category **A**, these stories do not directly address their audiences as consumers, but the context clearly brings a risk issue literally 'closer to home'. No direct solutions are offered to the problems they discuss, but in the latter examples a consumerist response is implicit: avoid salmonella by refusing to buy and eat eggs.

C – Expert advice

A further step along the continuum towards explicitly informative and advisory service journalism (and away from traditional systems-based news journalism) can be distinguished in those articles that present expert knowledge concerning the risks involved to the public:

The good cow guide

Is beef safe to eat? The *Sun* posed a series of vital questions to Professor Bernard Tomlinson, 75, a former Government Health adviser and an authority on brain disease. (Kay, 1996)[12]

Ministry denies threat to humans
Keith Meldrum, chief veterinary officer for the Agriculture Ministry, said in his reply to our questions [...]. (Fielding, 1994)[13]

The *Sun* article above continued with a series of questions and answers concerning the safety of different cuts of beef, while the following *Mail on Sunday* article focused on links between CJD and BSE. In both cases, the newspapers concerned are acting as conduits for information from experts and professionals; in Eide and Knight's (1999) terms a professional–client relationship is posited between the news source and the reader. The newspapers are effectively disinterested bystanders in this transaction, and take no responsibility for the information and advice provided. Instead, they act as proxies for the reader, facilitating the transmission of information from expert to client. Nevertheless, such articles are providing a clearer implication of, at least, a *potential* risk in the everyday lives of their readers. In each case, the articles accompany news items on the wider BSE issue. In the *Mail on Sunday*, no preventive actions are suggested; in the *Sun*, precautions such as avoiding offal and other '"less safe" pieces of the animal' are suggested by their expert. This latter example seems again to suggest only a relatively passive, consumption-based response to the BSE issue. Neither article refers to solutions that might be characterised by Eide and Knight (following Beck) as reflecting a 'collectivised subpolitics'; BSE and the risk to humans is, I would argue, consistently *de*-politicised in such coverage.

D – Columnists' advice

A further development involves those articles that give advice written by regular columnists. At this point, the newspaper begins to take on some of the responsibility for the advice and information given. For instance, an article in the *Express* headlined 'Should we really be frightened this time around?' by James Le Fanu (1996)[14] was published a day after the government's admission of a likely link between BSE and vCJD. The author of the article was a regular contributor to the *Express*; his by-line includes a photograph, and a final credit describes him as a 'London GP'. The article (which takes up the rest of page eight alongside the editorial column) suggest a need to 'place the new findings in perspective', arguing that such scares tend to have their risks 'exaggerated out of all proportion'.

In this example, the advice seems to be 'don't panic', and in effectively taking a government line on the issue this expert implies that the problem, such as it is, does not affect the everyday lives of his readers. It is therefore not a lifeworld issue, and can be (and indeed, via the government's precautionary policy measures, has been) dealt with via the systems of state and economy.

E – The newspaper speaks

Newspapers (particularly tabloids, where the news-comment division is not quite so clearly delineated) sometimes speak with their 'own voice' within their news pages. This is also evident in the service journalism aspects of food scare coverage: 'Daily Mirror answers the key questions you are asking' (Hay, *Mirror*, 1988);[15] 'Eggs are all white and that's no yolk' (Kay, *Sun*, 1988);[16] '10 tips for safe eating' (Carr, *Today*, 1989).[17] The *Mirror's* Q & A session follows on from a page one story concerning calls for Edwina Currie[18] to resign, while the *Sun's* egg advice is linked to a light-hearted piece on celebrity egg recipes, and includes hygiene advice among what seems to be egg industry public relations ('20 reasons to carry on popping your yolks'). *Today's* article follows on from a story on 'bad eggs from Europe'. All three offer advice for the reader about health risks concerning eggs, not via the presentation of outside expert knowledge, but from the newspaper's own perspective. This kind of service journalism relies therefore more heavily on the credibility of the newspaper itself. The examples here also seem to offer little in the way of progressive critique. Among the advice on how to store and cook eggs, number seven on the *Sun's* list of reasons argues that 'The chances of eating an egg infected by salmonella are more than 200 million to one AGAINST' (Kay, 1988).[19]

In each of the cases above, the only direct advice to readers concerns hygiene issues which, while addressing lifeworld issues, provides no link to collective sub-political responses.

F – Editorials

The most authoritative way for a newspaper to give advice is via its own editorial columns. In this way newspapers take on direct responsibility for the help they provide their readers:

> **Lay off**
> **Farm minister John MacGregor wants us to start eating eggs again.**
> He is worried that otherwise the egg industry will go under. Our advice is: **DON'T** eat another egg until someone gives you a cast iron guarantee you cannot get salmonella poisoning.
> **It is better that egg producers go bust than innocent people die from poisoning.** (*The Sun Says*, 1988)[20]

The *Sun* editorial above presents explicit advice for *Sun* readers on how to avoid the risks of salmonella poisoning. It therefore adopts an advocacy role and addresses readers as clients; but its advice reflects a second element of what Eide and Knight describe as the 'hybrid social subject' (1999, p. 525) of service journalism: the reader as consumer. By avoiding eating (and presumably therefore, buying) eggs, consumers might, as the *Sun* suggests, damage a section of the British food industry; but this is, for the *Sun*, an unfortunate by-product of the individual consumer's response to the risk. Any implied boycott is proposed not as part of a collective (sub) political response by citizens to (for instance) the structure of the food industry and its apparent failings; it is simply the relatively passive withdrawal of consumer support.

Risk, trust and public journalism

The extent to which service journalism addresses media audiences as citizens raises the possibility of a tentative comparison with the debates surrounding the theory and practice of public or civic journalism in the USA.

Concerns about the historical development of journalism in the USA, and (perhaps more pressingly) flat newspaper circulations and shrinking nightly TV news audiences in the 1990s led a number of senior newspaper and local TV journalists to confront the issue of public disaffection with news journalism (Cook, 1999, p. 1). 'Mainstream journalism' was argued to be failing to engage with the needs and interests of its audiences, who were treated as passive spectators in the political process; consumers of facts distilled by professional journalists rather than engaged citizens of a deliberative democracy. The response to these concerns generated a number of practices around the theme of reinvigorating American 'public life' (Rosen, 1999, p. 22) including convening (and covering) public 'town hall' meetings and forums, political debates and citizen panels, and employing polls, surveys and focus groups to organise reporting around the 'citizens' agenda' (Grimes, 1999, p. 9).

By encouraging public participation in the news production process, the adherents of public journalism argue that they 'reconnect' with the communities that they (supposedly) serve and generate a wider civic engagement in political and community issues. In doing this, public journalism rewrites a traditional understanding of the relationship between press and audiences: news should be about *forming* – rather than simply *informing* – the public (Grimes, 1999, p. 5). In this way, it challenges the notions of objectivity and impartiality that are cornerstones of the USA quality newspaper industry. In pursuing the ideal of objective news reporting, traditional journalism has, it is argued, encouraged the alienation of audiences from public life, and promoted cynicism and apathy in its place. Journalistic objectivity insists on a detachment that is impossible to achieve from a theoretical perspective, and corrosive in practice. It is impossible theoretically because journalism is almost by definition about taking a *stance*: a position on what is acceptable and what is not, what is right and what is wrong. There is therefore no such thing as 'morally neutral journalism' (Sanders, 2003, p. 43). On a practical level, the insistence on objective detachment means that news tends to present politics as a 'game' played out by experts and authorities, above the heads of the public, fuelling cynicism and disenchantment; it can therefore also be understood as being implicated in the 'primary definition' of issues (such as food scares) in terms of scientific rationality. Public journalism therefore insists on the news media taking on the role of the 'fair minded participant' in public life (Merritt, 1999, p. 369). Public journalism's critique of 'mainstream' USA journalism echoes Habermas' discussion of the 'refeudalisation' of the public sphere, and for some this link is made explicit (Rosen, 1999; Carey, 1999, p. 59). For other's, however, Habermas's concerns about the 'manipulation of public opinion through the mass media' and the consequent degradation of the public sphere in late capitalism (Habermas, 1989, pp. 168–9) are dismissed if not ignored (for example, Hardt, 1999, p. 208; Leonard, 1999, p. 86).

Public journalism can be criticised for being 'consumer-driven' in the sense that it sometimes relies on what people *say* they want to see and read, and thus may be especially susceptible to commercial imperatives. The forums, polls and focus groups that are intended to generate a 'citizens' agenda' may be little different to the market research that all commercial organisations (including newspapers) undertake in order to give their customers what (they say) they want. Following the citizens' agenda could therefore produce a journalism that is less, rather than more, 'deliberative' (see for instance, Grimes, 1999, p. 10 on the *Charlotte Observer's* 'Your Voice, Your Vote' project). It has been attacked by other USA journalists as abandoning journalism's traditional authority to become a form of partisan advocacy for particular interest groups, or 'civic stenographers' in Howell Raines's[21] phrase (cited in Rosen, 1999, p. 29). This criticism comes from the liberal mainstream, but could easily reflect Habermasian concerns with the encroachment into the public sphere of the economic imperatives of the system via the 'steering mechanisms of money and power' (Stevenson, 1995, p. 52). Certainly, public journalism has been argued to lack analytic depth, particularly with regard to the political economy of the press. As Hardt (1999) suggests, by failing to address the iniquities of the market-driven media system, public journalism is unlikely to generate a truly inclusive citizens' agenda, and instead 'many publics will remain silent and without representation' (p. 207). In other words, oppositional views, counterhegemonic discourses, are unlikely to emerge.

A brief comparison between the tenets of public journalism and the empirical evidence from the service journalism presented here suggests that in one sense the 'traditional' forms of news described in categories **A**, **B** and (in particular) **C** represent the 'mainstream' journalism that public journalism rejects. It adopts an ostensibly 'objective' position and presents information from official news sources and expert advice as an apparently disinterested observer rather than as a participant within a political culture. The latter categories (**D**, **E** and **F**), in which the newspapers speak in their own 'voices' (or those of their columnists), move towards a perspective closer to public journalism in that they assume some responsibility for raising and addressing the particular health issues involved. The impact of this is, however, limited for two reasons. Firstly, due to the principle of demarcation between news and comment that is still largely upheld (and notwithstanding the overt ideological positions of the tabloids in particular), service journalism in the UK is generally restricted to what US newspapers call the 'op-ed' pages. Secondly, and perhaps more importantly, I would argue that the civic engagement offered here is of a strictly circumscribed kind. The 'public' that is formed by service journalism is a collectivity of consumers, not citizens; individuals who at best act politically only as a by-product of their activities within markets.

Conclusion

I would argue that consumerist perspectives should not be dismissed as irretrievably individualised and depoliticised; it is possible that in the risk society such understandings can be part of wider critiques that offer alternatives to dominant definitions of such things as food scares. Previous research suggests that, in an admittedly limited sense, the 'traditional' forms of journalism can provide opportunities for non-official sources to voice these perspectives in a way which is critical of prevailing orthodoxy. Eide and Knight (1999), in implicitly dismissing traditional journalism argue that service journalism can offer a hybrid citizen–consumer–client subject position to audiences that might provide opportunities for collectivised subpolitical responses to risks such as food scares. The small case study presented here suggests, however, that service journalism is unlikely to provide such responses. As the categories progress from those most similar to 'traditional' journalism to those most clearly part of service journalism (that is, from category **A–F**), the potential for alternative perspectives is reduced rather than enhanced. I would argue that the newspaper coverage of food scares in service journalism either takes a wholly hegemonic position (in dismissing any concerns as baseless and expressing faith in the authorities, often via the views of scientists and other experts) or suggests only the most market-based, individualised consumer response: avoiding the product concerned.

Both service journalism and public journalism are (in part) intended to repair the damaged relationship between journalism and its audiences. The evidence that the practise of public journalism reduces distrust in the media is far from conclusive (Grimes, 1999, p. 14); certainly, it is clear that both service journalism and public journalism are seriously limited in their ability to generate genuinely deliberative and inclusive publics. Nevertheless, the debates around the latter suggest at least a recognition of the difficulties involved, whereas service journalism, as it moves away from traditional journalistic forms (of dispassionate presentation of 'expert' advice – that is, category **C**) towards a kind of participation in the debates and issues (via columnists' advice and opinions and editorials), offers only narrowly consumerist responses. In Habermas' terms, the limitations of service journalism represent a journalistic manifestation of the 'colonisation of the lifeworld' by the interests of the economy and the state (Pusey, 1987, p. 108). It may be presented as providing disinterested professional guidance and advice, but it offers only narrowly individualised, de-politicised and consumption-based 'technical' solutions (Habermas, 1971, p. 103) to public issues of risk and health. The newspaper audience is therefore poorly served by service journalism, being addressed primarily as consumers rather than citizens. Such journalism does not deserve the trust of the nation's citizens.

Notes

1. Bovine spongiform encephalopathy, and its human version, variant Creutzfeldt-Jakob disease.
2. Discussions of food scares as 'moral panics' have tended implicitly to reproduce the notion of such public concerns as in some senses at least irrational and in need of correction (Beardsworth, 1990; Gofton, 1990).
3. Certainly there is evidence that oppositional news sources were careful to restrict their own demands to that which could be characterised as 'moderate' and 'sensible' (Collins, 1999, pp. 216–7).
4. Stevenson for instance suggests that the 'pulverisation of the cultural sphere by the economy and the state' leads, according to Habermas's theory, to media cultures which are 'culturally hegemonic' and intent on limiting 'informed criticism' (1995, p. 52).
5. P. Wilenius, 'Gummer fights Mad cow boycott on British beef', *Today*, 23 January (1990) p. 4.
6. P. Wilenius, 'Gummer fights Mad cow boycott on British beef', *Today*, 23 January (1990) p. 4.
7. M. Hornsby, '"Mad cat disease" found by scientists', *Times*, 11 May (1990) p. 5.
8. D. Kemp, 'Egg peril in mum's cake at Christmas', *Sun*, 20 December (1988) p. 4.
9. W. Grant-Evans, 'Throw away cake if it's iced', *Today*, 20 December (1988) p. 1.
10. G. Greig, '"Don't use raw eggs if you ice the cake"', *Mail*, 20 December (1988) p. 9.
11. Many of these stories also gender food scares as a problem for (or in some cases caused by) 'mum' or the 'housewife' (see Fowler, 1991).
12. J. Kay, 'The good cow guide', *Sun*, 22 March (1996) p. 3.
13. N. Fielding, 'Ministry denies threat to humans', *Mail on Sunday*, 25 September (1994) p. 9.
14. J. Le Fanu, 'Should we really be frightened this time around?' *Express*, 21 March (1996) p. 8.
15. G. Hay, 'Daily Mirror answers the key questions you are asking', *Mirror*, 5 December (1988) p. 6.
16. J. Kay, 'Eggs are all white and that's no yolk', *Sun*, 6 December (1988) p. 16–7.
17. A. Carr, '10 tips for safe eating', *Today*, 6 July (1989) p. 23.

18. Edwina Currie was the government minister who effectively instigated the salmonella in eggs scare, and was accused of exaggerating the problem and causing
severe economic problems for egg producers.
19. J. Kay, 'Eggs are all white and that's no yolk', *Sun*, 6 December (1988) p. 16–7.
20. *The Sun Says* leader article, 'Lay off', *Sun*, 21 December (1988) p. 6. The editorial
is reproduced here in its entirety, and in approximately the same format.
21. Howell Raines was then the 'editorial page editor' of the *New York Times*. He
became executive editor in 2001 before resigning following the Jayson Blair scandal in 2003.

8
'Trust Me, I'm a Doctor': MMR and the Politics of Suspicion

Chas Critcher

From 2001 to 2003, controversy raged in the British media over the Measles, Mumps and Rubella (MMR) vaccine. This vaccine, which is administered to pre-school children, had been linked to cases of autism. No other country using this vaccine has experienced such a scare so the lessons of MMR may be specific to Britain. In particular, it may reflect the agenda-setting power of a small number of national newspapers and the broadcasting organisations that tend to follow their lead. Its wider implications may lie in the mechanisms by which trust in medical expertise can be deliberately undermined to the detriment of public health.

This chapter is based on the extensive secondary literature in specialist health journals plus a content analysis of all the MMR stories from 1998 to 2003 in the *Daily Mail*, a newspaper especially influential in campaigning against the vaccine. The discussion has four parts. The first section outlines the narrative of MMR briefly. The second section presents ideal types of views held by health professionals, the doubting public and the *Daily Mail*. The third section analyses the role of the media in the controversy, while the fourth part examines in detail arguments used in the *Daily Mail* to establish the issue as one of trust. The conclusion explores conceptual issues around trust and the mass media.

The MMR narrative

The MMR vaccine was introduced in Britain in October 1988, initially as one dose. MMR had already been introduced in many other countries, from Scandinavia to the USA. In the UK vaccination rates for three separate injections had been below the optimum level of 95 per cent. MMR was designed to improve them.

MMR's introduction caused little immediate media interest, even when in 1992 two brands of MMR were withdrawn because research suggested a distant link between the mumps component and aseptic meningitis. In 1994, 'Operation Safeguard' was launched by the government to vaccinate 8 million children with measles and rubella only, since there was a shortage of the mumps vaccine. A second pre-school booster injection was introduced in 1996 (Horton, 2004).

In 1995, a team of researchers at the Royal Free Hospital in London suggested a link between measles vaccination and Crohn's disease, a chronic bowel disorder (Thompson, Montgomery, Pounder and Wakefield, 1995). Reports by upmarket health correspondents were not followed up in the media. In the meantime, an organisation had been founded called JABS (Justice, Awareness, Basic Support) to promulgate ideas about adverse effects of childhood immunisation. A group of parents, convinced that their children had been damaged, were seeking to sue drug manufacturers.

Then, in February 1998, Dr Andrew Wakefield and 12 colleagues published a new research paper in *The Lancet* (Wakefield, Murch, Anthony et al., 1998). Its main focus was an apparent connection between autism and Crohn's disease. Wakefield also claimed to have found traces of the measles vaccine in his patients. Though the research paper did not seek to blame MMR for autism or Crohn's disease, Wakefield's subsequent statements and research papers (Wakefield and Montgomery, 2000) did suggest such a link. He advocated single vaccines as an alternative. In December 2001, Wakefield left his post for the USA, claiming he had been forced out for his views.

The media publicised Wakefield's claims immediately but otherwise coverage was low key throughout 1999 and 2000. Fresh interest was aroused in December 2001 and January 2002 when Conservative MPs persistently asked Prime Minister Tony Blair if his youngest child Leo had been vaccinated. Blair refused to answer on grounds of privacy. The *Daily Mail* was identified as leading the campaign against the government and in favour of single vaccines. Immunisation rates were immediately affected. By late 2003, they had slowly declined to levels where local epidemics, especially of measles, were being forecast. On 6 March 2004, 10 of the original authors signed a public retraction of the claims made on the basis of the research, barely reported by the *Mail* (Horton, 2004). Its columnist Melanie Phillips wrote in late 2005 that this was an issue which would not go away; but it already had, not least as far as her own newspaper was concerned.

The MMR story is in many ways a curious one. As Figure 8.1 shows, the peaks and troughs of the *Daily Mail* coverage were related less to significant events than to issues which the media themselves had created. The most obvious example was the controversy over whether Leo Blair had been vaccinated. The Prime Minster's refusal to answer prompted speculation that perhaps it had not been done, and he was therefore a hypocrite to advocate MMR for everybody else. Criticisms by political opponents clearly anxious to capitalise on the Prime Minister's discomfort sustained massive media coverage, even in the absence of any other events. The *Mail's* coverage of MMR thus peaked at the end of 2001 and the beginning of 2002.

Another notable peak at the end of 2003 reported the progress of the legal action by parents against the manufacturers of MMR. Supporters of MMR

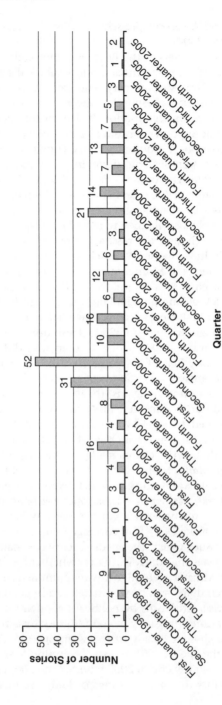

Figure 8.1 Number of Daily Mail stories by quarter 1999–2005.

were warning of impending measles epidemics. There were also accounts of published research, with comments from interested parties. As shown by Table 8.1 detailing the main topics of *Mail* coverage over the three main years, 'Leo Blair' and 'published research' accounted for a third of all stories from 2001–3. Third ranked were 'personal testimony' stories, often painful accounts of parents of autistic children and/or those agonising over whether to have their child vaccinated. However, little attention was paid to a major review of the state of knowledge about autism that denied any association with the MMR vaccination (Medical Research Council, 2001).

MMR is an unusual news drama. It has characters, themes and occasionally scenes but very little plot. It lacks a key event – death, disaster, enquiry – which often sparks interest in an environmental, health or social issue. Consequently much of the 'action' consists of accusations based on suspicion and innuendo and thus likely to encourage distrust. It is a case study in suspicion of both individuals and groups.

Among those in the front line were Dr Andrew Wakefield himself and his colleagues at the London Free Hospital; Richard Horton, editor of the *Lancet* when it published the original research paper; Sir Liam Donaldson, Chief Medical Officer of Health; the leaders of various anti-MMR pressure groups, notably Jackie Fletcher of JABS; and, briefly but intensely, the Prime Minster, his wife and his two-year-old son.

The most important overarching theme was the vulnerability of childhood. The potential victims were unable to make their own decision; adults had to do it for them. The controversy centred on whom had the right to make that crucial decision about immunisation. Detailed study of the debate in the media reveals three interest groupings. Each has its own distinctive view of the nature of the issue and the motives and duties of the other parties involved.

MMR accounts: Three ideal types

The three interest groupings are: health professionals, the doubting public and the *Daily Mail*. Each is characterised below as an ideal type.

Table 8.1 News stories in the *Daily Mail* 2001–3 by main topic

Topic	2001	2002	2003	**Total**	(%)
Leo Blair	15	15	2	32	18
Published research	12	9	7	28	15
Personal testimony	6	7	4	17	9
Measles outbreaks	0	10	2	12	6
Single vaccines	3	7	0	10	5
Legal action	1	3	6	10	5
Vaccination rates	2	2	6	10	5
Sub-total	39	53	27	119	64
All other	20	31	15	66	36
Totals	59	84	42	185	100

The health professionals' account

The health professionals' account defines the threat of these diseases as seriously damaging, even life threatening. The immune system must be developed to prevent their occurrence. Mass immunisation is regarded as the most effective means for their control or elimination. The government's immunisation policies largely work for the public good. The MMR vaccine is extremely safe, especially compared with individual vaccines. Allegations of an association between the vaccine and either autism or inflammatory bowel disease are regarded as scientifically unsound and morally reprehensible. The news media as a whole are seen as irresponsible in their coverage of MMR, pursuing their own agendas at the expense of assessing the scientific evidence. The subsequent decrease in vaccination levels is attributed to public ignorance of the seriousness of the diseases and the safety of the vaccine. Health professionals have a duty to maximise levels of mass immunisation. To achieve this, they need to become more effective communicators of scientifically sound information in order to overcome the misrepresentations of the media and the ignorance of the public.

The child, in this account, is an organism susceptible to damaging invasion from which it needs to be protected by medical intervention. It is an account characterised by impatience with those who doubt its premises and certainty about the validity of its views. In broad terms, this might be classed as a *professional/scientific* account. 'Professional' here implies expert status, ethical propriety and the disinterested pursuit of patients' best interests. 'Scientific' connotes that their views are based on hard evidence, objectively collected and analysed.

An example of this perspective is an article published in the *British Medical Journal* just as the controversy was gaining pace (Bedford and Elliman, 2000). The authors begin by advocating mass immunisation that 'has probably saved more lives than any other public health intervention, apart from the provision of clean water' (p. 240). The authors then outline and refute each of the objections against MMR: that measles is not serious, that such diseases are uncommon, that the vaccine does not work or is unsafe. MMR does not cause autism; it is just coincidence that the vaccine is administered at the same age as autism is diagnosed, around two. Wakefield's original paper did not claim to have established such a causal link – that which no serious scientists accept:

> This minority view has received disproportionate publicity, giving the impression that a substantial body of medical opinion shares this concerns. Sensational newspaper headlines and coverage in television programmes give the theory undue prominence, and it is no surprise that the uptake of the MMR vaccine has declined. To counter this it is necessary to explain to parents why the research is flawed and that there is no evidence of a link between the vaccine and autism. (Bedford and Elliman, 2000, p. 242)

The whole article is eminently rational, a rebuttal of the arguments against MMR. The long-term solution is to take parental concerns 'seriously and sympathetically', by providing 'accurate information' (Bedford and Elliman, 2000, p. 242), so that they will accept MMR.

A few dissented in the *BMJ*, mainly on ethical grounds. More significantly, those working alongside General Practitioners (GPs) were less convinced. An early survey of health care professionals in North Wales showed that half of all front-line groups had some reservations about the second dose. Practice nurses were more likely than health visitors or GPs to share the scepticism of the lay public. 'Despite expert advice to the contrary, a substantial proportion of practice nurses believed that autism and Crohn's disease may be linked to the vaccine' (Petrovic, Roberts and Ramsay, 2001, p. 84).

The doubting public's account

The doubting public's account differs on almost every issue from that of the health professionals. The three diseases are not necessarily serious but a natural part of growing up. The body should develop natural immunity through exposure rather than contrived immunity through vaccinations. Government says it has the interests of the public at heart but its political and economic motives are suspect. Assurances that the MMR vaccine is safe are treated sceptically, with supporters suspected of pursuing their own economic interests and those of the pharmaceutical industry. The scientific debate about the safety of the MMR demonstrates that the experts cannot even agree among themselves. The media are not wholly believed or disbelieved but their interest is taken as an indication that the issue is genuinely controversial. Whether or not to immunise is a highly personal dilemma. Those who should provide disinterested advice are unable or unwilling to give a balanced view, often because they are under pressure to achieve targets for immunisation. As a consequence, parents feel harassed by health professionals who ought to be providing balanced information for parents to make an informed decision that should then be respected.

The child in this view is a unique and precious individual whose health is paramount.

This account is characterised by doubt about the information provided by experts and uncertainty about the effects of any decision they might make. In broad terms this might be defined as a *sceptical/consumerist* account. It is sceptical about the motives of all those involved in the debate: government, health professionals and media. It is consumerist because it wants information to enable individual choices that are indifferent to the common good.

An example of the views of doubting parents was provided in the *BMJ* by a radio journalist (Alcock, 2002). Working for *BBC Radio 5*, she had taken an undecided couple to talk to various experts on both sides about the MMR vaccine. Darren and Carol Warburton were uncertain about the vaccine and could not 'decide where to draw the lines between government and medical professionals' advice' (Alcock, 2002, p. 492). While they wanted to trust their doctor and health visitor, they 'felt they were being spun a political line'. Such parents were 'most convinced by the personal touch', such as experts talking about their own children. This made Tony Blair's refusal to talk about his children a mistake. 'If Tony Blair had been able to talk personally of his and Cherie's dilemma over vaccination, it would probably have held much more sway with undecided parents than any medical research'. Press conferences citing expert opinion were irrelevant. The available evidence favoured MMR but 'the decisions we make about our children's health are, in the end, a lot to do with individual emotions – confidence, trust, fear'. That this couple eventually opted for single vaccines illustrated that parents needed to 'feel as though the medical profession isn't pulling rank and dismissing their concerns' (Alcock, 2002, p. 492).

Not all doubters thought like this and not all parents were doubters. Throughout the controversy the vast majority of parents of two-year-olds maintained trust in the health profession as a whole. A study of parents of young children undertaken in the West Midlands during the first half of 1992 concluded that: 'Media discussion of MMR has served to worry and has challenged embedded understandings of the value of immunisation, but for our participants it does not seem to have irreparably damaged a positive culture' (Petts and Niemeyer, 2004, p.19).

The *Daily Mail*'s account

The *Daily Mail* does not deny the seriousness of the diseases. The need for mass immunisation is recognised but the political means are disputed. The MMR vaccine cannot be regarded as wholly safe in view of the level of dissent within the scientific community. Experts' financial links with the pharmaceutical industry and GP payments for vaccination levels reveal economic motives. The government is inept and motivated by the cheapness of MMR. The views of parents, as they agonise over the decision or cope with children's illnesses, are constantly foregrounded. Tony Blair's refusal to say whether his son Leo had been vaccinated is at best evasive and at worst hypocritical. Potential epidemics are blamed on the government's intransigence. Genuinely independent research is needed. In the meantime, parents should be given the choice of separate vaccinations.

The child in this account is a vulnerable being whom parents are entitled to protect.

This account is characterised by hostility to government and medical establishment and clarity about the apposite policy. In broad terms this account might be termed *political/populist*. It is political because it is part of the paper's general antagonism to a New Labour government. It is populist because it sides with the plight of 'ordinary' parents against the interests of government, experts and industry.

In a *Daily Mail* editorial at the height of the Leo Blair controversy virtually all elements of the ideal type are present (Editorial, 2002, p. 12).[1] The editorial begins with a habitual concession, that the three diseases are dangerous. Yet 'at the same time' parents are genuinely troubled because the row 'has generated more heat than light'. The Chief Medical Officer of Health is accused of 'apocalyptic' language but the issue cannot be resolved by 'New Labour propaganda'.

The 'government and the medical establishment' are to blame, victimising doctors who favour single jabs and offering GPs financial incentives to 'bully' parents. 'And it certainly doesn't help when Tony Blair won't give a straight answer over whether baby Leo had had the jab'. By contrast, 'parents are not fools'. They know, 'as this paper has always made clear' that the vaccine is safe, that autism rates are rising and that 'science is not infallible' since all remember BSE. Their judgement is more to be trusted than that of shifty politicians 'who are now trying to demonise the media for articulating the quite legitimate concerns felt by millions of Britons'. The ending is startlingly rhetorical:

> But this is not Stalinist Russia. Neither the Government nor the medical establishment has the right to behave like some all-powerful Victorian nanny. Ordinary people work for nearly half a year to pay the taxes that support the NHS. Their views deserve to be respected. (Editorial, 2002, p. 12)[2]

The *Daily Mail* did establish leadership of this issue but other media did not automatically follow. Upmarket newspapers, with health correspondents well networked into the health establishment, took a more sanguine view, even those hostile to the government. Broadcast media are forbidden to editorialise and supposed to remain objective. However, in practice 'balance' involves giving equal weight to both sides of the argument, so opponents of MMR gained rather more publicity than their case may have warranted. But not all media were as distrusting and suspicious as the *Daily Mail*.

No news is good news: The role of the media

The consequences of the public debate about MMR were from a public health point of view detrimental, 'a case of media coverage affecting public behaviour in ways that may increase rather than reduce health risks' (Harrabin, Coote and Allen, 2003, p. 4). Surveys conducted by Cardiff University (Hargreaves, Lewis and Speers, 2003) suggested that the public's trust in the safety of the vaccine declined in the six months between April and October 2002. In April, 25 per cent thought that scientific evidence showed a link between MMR and autism, 30 per cent that it did not and 39 per cent that there was equal evidence on both sides of the debate. In October, the respective figures were 20, 23 and 53 per cent. The public debate had caused more to believe that the evidence was equally balanced, decreasing the proportions whose views were clear-cut. There was a decrease in those who would allow the MMR vaccination (from 53 per cent to 47 per cent), a steady rate of those who would opt for single jabs (30 per cent to 31 per cent) and an increase in the undecided (13 per cent to 18 per cent). Hargreaves et al. (2003) see such trends as accurately reflecting media coverage that assumed that there was equal merit in both sides of the argument.

It seems clear that 'the coverage clearly shaped the way many people understood the issue, and appear to have led to a loss of confidence in the vaccine in Britain – while confidence remains high elsewhere' (Hargreaves et al., 2003, p. 44). Changes in attitudes produced changes in behaviour. 'Take-up of the MMR vaccination declined by up to eight per cent in England and Wales between 1995/6 and 2001/2'(Harrabin et al., 2003, p.24). Figure 8.2 issued by the Department of Health showed both confidence in the vaccine and its uptake to decline slowly from 1994 onwards, then sharply throughout 2002 and 2003.

This loss of confidence occurred partly because the issue and its coverage were highly emotive:

> A TV report, for instance on MMR, containing evocative images of autistic children, may leave a more lasting impression on the viewers' minds of the dangers of the vaccine, than a carefully worded, circumspect report, complete with scientific data, that points to its relative safety. (Harrabin et al., 2003, p. 23)

The media cannot simply tap into a well of public suspicion. They have to construct a credible account of the issue, which discredits other versions. Hargreaves et al. argue that the media as a whole misled the public by: giving

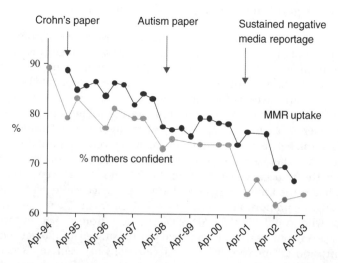

Figure 8.2 MMR uptake at 16 months and proportion of mothers believing in complete or almost complete safety of MMR vaccine.
Source: Department of Health in-house research.

the impression that there was equal evidence on both sides about the safety of MMR; representing the views of only those parents anxious about or opposed to the vaccine; ignoring the problems in providing single jabs; exaggerating the rate of decline in vaccination rates; and assuming that this was directly attributable to anxiety about the vaccine's safety. 'The problem in retrospect was that the debate was *not*, on the whole, about the key scientific aspects of the controversy' (2003, p. 44).

What it was about was a story, with its villains and heroes: Wakefield as martyr, squabbling scientists, duplicitous politicians, confused and angry parents: 'the consistent telling of a story – particularly one with echoes of other stories – clearly influences public understanding' (Hargreaves et al., 2003 p. 51). The high point of this drama was the Prime Minister refusing to disclose whether his son had had the vaccination, which obsessed the *Daily Mail*.

As it often does in its more successful moments, the *Mail* convinced the rest of the media to adopt the story, if only to report on its own campaigning. Without this editorial decision, the whole MMR furore might have been a local debate among health researchers, little reported in the media or noticed by the public, with negligible effects on vaccination rates. Psychologists of risk are wrong to reduce the role of the media to that of 'a conduit of information between information sources and the general public' (Frewer and Miles, 2003, p. 268). The *Mail* actually played a key role in undermining trust in those who would normally be regarded as expert authorities on health.

Suspicious minds

A working definition of trust is the 'confident expectation about another's motives with respect to oneself in situations entailing risk' (cited in Alaszewski, 2005, p. 243). Hobson-West (unpublished work) adapted lengthier typologies to provide three dimensions of trust: faith in the judgment of experts; interest promotion, that those experts will seek to pursue the common good; and role performance, that experts are competent to carry out their agreed function (Hobson-West, 2003). Each dimension has to be applied to three actors in MMR: the vaccine itself, health professionals and government. The task facing the opponents of MMR was to undermine trust on all three fronts.

The *Mail* tackled the issue head on: 'we are witnessing a collapse in public confidence over the Government's soothing assurances over MMR' (Editorial, 2002, p. 1).[3] For a substantial minority of the public, the *Mail* and other media succeeded in establishing doubts about MMR by discrediting political and medical authority. Politicians were easy to discredit:

> Trust grows out of mutual understanding and respect. These qualities are not always evident in political relationships, where governments and their advisors have often tended to treat citizens as though they cannot be relied upon to respond in a mature fashion to complex or uncomfortable

information and must be shielded from it with half-truths or denials. Once the media get a whiff of a cover-up, headlines are guaranteed that may precipitate a full-scale panic, suggesting an even greater risk than the one the government is trying to play down. (Harrabin et al., 2003, p. 38)

Tony Blair's refusal to disclose his own son's vaccination status was successfully presented as 'an important indicator of the government's faith in its own position'. Whatever his rights to privacy, his decision meant that he had failed a test of trust (Hargreaves et al., 2003, p. 42). His hypocrisy is for the *Mail* accompanied by arrogance, that the government knows better than parents. 'There is no question of choice. The public is expected to do as it is told' (Editorial, 2001, p. 12).[4]

Politicians are by definition suspicious characters but it was harder to shift the authority of medicine. Health professionals consistently enjoy a higher degree of trust than either politicians or the media (Frewer and Miles, 2003; Hargreaves et al., 2003). Medical authorities closest to government, like the Chief Medical Officer of Health, were portrayed as having adopted its questionable agenda. His position was in effect politically compromised. For other medics, however, the corruption was not political but economic. They were favouring MMR because they were being paid to do so. GPs who might otherwise be trustworthy were receiving bonuses for hitting child immunisation targets. They were not to be trusted, as they were not disinterested.

It was straightforward to demonstrate, because largely true (Gale, 2003), that many specialist researchers were funded directly or in kind by drug companies. This could be used to discredit both researchers and members of review committees appointed by government or other organisations. The *Mail* thus revealed gleefully that

at least 19 of the experts behind the Government's stubborn insistence on the safety of the MMR jab have links with the manufacturers, including shareholdings, donations to university departments and the funding of research projects. (Editorial, 2003, p. 12)[5]

The same editorial argued that 'In any other profession or public sphere even the possibility of such an obvious conflict of interest would not be tolerated'.

For the *Mail* then, government, politicians, medical scientists and GPs all have suspect motives:

At the heart of this issue is the question of trust. If parents are to accept the Government's word on the safety of the vaccine they must be able to believe that official assurances are based on expert opinion untainted by even the merest hint of social pleading.

That the views of some advisers might be considered suspect in this regard is cause for concern. At the very least it will lead more parents to determine that their children will not have the jab – a decision which courts the danger that their offspring will be vulnerable to measles. (Editorial, 2003, p. 12)[6]

The paper managed to maintain a complex position. It thought the vaccination was safe but its advocates were suspect, so parental doubts were legitimate and justified the choice of separate vaccines. The paper too argues that if vaccination rates fall and there are epidemics, the fault will be not with them but with the government for its high-handed conduct. It could even sympathise with some of the more extreme claims against MMR, that a triple injection was too much for a small child's body or that it was the only available explanation for the rise in autism. This is a position of some sophistication, albeit self-serving.

Conclusion: Beyond reasonable doubt

For social science, the key questions are not about whether a claim by a doctor such as Wakefield is technically right or wrong but why, when doctors, other scientists and the government repeatedly claim that he is wrong, this does not seem good enough for some people. (Hobson-West, 2003, p. 8)

Drawing conclusions from a single case study is always hazardous. The real need is for comparative study. Similar to MMR was an earlier scare over vaccination against pertussis (whooping cough). That vaccine had been linked in the early 1970s with brain damage. Media and public reaction caused a dramatic fall in immunisation rates from 80 per cent to 30 per cent. In the 12 years after 1974 there were three epidemics, 300,000 cases of whooping cough and 70 deaths (Griffith, 1981; Nicoll, Ellman and Ross, 1998). Unlike MMR, this scare was reproduced in other countries (Gangarosa, Galazka, Wolfe et al., 1998).

A rather different kind of health issue, though it could also involve injections, occurred alongside the MMR issue. In 2003, 2004 and 2005, research articles were published which suggested that specific forms of Hormone Replacement Therapy slightly increased the possibility of contracting breast cancer, especially among women with previous incidents.[7] Media interest was immediate but short-lived. Many women of late middle age testified that HRT had so transformed their lives that any slight risk attached was acceptable.

An older but much better documented case for comparison is AIDS. AIDS was a different type of issue, clearly life threatening, mainly for gay men. AIDS provoked a formidable lobby on behalf of the potential victims. Government had no established policy, unlike that of mass child vaccination. Common to both AIDS and MMR was a clear consensus among medical and scientific opinion about what should be done. The outcomes, however, were different.

On AIDS, the medical and scientific consensus prevailed. 'In general, the British media followed the liberal/medical orthodoxy on AIDS. Television news exclusively so' (Miller, Kitzinger, Williams and Beharrell, 1998, p. 163). This was not an automatic outcome; it had to be fought for, a process that has been analysed in some detail (Miller et al., 1998). Convincing specialist health correspondents on leading upmarket newspapers and later broadcasting organisations helped to curb the news agendas of conflict and drama. Opposition to AIDS policy remained among some newspapers, including the *Daily Mail*. As I have argued elsewhere about moral panics (Critcher, 2003), a campaigning newspaper only gets to set the media agenda if other papers and then broadcasters follow suit. In the case of AIDS, these tendencies were countered by careful briefing of selected correspondents. In the case of MMR, this either did not happen or happened too late. On AIDS, broadcasters did not take their lead from the *Daily Mail* or other press sceptics. 'TV news had no doubts, embracing the liberal orthodoxy of "expert" opinion as if it was an unchallengeable scientific consensus throughout the period 1987–90' (Miller et al., 1998, p. 74). On MMR, by contrast, the liberal orthodoxy was resisted by influential sections of the press which broadcasters reported as if a genuine controversy over the vaccine's safety existed.

Interventions can change the course of media coverage. It remains true that the press operate in a vein that is inimical to scientific discourse. The preference for the personalised over the generalised, the anecdote over the statistic, the maverick over the establishment, the extreme position over the moderate opinion – these are all daily characteristics of the mass circulation newspapers. The media discourse about MMR was especially affected by hostile newspaper columnists. Fitzpatrick (2004, p. 170) lists seven of them, even without Melanie Philips, the *Mail*'s chief writer on MMR, who maintained the belief into 2006 that Wakefield is right and everybody else is wrong. That no more than perhaps a dozen journalists and their editors could steer the whole issue is simply a measure of the unaccountable power of a formally free press in a democracy.

These are still tendencies, not fixed processes. News values push coverage towards drama, conflict and distrust of authority; but reliance on news sources can favour reasoned response and the validation of expertise. The political context is important. MMR was an issue over which a Conservative press could berate a Labour Prime Minister, especially when highly personalised. AIDS occurred in the heyday of the untouchable Margaret Thatcher.[8] So we need to understand both the specificity of each health issue, as well as the media processes that are common to them all.

'What is important is not the generalities of media production (although these exist) but the specifics that explain the different profiles, trajectories and evaluations of specific social issues in their political and social context' (Miller et al., 1998, p. 224).

As an issue MMR had its own peculiar characteristics, notably its exceptional emotional pull because it involved very young children. The close relationship between the medical profession and the pharmaceutical industry almost invited distrust. The coincidental rise in diagnoses of autism was a propaganda gift to the vaccine's opponents. In skilful hands such elements can be mixed into a powerful brew. Journalists – whether news gatherers, leader writers or controversial columnists – can create uncertainty and distrust in the face of all published evidence and all expert opinion. The tricks are simple to describe although difficult to bring off. Discredit medical expertise and political authority by revealing the venality of their motives; counter science with an appeal to commonsense to 'explain' the coincidence of MMR vaccination and autism diagnosis; and, finally, claim in the name of the consumer the 'right' to choose, in this case separate vaccines.

On this issue, for some time and with a significant minority of its audience, the press wittingly, and then broadcasting unwittingly, sowed the seeds of distrust of a vaccine and thus those who advocated or promoted it.[9] Perhaps they did, as some would argue, mobilise public anxieties endemic in the Risk Society, but that may be too simple an explanation:

> Trust as a category is made up of a series of composite factors, such as authority, perceived ability to act, previous competence and informational credibility. As with risk, we can expect particular dimensions of trust to be accentuated and reduced in different spaces and places. (Mythen, 2004, p. 152)

In the space and place of AIDS (and probably HRT), trust was given by the majority, despite scientific uncertainties. In the case of MMR (and probably whooping cough), trust was withheld by minorities, despite scientific certainty. Risk, trust and suspicion are not ontological states but discursive formations. The media remain central to their generation and reproduction.

Notes

1. Editorial, 'Vaccination and Public Concern', *Daily Mail*, 8 February (2002) p. 12.
2. Editorial, 'Vaccination and Public Concern', *Daily Mail*, 8 February (2002) p. 12.
3. Editorial, 'Comment', *Daily Mail*, 6 February (2002) p. 1.
4. Editorial, *Daily Mail*, 14 December (2001) p. 12.
5. Editorial, 'MMR, Experts and a Question of Trust', *Daily Mail*, 11 March (2003) p. 12.
6. Editorial, 'MMR, Experts and a Question of Trust', *Daily Mail*, 11 March (2003) p. 12.
7. See for example: J. Weldon, 'HRT: How Many Women Will Now Take The Chance?' *Daily Mail*, 1 December (2004) p. 7; J. Meikie, 'HRT Raises Risk of Cancer, Says New Study', *The Guardian*, 29 April (2005), p. 5.
8. Margaret Thatcher was Conservative Prime Minister of Britain from 1979 to 1990.
9. As late as June 2006, 30 medical experts warned in an open letter that MMR immunisation rates (83 per cent nationally, 70 per cent in London) were low enough for a measles epidemic to be imminent. See: I. Sample, 'Draw Line Under MMR Scare, Plead Top Doctors', *The Guardian*, 27 June (2006) p. 3.

9

New Media Enterprise in the Age of Suspicion

Gillian Allard

This is a study of individual economic struggle. Its subject is an Internet pioneer based in a British provincial city who bears little resemblance to the stereotype of the trendy young metropolitan entrepreneur that was beloved of investors in the 'dot.com' boom of the closing years of the 20th century. From the mid-1990s, when the potential of the Internet for distributing and downloading music was only beginning to be recognised, this middle-aged woman, whom I shall call Joan, was using it to give a platform to minority-interest music. She received plaudits for her innovative work, but she could not make money from it.

I frame Joan's experiences by reference to the dialectic between two explanations of economic behaviour that take a contrary approach to trust. As I shall demonstrate, the argument that economic networking is the most efficient means of regulating a flexible 'new' economy is predicated on the assumption that social interaction between and among connected participants conveys information about who is, and who is not, 'trustworthy' and obviates the need for hierarchical and bureaucratic mediating structures. Counter to this, the 'new institutional economics' maintains that there is a continuing need for formal governance infrastructures to substitute for trust among utility-maximising individuals.

As will become apparent, Joan attributed her problems to the investment behaviour of public and private institutions – the kind of supposedly impersonal bodies that mediate economic relations, according to the new institutional economics – and, indeed, by reference to the corruption of the capitalist system in general. My own interpretation of her plight favours the network explanation of economic organisation, while acknowledging the network's inevitable exclusion of groups and individuals whose confidence in self and others has been eroded by past experiences. I shall argue that her own lack of trust in the local and the global conditions in which she worked contributed to her inability to develop the reciprocal ties with others upon which the development of her business depended.

The Internet: Network of networks or virtual supply chain?

During the dot.com 'bubble' of the mid-to-late 1990s, the get-rich-quick guides to how to exploit the commercial potential of the World Wide Web (for instance, Cronin, 1994, 1995; Kiam, 1995; Levinson and Rubin, 1995; Bickerton, Bickerton and Pardesi, 1996; Bayne, 1997) rarely paid much attention to the structuring of the Internet. However, a more thoughtful approach to the Internet as a 'network of networks' was focusing on its potential to bring together individuals and small organisations collaboratively to produce, promote and distribute items for custom or niche markets, perhaps regardless of their physical location (for instance, Hamill and Gregory, 1997; Poon and Jevons, 1997). That is unsurprising, given that 'networking' had emerged as a favoured metaphor for the characteristics of a 'new' economy.

Networks have been promoted as an efficient means of increasing the speed and accuracy with which knowledge and learning could be transferred, disseminated, interpreted and shared in a knowledge-based economy (Powell, 1991 [1990]; Senge, 1992; Cooke and Morgan, 1998). As part of that economy, the organisation of cultural and creative industries has received critical attention, particularly in respect of the distinction between districts that are characterised by networks of innovation and mutual support and those that are not (Bianchini and Schwengel, 1991; Bianchini, 1993; Florida, 2002; Miller, 2004; Oakley, 2004). Such analyses have clear (but not always articulated) affinities with the 'flexible specialisation' thesis originating in the findings of Piore and Sabel (1984) that artisanal, craft-based, small-scale but technologically advanced and productive economic activity in north-central Italy rested upon the reinvigoration of 'community'.

Such social arrangements are said to overcome the problem of opportunism in market settings while offering an alternative to inflexible, bureaucratic hierarchies. An intervention by Mark Granovetter is notable here. He accused mainstream economic argument of abstracting human behaviour 'out of social context' and atomising it 'from that of other groups and from the history of its own relations' (Granovetter, 1985, p. 486), arguing that economic behaviour is embedded in historically contingent social practices rather than simply the rational action of utility-seeking individuals. Granovetter challenges what he calls 'undersocialised' theories of human behaviour in which clever institutional arrangements – rather than the obligations inherent in concrete personal relations – make it too costly to engage in malfeasance. 'Oversocialised' explanations of human behaviour are equally unsatisfactory. They view the individual as the sum of a set of internalised social influences which take no account of the specificities of ongoing 'concrete personal relations and structures (or "networks") of such relations in generating trust and discouraging malfeasance' (Granovetter, 1985, p. 490).

Aldrich and Zimmer have applied Granovetter's thesis to entrepreneurial action. They criticise undersocialised views of entrepreneurs as free agents, 'operating atomistically in an environment where their cognitions and beliefs drive their behaviour' (Aldrich and Zimmer, 1986, p. 4). 'Trait' theories, which assume that some people are more likely to succeed as entrepreneurs because of their personality, fall into that category; economic, 'rational actor' models of entrepreneurship also focus upon individual decision makers at the expense of considering the wider social context for their actions. Oversocialised models of entrepreneurship are equally inadequate. That approach assumes that certain groups possess beliefs, values and traditions – rooted in, for example, national origins, culture or religion – which predispose them to be entrepreneurial. Aldrich and Zimmer prefer an alternative way of considering entrepreneurship: as being embedded in networks of continuing social relations.

Johannisson (1995) takes a more critical approach to entrepreneurial networks, observing that they might sediment over time, support asymmetrical power relations and, in effect, resemble institutions. Some studies of social networks certainly confirm that a 'rational actor' might simply objectify a network and use it instrumentally to access and manipulate resources – as when 'brokers' occupy the intersections of networks (Boissevain, 1974) or connect the potential contacts that accumulate around 'structural holes' (Burt, 1992). Specifically in relation to 'flexible specialisation' networks in the music industry, Hesmondhalgh (1996, 1998) has challenged the assumption that they necessarily enhance the power of small independent producers, suggesting that their lack of financial and legal 'muscle' will oblige them to defer to contacts that are better resourced to access major promotional and distribution channels.

Granovetter presented his argument about the social embeddedness of economic action as a direct challenge to the 'new institutional economics', which takes a contractual–transactional view of economic behaviour. From such a perspective, hierarchical institutional arrangements – for example, a vertically integrated supply chain – exist to mediate economic transactions where the costs to a firm of external contracting are too high; they also check the self-interest, malfeasance, inefficiency and disorder that arises when transactions are left to the market.[1]

Amidst the hype about the potential of 'e-commerce' from the mid-1990s, some economists were employing the principles of the new institutional economics to challenge the assumption that new information infrastructures would inevitably lead to the elimination of intermediaries in electronic markets and the flattening of business hierarchies (Sarkar, Butler and Steinfield, 1995). They envisaged systems of online trade in which intelligent software agents, or 'cybermediaries', would take over the co-ordinating functions that are provided by intermediaries in traditional distribution channels (Gazis, 1998; Vulkan, 1999). Less than a decade later, such preference agents are an integral part of online commerce. Meanwhile, the Internet's potential to dis-intermediate the channels that distribute recorded music has been realised insofar as it is possible to easily download a piece of music from the Internet directly onto a computer, MP3 player or mobile telephone. The same process-es make it possible – theoretically, at least – for a musician or small record label to bypass established distribution and promotional channels by selling music directly from a web site. Moreover, the storage and distribution effi-ciencies offered by Internet technology mean that longer and more varied product lines can be developed to serve tiny and refined taste segments so – again, theoretically – it is also possible for small labels and individual artists to develop and serve a demand for special-interest genres that bigger labels decline to take up. But if they are ambitious, they will have to bear the risks and costs of producing the music, designing and maintaining a web site and testing and developing the market before their product (and the rights in it) is taken up by larger companies.

In any case, there is a cost to both parties – the music producer and the music consumer – of using direct, disintermediated, channels. The cost to the producer of designing, maintaining and promoting the type of web site required to take, process and dispatch orders is substantial in time, if not in cash, and a greater cost might be feared if there is no trust in the arrange-ments for copyright protection of work distributed via the Internet. Equally, for the fan unwilling to engage in extensive web surfing, the time required to search for and identify music – as well as the perceived threat of misap-propriation of financial and other personal information registered via online payment mechanisms – might be too great. It would have been sur-prising if the efficiencies that accrue to both artist and fan from established (and hierarchical) production, marketing and distribution channels within the 'traditional' music industry had not also been sought from digital trans-actions.

A life in music

The accumulation of ties between connected individuals through which flow information, trust and mutual obligation is sometimes conceptualised as 'social capital' in the context of strategies to drive collective economic and social development (Putnam, 1993, 2000; Fukuyama, 1995; Durlauf and Fafchamps, 2004). In his study of the *personal* consequences of work in the 'new economy', Richard Sennett gives a different twist to social capital, arguing that it helps to uproot people from concrete attachments to place in late, flexible, capitalism. A fund of social capital – 'shared past experiences as well as individual achievements and endowments' (Sennett, 1998, p. 85) – enhances people's ability to navigate loose networks and to take risks. Risk is corrosive both for society and for the individual: the certainties of hierarchical bureaucracies have paled, to be replaced by flexible networks and 'teamwork of demeaning superficiality' (Sennett, 1998, p. 99). Sennett insists that the idea that those networked relationships have any ethical grounding is a fiction. Such is their transitory and discomfiting nature that the individual can no longer build for herself or himself any coherent life narrative.

Joan's case certainly suggests that it is not possible to survive indefinitely in the present by clinging to the affiliations of the past. Her plight might be elaborated by reference to Giddens's definition of 'ontological security' as the 'confidence or trust that the natural and social worlds are as they appear to be, including the basic existential parameters of self and social identity' (Giddens, 1984, p. 23). Giddens has explained how globalisation changes the texture of social life and our conception of who we are and how we live. It disturbs the balance between social structure, human agency and reflexivity: that is, it undermines the confidence that a social actor has in her knowledge of the conditions in which she acts and her own contribution to them (Giddens, 1990, 1991, 1999). Joan was working in conditions of flexible capitalism, but she did not seem to *want* to understand them.

I interviewed Joan in June 1998 at her home, where she ran her web site with her husband, as part of a wider research project on cultural enterprise in the Internet. The account that she gave me of her experiences was riddled with contradictions – although, of course, what follows has been doubly shaped by me, first as interviewer and second as editor. With regard to the first shaping, at the time of our meeting the interviewer (namely, myself) and the interviewee had different agendas. The interviewee wanted to talk about the technology, and she wanted me to tell her how she could access funding for what she was doing. I wanted her to talk about her markets and the online and offline networks that she belonged to. The result was quite a fragmented, digressive conversation. I have tried to maintain a sense of that here, although the presentation of excerpts from transcripts of a three-hour discussion has necessarily been selective.[2]

Notwithstanding the observations above about self-confidence, trust and the coherence of an individual's life narrative, an opening question from me about the company's background did elicit a story with a beginning, a middle and an end (although no resolution). I reproduce it below (paragraphs 1–7):

1. ALLARD: Could you say a bit about the background of the company and how long it's been trading and what ways it's changed since its foundation?
2. Right. [*Husband*] and I have always worked in the cultural field. He's a composer and a musician and he was a professional composer and musician for, well, a musician for 15, 16 years in London working on West End shows and things like that. We formed a publishing company in 1972, I think, and we've had other cultural things that we've either

been running, been organising or been associated with right the way through. Let's see, we moved to [*place name removed*] in '79, he started working at [*name of institution removed*] in '81 and he more or less stopped being a musician but not a composer. There wasn't much music work in [*place*]. Well, more-or-less nil. Certainly nothing he could earn a living at. It was, um, it was one of the little shocks we had.

3. ALLARD: Uh huh. It's not, not what you'd expect.
4. No, no. And what there was minimal, and what there was was very tied up. I don't think there are very many professional musicians, I mean people exclusively earning money from playing music.
5. ALLARD: Right, right.
6. Right, so that was that. We've always produced things; it has always been very difficult producing things. We've never produced CDs; we've never had the money. We've always produced cassettes and things like that.

The observation that the lack of music work 'was, um, it was *one* of the little shocks we had' (paragraph 2) is an early clue to the wealth of experienced and expected disappointments that inform this account. Having set out the background to the company, my informant signals that she is ready to move onto its current difficulties with her 'Right, so that was that.' Note the use of the always–never comparator in paragraph 6 as she summarises the problems that she will reveal. She implies a creativity that is 'always' frustrated by lack of resources: 'We've *always* produced things; it has *always* been very difficult producing things. We've *never* produced CDs; we've *never* had the money. We've *always* produced cassettes and things like that.' She continues:

7. In 1981, a friend of ours got killed and in 1991 we wanted to bring out the later piano music that he had done because most of the Arts Council funding for any of his music is always the *avant-garde* music which he didn't want to be associated with towards the end of his life. And the only way of getting the other music heard was to do it as a CD. So we formed initially it was [*name removed*] Records, then in 1981 we registered that with, in 1991 we registered that with PPL.[3] So the publishing company has been registered with everything since '72, MCPS.[4] So we registered with PPL, we registered [*name of record company*], produced that [*title*] CD, and then we had plans to do some other things. [*Husband*] was still working at [*name of institution*], just money and time, it takes a long time to do anything. I mean [*title*] was easy, we had tapes, historical tapes. And we have a lot of tapes which we would like to do but it still costs a lot of money to produce a CD.

There is stumbling over dates in paragraph 7 – the events she was recounting were troubling, although at the time of the interview I did not know the full details – and shortly afterwards the temporal structure of the narrative broke down. I later discovered, after conducting my own research into the music in question, that the friend who had 'got killed' had been the founder of an experimental music collective with which Joan and her husband had been involved in the late 1960s. Inspired by its founder's Maoist political affiliations, this 'orchestra' had repudiated what it perceived to be an elitist and bourgeois musical avant-garde. Its improvisations seem to have involved all the participants – at the same time and according to their own individual interpretations – playing either especially composed music or well-known classical pieces. It thereby produced a music in which everybody accompanied everybody else, accepting everything that happened in the process. The collective split up into factions rather quickly and collapsed; some of its members, including Joan's husband and the founder of the original collective, formed a second radical music group. Some years later, the founder – the friend of Joan and her husband – died after a hit-and-run accident near his home.

Referring back to the earlier discussion of 'undersocialised' and 'oversocialised' explanations of behaviour, the social organisation of the music collective seems to have collapsed into a kind of anarchical no-man's land in which individual interpretations of music were neither co-ordinated among its members nor orchestrated by an authoritative conductor. It is unsurprising that it split into factions, but it provides an interesting insight into Joan's background and her present situation. Like the music collective to which she once belonged, Joan now seemed to eschew both the regulation of the social network and the authority of established hierarchical systems.

After she had sketched out the company's background, Joan and I talked for several minutes about the process of forming the company, the difficulty of raising finance from banks and the barriers to accessing retail distribution channels. I suggested to her that the Internet must be a great opportunity for opening up new distribution channels. She responded by talking about Internet service providers. I persisted:

8. ALLARD: So basically you got in there as soon as it was available in a cost-effective way.
9. Right, right. And we were thinking of doing it for e-mail and things like that. I found the Web very early on and I thought it was very exciting. [*Husband*] took a little convincing but I thought it was really exciting and was going to explode as soon as I found it. It had to.
10. ALLARD: Yeah? Did you realise fully its potential as a medium for direct distribution?
11. Oh yes, oh yes. And being able to talk to people. I mean, it was, I was very, very clear about it as soon as I, as soon as I found it. We did the web-site immediately.

Note the expressive language in paragraph 9 – 'I thought it was *very excit-ing* [....] I thought it was *really exciting* and was going to *explode*' – and her certainty: 'it had to'. That clarity of thought ('I was *very, very* clear about it *as soon as I, as soon as I* found it') is linked with decisive action: 'We did the web-site immediately' (paragraph 11). The conversation turned for sev-eral minutes to matters of html, modem speed and bandwidth. I brought the focus back to music by asking her how she would sum up her mission. She said that she wanted to ensure that more British composers were heard. I asked her how the Internet could help her to achieve that. She replied:

12. The possibilities with the 'Net are that we don't have to make CDs. CDs are expensive to make – less expensive than they were, but they're still expensive to make. You have to put them somewhere when you've made them. If you make 500 or 1,000, they have to go some-where.
13. ALLARD: Yeah, yeah.
14. And you're probably going to have to store them for 10 years. Because it's going to be slow sales always in this area. It's a niche market, a very small niche market in every country in the world. And most of the time we have no access to the rest of the world, because we're not big enough. For the moment there is a little window on the Internet until it becomes more controlled by somebody.
15. ALLARD: And you think that's going to happen?
16. No idea. But looking at the way things go in life, it's a possibility. I mean, I think the window will be there for a period of time. It may con-tinue, and it may not.

The enthusiasm for the Internet that she expressed earlier was now being qualified by a more pessimistic (or realistic) evaluation of its possibilities given the nature of her markets – small niche markets across the world – and the size of the company. She was able to evaluate what was possible with what was to hand, and she understood the constraints. The Internet pro-vided a 'little window' on the world 'for the moment' (paragraph 14).

Joan was well aware that big companies dominated traditional distribu-tion channels in the music industry, telling me that 'most of the small record shops that would take our product have closed' and that large stores would not deal with her because she did not have a big enough product. She had tried to find a distributor, but most distributors wanted to pay her less than her CDs cost to produce and her experience of using smaller dis-tributors had been unsatisfactory. I asked her what information she had about the markets for her work. She was not interested. She replied, 'I haven't got time to be bothered. I don't really care. I mean, I would just like ..... want people to buy'.

Later in our discussion, Joan returned to the subject of the Web's future after another long digression about how she could obtain finance for her work:

17. When I saw the Web, not the Internet, when I saw the Web, even with its 'Browser One', and the fact of the way it had been developed by the physicists and that they weren't money orientated, that they had done it on the basis of communication ..... I mean, I'd never done programming or anything like that ..... [*tape change*] ..... Because it had come from the physicists, from Berners-Lee, it was just, it was just so exciting. I mean, I looked at it, and I wondered how long the money people would take to get hold of it.

Once again, she expresses her excitement about the Internet. She extinguishes it, almost with bathos: 'it was just, it was just so exciting. I mean, I looked at it' (here comes the anti-climax) 'and I wondered how long the money people would take to get hold of it.' It is as if money devalues the Internet, makes it less authentic. As she says, physicists had developed it and 'they weren't money oriented [...] they had done it on the basis of communication'.

Elsewhere in our interview, Joan expressed similar sentiments about other aspects of the information and communications infrastructure. By the time I met her in 1998, her web site was hosting an experimental 'micropayment' system that allowed customers to pay for individual tracks with their credit card and to download the music, a pioneering feature at the time. Joan had been forced to resort to this system because her lack of trading history and low turnover prevented her from obtaining a credit card merchant facility. A third party, the telecommunications company BT (previously known as 'British Telecom'), operated the micropayment system and took a substantial margin on each sale (something I found out not from Joan but from my own background research later). Joan was, in effect, paying to product test the technology for the telecoms giant – which was also acting both as network broker by facilitating connections between otherwise disconnected participants *and* as trusted intermediary in a musical supply channel.

I asked Joan to tell me about her experience with the BT micropricing experiment. She replied:

18. BT were an old state company. There are still people in BT who think in that way, like there are still people in the BBC who think in that way. They are technologically trained, so we could talk to them. We've only been dealing with their technical people.
19. ALLARD: And do you feel that there's an empathy?
20. Oh yes. But we've had hardly anything to do with product managers, who I think are shit.

21. ALLARD: What are the product managers trying to do? Sell?
22. Product managers are trying to please accountants and make money.
23. ALLARD: Right, okay.
24. The technical people are trying to make something work. That's the difference.

Unsurprisingly, she has similar sentiments about art and she was quite clear that the state should fund her work. Towards the end of the interview, I asked Joan what she thought was the role of bodies that were connected with supporting and promoting the arts, and what they could do for her. She replied:

25. They could do a lot, but they actually require you to go cap in hand, a bit grovelly. They all want, they all want.]
26. ALLARD: Do you think they should do something?
27. They all want, they all want you to say that you're going to make a lot of money. Unfortunately.
28. ALLARD: Right. Do you think that they should do something which doesn't, is not necessarily contingent upon you making a lot of money?
29. Yes. I think they should support the composers from here on the basis of supporting the [...] culture. I think it's that important. You know, like I think British composers should be supported. The American composers get subsidised in this country all the time.

She was also critical of the copyright collection societies that administer and distribute royalties on music. Indeed, at several points in our discussion she criticised Performing Right Society (PRS) and MCPS (and their computer systems) as being 'crap', 'very inefficient' and 'totally incompetent'. Her frustration was born of concern that such agencies – typical of the kind of bureaucratic structures that the New Institutional Economics would have in place to safeguard against malfeasance – were restricting the potential of the Internet.

At one point in our discussion, Joan stated that she saw the future of herself in the Internet in terms of links with other people who are producing on the Internet, but she felt that her skills base would be so high that other people would be unable to reciprocate. I kept asking her about the types of network that she would work with, and she kept telling me that although she was prepared to work across artistic genres, her skill level was so high that she would end up teaching and 'on the reciprocal level ..... would be doing all the giving' – a prediction which seems indicative of her lack of trust in the skills, experiences (and, indeed, capacity to reciprocate) of others. In effect, she appeared to be suspicious of the dynamics of the networks she aspired to join.

Some months after our meeting, Joan's web site won an award in a UK-wide competition, sponsored by BT and a national newspaper, to identify innovative e-commerce initiatives by small business. In an e-mail to me to announce the award, she commented that sales were still not good and that not enough people yet had the technology to download the music. However, it is unlikely that infrastructural limitations were the only reason for the lack of sales; nor can the other problems facing the business be attributed simply to a lack of funds.

To paraphrase an argument inspired by Giddens (1984, 1990, 1991, 1999) and cited earlier, Joan seemed unable to weigh the relationship between human agency (her own and others') and social structure in the local and global contexts in which she was trying to work. Her 'ontological insecurity' revealed itself in her suspicion of the people in the concrete networks and hierarchies that support 'online' commerce, a suspicion that was mutual. While I was carrying out the research of which my interview with Joan formed a part, I became aware that she was the cause of some exasperation among local administrators.[5] An arts support worker told me that she had been to meetings in which Joan had harangued the local arts council for its shortcomings and that she seemed not to understand that 'times had changed' and the state did not fund art in the way that it used to. A representative of a local economic development project told me that he had tried to recruit her to an employment bank that matched skilled people with employers' needs on a freelance basis, but she would not participate.

Conclusion

A number of contradictions emerge from Joan's account of her experiences as an Internet pioneer. She was extremely hostile to capitalism and all its works, yet she wanted to make money out of what she was doing. She was a stern critic of the state and of its organisational bureaucracies; nevertheless, she believed that the state should fund both art and technology. She understood that her future lay in being able to reach a global niche market for her music, but she was unprepared to find out what the characteristics of that niche were in order that she could adapt to it. Worse, she had isolated herself from local producer networks because she felt that her skill level was so high that other group members would not be able to reciprocate; at the same time, she had alienated arts administrators whose bureaucratic function was to administer funding at 'arm's length' from governments seeking to avoid the appearance of direct influence on, or interference in, a country's culture.

It could be argued that Joan's musical past had endowed her with a fund of 'social capital': so much so that she had devoted considerable effort to promoting the commitments associated with that past on her web site. But if her predicament were to be conceptualised by reference to social capital as a nexus of information, trust and mutual obligation for *commercial* ends, it would be an exemplar of Sennett's (1998) warning about the corrosive effects of risk. As noted previously, Sennett argued that risk-taking is facilitated by the transitory networks that characterise 'flexible' capitalism and disrupt the coherence of individual experience and understanding. Joan took risks with the Internet as a new medium, but she had very little confidence that the institutions and people associated with it would remain uncompromised by commercial imperatives. In effect, she was deeply suspicious of the conditions that would in logic have justified her taking the risks that she was taking. It is unsurprising that there were so many anomalies and contradictions both in the self-narrative she presented to me and in her actions as an aspiring cultural entrepreneur.

Notes

1. See Williamson (1975, 1985). Milgrom and Roberts (1992) provide an authoritative account and assessment of the new institutional economics.
2. There is no space here for a detailed discussion of transcription methodologies other than to describe the editing techniques used here. False starts have been removed where they are not relevant to the analysis. Where a thought trails off and a sentence or phrase is not completed, that is indicated by a row of five points. Punctuation has been used to indicate the speaker's intonation as it would in, say, the script for a play. A brief omission or excision is indicated by a 'three-point' ellipsis, [...], if it is simply part of a sentence. A more substantial excision is indicated either by a 'four-point' ellipsis, [....], or by a brief description of the missing element, italicised to distinguish it from the spoken words. Underscoring indicates some form of stress in pitch or amplitude; a left hand square bracket, [, indicates an interruption by one speaker of the other.
3. Phonographic Performance Limited (PPL).
4. Mechanical Copyright Protection Society (MCPS).
5. The comments reported here were made during discussions in a regional policy forum in which I was a participant observer. They were made in response to my citing Joan as a case of someone who seemed to be making innovative use of the Internet to promote and distribute cultural work.

10
Trust, Data-Mining and Instantaneity: The Creation of the Online Accountable Consumer

Andrew McStay

The concept of trust is central to studies of e-commerce as it is arguably the largest barrier to the wider adoption of online commerce in terms of purchasing goods. While the vast majority of consumers do not hesitate to give out credit card details over the phone, in stores and elsewhere, many consumers are averse to giving out credit card details and personal information over the Internet (Armstrong, Barr, Coutts et al., 2003). To explore consumers' lack of trust further, this chapter is structured into three sections. These are: social ontology, trust and its relationship to technology; dataveillance and theoretical implications of Customer Relationship Management (CRM) strategies; and real-time feedback and the commercial environment of instantaneity.

Although identity and communicative facets of the Internet remain important and worthy areas of study, we should not neglect the developments of the commercial facets of the Internet and the Web. This is an arena that is only set to grow. Rather than focussing on utopian Rheingoldian (1998) global communicative 'love-ins', or dystopian Virilioesque styled (2000) neo-Luddite accounts of cyberspace, this chapter's theme stems from the events and material practices occurring today – specifically users' orientations towards computers with which they check their morning e-mail (among other things) and the commercial and advertising practices that occur in the contemporary period of ubiquitous computing. Furthermore, this chapter only examines the period following the dot.com crash of the late 1990s and early 2000s. This is because the market has shown maturity unseen in earlier stages of online commerce, whereas formative stages were characterised by hype and spectacular over-speculation of what the electronic commercial environment was worth financially. Arguably both business and other users have re-evaluated the market of online commerce as a space for acquiring goods and services and as a place for advertising and marketing wares. Online advertising currently holds 3.9 per cent of the UK advertising media spend (BBC, 2005)[1] although users spend 12 per cent of their time online – three times as many hours than with newspapers and six times than with magazines (Internet Advertising Bureau, 2003). Research from Jupitermedia (2006) also notes Americans spend as much time online as watching television at 14 hours per week, and online media are displacing all varieties of print media. However, although the commercial aspect of the Web has settled and now displays more realistic business practices (Oser, 2004), users are often reticent to engage with commercial sites as readily as they do offline stores. This is primarily to do with perceived risk of safety online and lack of inclination to offer personal details across the Internet (MORI, August, 2000; Germain, 2004).

Social ontology: Trust and its relationship to technology

In examining the role of trust with regards to users' consumption of advertising online, this chapter extends the work of Ulrich Beck (1992b, 2002) and his thesis of risk society. Beck defines this as 'living in an uninsured society' (Beck, 1992a, p. 101) – that is a world with no guarantees of safety, a world where 'the hidden central issue in world risk society is how to feign control over the uncontrollable – in politics, law, science, technology, economy and everyday life' (Beck, 2002, p. 41). Trust by necessity involves an element of risk and both sentiments, I argue, play a large role in consumers' use of online commerce and the surrounding discourses that fuel the technological imaginary in the post-dot.com crash era.

The issue of risk and trust is one that is central to the developing modern western world. As Lupton (1999, p. 5) notes, risk as an idea and management activity changed through the emergence of modernity in the 17th century and gathered momentum in the 18th century. As opposed to risk issues being derived from an external deity and thus involving an element of abdication of responsibility due to fate and pre-destination, risk instead became a human concern upon which responsibility lay.

Giddens (1990) stresses that risk today is an accentuation of modernity that has become more universalised in the face of globalisation. As a corollary, trust for Giddens (1990, p. 26) is involved in the wider belief in the modernist project. It is not invested in individuals but in wider machinations. In short 'it is a form of faith' (1990, p. 27) which expresses something akin to a pledge as opposed to a cognitive understanding. Here we depend on persons and more importantly structures upon which we have no intimate relationship. Pertinently Sztompka (1999, p. 82) also notes that the lack of trust regarding transactions on the Internet and the lack of face-to-face interaction is amplified by 'dilemmas of anonymity as limiting trust'. In addressing this, Sztompka (1999, p. 82) points to security measures such as firewalls, intrusion detection programs, digital certificates and encryption techniques as possible methods of resolving this sense of insecurity. However, he recognises that these technologies will never resolve the need for person to person interaction or the importance that users' place on knowing who they are communicating and transacting with; he also states that 'risk will never be eliminated completely to the levels acceptable for any "normal" transactions' (1999, p. 82).

Given the risk and trust factors in the online commercial environment, what mechanisms exist to reassure online consumers and how do they work? In exploring these mechanisms, it is useful to return to Giddens (1990, p. 27), who, after investigating the relationship between agency and structure makes the distinction between 'expert systems' and 'symbolic tokens' in his discussion of abstracted forms of trust. For Giddens, trust is something that operates in the face of risk in which there are varying degrees of safety measures that can also be taken. Both expert systems and symbolic tokens are reliant on what Giddens (1990, p. 53) describes as the 'development of disembedding mechanisms'. These are mechanisms that extend social practices outside the context of the local and instead reorganise social relationships across greater expanses of time and space in the drive to further globalisation.

'Expert systems', as Giddens (1990) notes, are akin to being able to walk upstairs to a bedroom secure in the knowledge they will not give way, or to use a more contemporary example, surfing the Internet with a virus guard on. They are a consequence of scientific advances and the resulting increase in technical knowledge. They create a distance between the practitioner or expert, and, layperson or user. Giddens (1990) argues that as modern societies become reliant upon expert systems, trust increasingly cements this relationship together. Where trust is ruptured, ontological insecurity ensues. As Sztompka (1999, p. 39) notes, there is a growing recognition of the limitations of expertise and repeated faults in operation of 'abstract systems'. Examples include: online (and offline) banks managing identity theft, holes in Microsoft Windows' operating systems and programs downloaded from apparently reputable web sites that contain micro-programs that utilise users' data without their knowledge. Furthermore, the absence of real world referents (such as brand longevity or lack of personal characterisation) in Internet space exacerbates the problem of trust online.

The question for marketers is how to create and manage trust in light of consumer suspicion. Ultimately, trust for Giddens (1990) is related to absence in space and time whereby an individual has certain structural functions removed from their view yet still has enough faith invested in the structure to carry out the transaction.

Faced with building consumers' trust in e-commerce, security measures have been developed such as surveillance (the capacity to detect intrusion on a users' machine which may activate in response to suspicious activity); transparency of identity (identification of localised identity through such systems as biometrics[2]) and access control (the use of cryptographic barriers to keep unwanted threats outside and information inside). For scientists and engineers, the closer they can get to perfecting a suite of mechanisms for controlling risk of access to systems and information, acquiring suitable markers of identity, and watching users for unruly actions, then the closer we get to an online world in which we can trust. That is, the closer we get to the inculcation of 'expert systems' (Giddens, 1990) upon which users' can depend to provide order and safety online.

However, Nissenbaum (2001) argues that such security measures are merely a panacea in tackling the issue of user trust. She further notes that the fulfilment of trust online cannot be found in security measures, pointing out that reliance on such measures is tantamount to living behind prison bars, under surveillance cameras, body frisks and padlocks offline. Furthermore, the security industries' perspective of the problem of trust is too narrow: they tend to view users in terms of 'insiders' and 'outsiders' worrying that malicious attackers from outside may break into legitimate users' online space, compromise or steal information and destroy or compromise systems. Yet, Nissenbaum (2001) points to 'unrespectable' insiders who have access to our data and machines as an equally powerful force in creating resentment and harm in the fostering of distrust online. Security measures do not protect against unrespectable insiders generating spam,[3] flaming,[4] chain mail[5] and even virtual attacks[6] on users. Neither do they protect online users from legal intrusions, for example, marketers and data collection companies who collect information about online inhabitants for the purpose of selling such information to third parties (McStay and Bakir, 2006). Thus a climate of suspicion and distrust online ensues even if the online world is secure from 'outsiders', as there is little or no defence against unruly inside members of the online world who Nissenbaum argues are 'chipping away at trust just as surely as the allegedly amoral hackers' (2001, p. 12). As such it is Giddens's (1990) experts systems that exacerbate the problem of trust and risk online. Although users are growing increasingly comfortable with using e-commerce (Fusaro, 2002) and the symbolic systems that these entail, there remain user issues with invasive expert systems that facilitate these mechanisms. Those explored below are user agency with regard to specific risks, user actions in the face of specific risks, and user fears of the electronic environment *per se*.

Sztompka (1999, p. 25) defines trust as 'a bet about the future contingent actions of others'. It involves trust through action and the expectation that other's actions will have a contingent influence on the outcome of the 'bet'. Online commerce and the personalised nature of one-to-one interaction with the computer screen by necessity involve an element of risk and its corollary, trust, in the technocratic virtual condition. Risk here is considered as being activated by our own actions. For instance, downloading software from the Web opens oneself up to the risk of adware[7] and spyware.[8] We trigger off/recognise threats by unintentionally and intentionally making them relevant to us. Sztompka (1999, p. 30) further notes that risks are not just 'out there', but are taken and faced. In this sense, 'risk belongs to the discourse of agency, rather than the discourse of fate' although humanly created risks are still bound to the same uncertainty principle as with natural hazards (Sztompka, 1999, p. 39). He describes this as 'manufactured uncertainty' (Sztompka, 1999, p. 39). The significance of trust comes to the fore as a means of taming risk and countering uncertainties. Giddens similarly notes that given the expansion of abstract systems, 'trust in impersonal principles, as well as in anonymous others, becomes indispensable to social existence' (1990, p. 120). Luhmann, preceding Giddens, argues that we should expect trust to be increasingly in demand as a means of 'enduring the complexity of the future which technology will generate' (1979, p. 16).

So although as consumers of online advertising media we are aware of risks and potential hazards such as computer viruses, we continue to carry out our daily routines such as checking email. Arguably it is only when we are attacked by viruses, adware or spyware that our ontological status of low level fear becomes something much more; it becomes distrustful of online advertising *per se* including reputable advertisers. As Giddens notes:

> The predictability of the (apparently) minor routines of day-to-day life is deeply involved with a sense of psychological security. When such routines are shattered – for whatever reason – anxieties come flooding in, and even very firmly founded aspects of the personality of the individual may become stripped away and altered (Giddens, 1990, p. 98).

As the following section explains, the tools that advertisers use to target online consumers work to fuel discourses of mistrust and fear of online space.

Dataveillance and theoretical implications for trust of CRM strategies

Strategic hindrances for marketers and risk/trust anxieties of users stem from data-miners' legal use of adware and spyware as well as surveillance of personal information. As an expert system, adware is used to feed tailored adverts to users and make the overall user experience more personalised. One-to-one and personalised advertising does not broadcast to undifferentiated masses, but is instead customized for micro-targeted market segments. As opposed to traditional big brand advertising that works on a broadcasting model with the knowledge that there will be a large degree of wastage, one-to-one advertising aims to go still further than the narrowcasting model and engage users on a more-or-less individual basis tailoring advertisements and methods of delivery.

This requires information about users' activities and many companies offer incentives in exchange for information. To elicit such information marketers offer access to services and information. Alternatively, they may use adware and spyware that do not offer such incentives but instead covertly install themselves on users' machines. Issues of risk via lack of control of one's machine and the threat to trust arise when privacy is encroached upon through dataveillance, that is, 'the systematic use of personal data systems in the investigation or monitoring of the actions or communications of one or more persons' (Clarke, 1999, p. 2). Arvidsson (2004) notes that data-mining is not exclusive to the Internet: through the use of credit card records, mailing lists, customer benefit programs and barcode scans, 'our flaneuring life off-line also generates its virtual double in the form of a data trail to be processed and commodified' (2004, p. 457). This data double then enters into the circulation of a capitalist economy as raw material for information as commodity.

Disciplining practices of consumer profiling and data-mining initially find their theoretical expression in Foucault's (1977) investigation of the panoptican. However, as Haggerty and Ericson (2000) note, within surveillance studies there is a protracted reliance on Foucault's (1977) thesis of Bentham's 18th century panoptican. This finds expression today in Closed Circuit Television (CCTV), and, as Lyon (1994), Koskela (2003) and Yar (2003) note, when surveillance is conjoined with computerized tills and video cameras then we have entered a period of the panoptican without walls. However, as Wood (2003) points out, surveillance is not contingent upon 'sinister forces' wishing to do us harm. Wood (2003, pp. 237–8) states that surveillance can be used: '[...] in the name of the efficient servicing of consumer demand, society and sociality that has moved beyond the modernist project so accurately described by Foucault, towards a new situation of "unintended control"'.

For online services to be efficient it is necessary for expert systems, web site publishers and online stores to hold personal information about users in the name of protecting the interests of users and to streamline their experience. This issue becomes somewhat more complex when information is passed on to interested third parties. Dataveillance, although not so reliant on the surveillance-based panoptic model, still utilises disciplinary notions. Rodowick (2001, p. 222), in his discussion of Foucault (1977), Deleuze (1992) and electronic media argues that 'control societies organize power through the invisible or virtual architectures of computer networks and telecommunications'. He acknowledges the benefits that digital culture offers but asks at what price in terms of restructuring of power relations with the advent of digital technologies and accompanying dataveillance. Elmer states that

> [...] dataveillance entailed decentralizing the panoptic mode of surveillance calling into question the production of risk management tools – computer matching or profiling techniques that attempt to attribute general characteristics to individuals. (Elmer, 2003, p. 236)

Clarke (2001, p. 2) distinguishes between surveillance and dataveillance by pointing out the simple fact that watching people is expensive. It is far more cost-effective to monitor people through their data-trails than to watch them directly.

The situation is somewhat less one-sided than it may appear. As Elmer (2003, p. 237) notes there remains the issue of users and consumers being willing participants in the dataveillance process receiving both prizes and punishment. For example, when ordering products online, clicking on an advert, or filling personal details online there is often a reward or prize for delivering such information. For those who decline they may have to pay more for the same artefact or service, or be unable to access certain information or news services, like *The New York Times*. Thus the situation is somewhat more complicated than users being gazed upon by identifiable organisations. Instead data collection companies are not readily identifiable and take on a more abstract, ethereal form less easily identifiable and certainly more difficult to contact for the unaware user of a personal computer. Deleuze (1992, p. 4) states control mechanisms no longer operate through such unidirectional forces as the gaze, instead noting that 'Enclosures are molds, distinct castings, but controls are a modulation, like a self-deforming cast that will continuously change from one moment to the other, or like a sieve whose mesh will transmute from point to point'.

This ephemerality is readily notable when one looks at the workings of adware and spyware – the tools of insider data-gatherers. They install themselves (or the user unwittingly installs them) on a personal computer and when (and if) the user discovers them and tries to delete the programs they reinstall themselves via 'trickler' type programs that contact the host machine and download and reinstall the deleted adware program. Or, as Elmer (2003, pp. 241–2) puts it, societies of control depart from 'molds' of confinement that boxed 'deviants' into a wider system of control that attempt to 'account for the systemic modulations of populations by technological machines and information flows'.

These 'systemic modulations of populations' find expression in the identification of users online and the speed in which information can be gathered about users' activities. Rather than data collected from users being filed and used for later purposes, data are generated and put to commercial use immediately. However, as Deleuze (1992, p. 5) notes, in a 'control society' we are no longer designated by a signature or a number but instead a code. In terms of PC dataveillance, the code is a user's Internet Protocol (IP) address. It is not a signature, as it reveals nothing about the individual, but instead the activities of the IP address (such as where on the Internet does it go, how long does it stay for). As Deleuze (1992, p. 5) notes we have 'become 'dividuals, and masses, samples, data, markets, or "banks."' That is, users lose markers that form the individual as a social being and instead are reduced to a figure or variable. This becomes especially relevant when one considers that data are never held by one source. It is sold, diffused and used over and again, refined and redefined endlessly as programs on users' computers send information back to remote computers with the consequence being that matrices of users are reconfigured. The user is an ongoing impersonal assemblage utilised primarily for the purposes of marketing and governmental surveillance.

The user is reduced to a configuration of algorithms that have no reference outside of a weak simulation of the user. For Customer Relationship Managers, users are understood in terms of probability garnered from previous activities in offline and online social and commercial nodes, such as the use of store cards, magazine subscriptions and types of web sites visited. Hier (2003) also points to Haggerty and Ericson's (2000) extension of the notion of assemblage into 'surveillant assemblage'. This notion points to the assemblage of control, governance, security and profit that bear upon the gaining of users' personal details (or assemblages of which), especially given the fall-out from the '9/11' strike on the USA and the wider ramifications of the 2001 USA Patriot Act[9] introduced 45 days after the attacks (USA Congress, 2001). Hier describes these assemblages as a 'mechanism of visualisation' that bear upon users as 'a cyborg flesh/technology amalgamation comprised of pure information' (2003, p. 402) that is then targeted back at the user for a number of reasons including sales of products and advertisements. Furthermore, Lessig (1999) presciently points to contemporary online environments and future cyberspaces as a collection of coded architectures that are employed for one thing – control. The capacity to control from afar is the purpose of cybernetics. As early as World War II, Wiener (1961 [1948]) was working on cybernetics introducing terms such as 'feedback', 'input' and 'output' in describing the actions of both machine and animal. Indeed Hayles (1999, p. 91) notes that Wiener (1961 [1948]) chose to reject humanist ideas of subjectivity and instead focused on humans as simply being parts of systems with actions measured through behaviour rather than introspection. Control and demarcation of cyberspace is vital to advertisers and marketers because of their needs for an identifiable target audience receptive to commercial messages. This process of authentication is fuelled by both the willing and unwilling offering of data to data-miners, collectors and marketers.

Real-time feedback and the commercial environment of instantaneity

Authenticated information on users gathered by data-mining/collection companies, such as DoubleClick, Trice, BidBuddy and GoldLadder[10] reify discourses of instantaneity. They create collective market consciousness and the notion of instant data for instant application, whereby marketers and advertisers can, as the data-mining company *Insight* describes, 'Capture customer feedback, perform real time analysis and take action immediately' (2002). As Gandy (2003, p. 26) notes, the depth and extent of information is many times greater than that which can be extracted from what Lindstrom (2001) describes as offline bricks and mortar stores. Here data-mining and advertising converge into a synergy of real time feedback powered by information. Discussion of instantaneity and digital spaces is far from new: Virilio (1997, 2000), in a non-advertising context, has written extensively on the topic of immediacy. Virilio (1997, p. 16) describes instantaneity as the 'accident of the present', the abolition of the chronologically bound journey into a perpetual present where there is only the timeless exchange of information in a perfect surveillance-bound network.

The Internet has long since moved from being an unregulated arena of anonymity to one where control, authentication and tracking become implicit within the code and architectures of the Web. It is in this arena of control and instantaneity that marketers and advertisers seek an audience that are comparable to 'objects' in software programs (Fuller, 2003, p. 139). 'Objects' in software terms are bundles of data and related procedures that can both process and receive information. This means that companies and advertisers ask users to input personal data and therefore become part of a cybernetic informational loop – more often for the benefit of access to sites, product offers, discounts and favourable credit ratings. What this means is that the relationship between programs and users change. Computer software programs are not so much tools of users, but rather part of a symbiotic relationship in which the user is the tool of the program and the program is the tool of the user. This is manufactured through the mechanics of the Human Computer Interface (HCI). In this sense the user is the product of functionalist training from the HCI and thus constrained by the tools at hand. The user points, clicks, sends, receives and thus experiences erasure in the face of the Boolean logic of the machine, the Internet, and the profit-driven motives of the business that supports most private media – advertising. This sense of erasure contributes to the key problems that online advertisers and more generally CRM, face in their task of building trusting relationships in the arenas of online advertising and online consumption. That is, in their endeavour to get closer to their target audiences they in fact alienate them. In attempting to create one-to-one relations with their audiences, marketers and advertisers do not dispel distrust but instead amplify distrust by utilising the same mechanism that users are distrustful of, that is, the surveillance of users' activity and the positioning of users as information providers.

This issue of instantaneity and advertising delivery is only set to grow. Advertisers, marketers and Web publishers are increasingly tiring of poor feedback from banners, pop-up adverts and email marketing (Durkin and Lawlor, 2001). To some degree one may even argue that we are seeing the realisation of McLuhan's (1964) prophecies of the technological simulation of consciousness itself. McLuhan (1964, p. 3) famously predicted that the future of media involves '[the] technological simulation of consciousness when the creative process of knowing will be collectively and corporately extended to the whole of human society'.

This prophetic realisation is not in the holistic or planetary communicative fashion that McLuhan envisaged, but instead to serve the wants of advertisers and marketers. This 'creative knowing' is not so much a transcendence of embodied captive consciousness as much as totally targeted communications, understood and utilised by the 'experts' at the expense of users and consumer trust.

Conclusion

This chapter has elucidated key problems in the building of trust as it relates to e-commerce and online advertising. It is precisely the tools employed to build trust and relationships with consumers that users are arguably most concerned about. Thus marketers and advertisers find themselves in a negative feedback loop. The more precisely consumers are targeted, the more likely they are to turn away from the 'expert system'. This poses a real problem for advertisers trying to garner consumer trust: how do they allay consumer concerns about information privacy while at the same time generating greater levels of data to target consumers? Meanwhile, users have cause for concern, for as data-mining grows ever more pervasive, the architecture of the commercial Web is becoming ever tighter and accountable. Central here is control, and how the online environment is being refined to serve the informational needs of advertisers and corporations. This is not so much one-to-one advertising or interactive trust-oriented relationships. Instead this is the configuration of the user as a dependable and quantifiable variable whose program parameters have been mapped and thus is part of a wider package that can be delivered to businesses that seek the ultimate consumer – the truly accountable consumer.

Notes

1. BBC, *Online Ad Spend Trumps Airwaves*, (2005). Retrieved 11 November 2005 from the World Wide Web: http://news.bbc.co.uk/1/hi/business/4413461.stm
2. Biometrics is an authentication protocol usually based on users' fingerprints or retinal recognition.
3. Spam is unsolicited 'junk' e-mail sent to large numbers of people to promote products or services. It also refers to inappropriate promotional or commercial postings to discussion groups or bulletin boards.
4. Flaming is the practice of posting messages that are deliberately hostile and insulting to a discussion board usually on the Internet.
5. Chain mail is email that requests the user to forward said mail to fellow users. These usually take the form of a request, threat or a hook.

6. Virtual attacks are attacks on another user that cause mental distress.
7. Adware is programming that is put in someone's computer for the purposes of gathering information. Often it is used for the purposes of data-collection for marketing ends.
8. Typically, spyware is a separate program that is installed at the same time as shareware or similar program, and will usually continue to generate advertising even when the user is not running the originally desired program.
9. The USA Patriot Act (its full name being 'Uniting and Strengthening America Act by Providing Appropriate Tools Required to Intercept and Obstruct Terrorism Act of 2001') was enacted by the US Congress on October 26, 2001, at the request of President George Bush in response to the terrorist acts of September 11.
10. See http://www.doubleclick.com; http://www.triceuk.com/pp/; http://www. bidbuddy.co.uk and http://www.goldladder.co.uk/.

Part III Media and Building Trust

11
Risk Communication, Television News and Trust Generation: The Utility of Ethos

Vian Bakir

This chapter examines how international Non-Governmental Organisation (NGO), Greenpeace, and multi-national oil and gas corporation, Royal-Dutch Shell, attempted to generate trust from various audiences through news-oriented rhetorical strategies. Two risk issues are explored where Greenpeace sought international attention in the 1990s and which generated 'reputational shocks' (Wheeler, Rechtman, Fabig and Boele, 2001, p. 194) causing Shell to reassess its corporate reputation management. The risk issues comprise the disposal of Shell-UK's North Sea oil rig, the Brent Spar (hereafter referred to as the 'Spar') and Shell-Nigeria's pollution of Ogoniland, Nigeria.

In seeking to influence the public (and thereby, decision-makers), gaining media attention has been Greenpeace's paramount strategy since its creation in 1971. Increasingly, 'big business', targeted on its environmental record, has retaliated. By the early 1990s, Royal-Dutch Shell was frequently regarded as a model for Multi-National Corporation (MNC) managers (*The Economist*, 1995),[1] having worked assiduously with conservationists to promote its green image (Ketola, 1993; Elkington and Trisoglio, 1996). Arguably, for organisations like Greenpeace and Shell, generating trust with multiple audiences such as journalists, the public and governments, is particularly important given Beck's (1992b) observation on the risk society's private and political mood swings. Since environmental risks are largely invisible, generally recognisable only through scientific theorising and experimentation, they are susceptible to divergent interpretations: 'The risk society shifts from hysteria to indifference and vice versa' (Beck, 1996a, p. 37).

In looking at the construction of mass-mediated trust in the risk society, this chapter utilises, and thereby examines the utility of, Aristotle's (384–322 BC) rhetorical concept of 'ethos' (persuasion through 'stance', 'moral character' and 'personality') (Aristotle, 1965). Aristotle saw ethos as the most important of the three main rhetorical structuring principles, the others being 'pathos' (persuasion through emotion) and 'logos' (persuasion through reasoning) (Aristotle, 1962, 1965). In other words, persuasion through targeting hearts and minds necessitates the rhetorical structuring principle that allows us to *trust* our hearts and minds – ethos. It is expected that with risk issues, where interpretations are plural, utilising ethos to generate trust is vital to those seeking to influence the public or policy-makers.[2] As Aristotle (1965, p. 60) says: 'we trust men of probity more, and more quickly, about things in general, while on points outside the realm of exact knowledge, where opinion is divided, we trust them absolutely'.

The risk issues

The battle over Brent Spar

The Spar was the first oil platform to be disposed of since North Sea oil drilling began in the 1970s. In spring 1995, Shell-UK and the UK Government agreed to dispose of the Spar by dumping it in a deep trench in the North East Atlantic. Greenpeace's three strongest organisations in Europe – Greenpeace-UK, Greenpeace-Netherlands and Greenpeace-Germany – objected and in time-honoured fashion, captured media attention through direct action, boarding the Spar on 30 April 1995 and remaining there intermittently until 20 June. Greenpeace's media campaign generated widespread boycotts of Shell across Northern Europe, particularly in Germany (Tsoukas, 1999), and denunciations by prominent European politicians (Löfstedt, 1997), while Shell itself became publicly divided over the issue (see Bakir, 2005). Given this mounting pressure, Shell-UK made an unprecedented 'U-turn' on 20 June 1995, cancelling the deep-sea disposal.

The battle over Ogoniland

In 1958, Shell-Nigeria discovered oil in Ogoniland – 404 square miles of fertile Niger Delta land, home to 500, 000 Ogoni people out of approximately 100 million Nigerians (Brock, 1999). While oil became the fiscal basis of the Nigerian state (Obi, 1997), the oil-producing areas have minimal infrastructure and suffer massive environmental degradation. Nigerian writer and campaigner, Ken Saro-Wiwa, helped create the Movement for the Survival of the Ogoni People (MOSOP) in 1990, which adopted the Ogoni Bill of Rights in 1991, demanding ethnic self-determination, greater national representation, fairer shares of oil revenues and control over their environment. An 'Ogoni Day' demonstration in Nigeria on 4 January 1993 led to the Nigerian military regime decreeing that demands for self-determination and disruption of oil production were punishable by death under treason laws. Greenpeace's (among other NGOs') involvement with MOSOP also started in 1993 (Bob, 2005). On 21 May 1994, four pro-government Ogoni leaders were killed by a mob. Saro-Wiwa and eight other Ogoni activists were arrested, accused of complicity in these murders (Idowu, 1999): they were sentenced to death on

31 October 1995, and executed 10 days later. As with the deep-sea disposal issue, appeals were made for boycotts, with Greenpeace helping to organise anti-Shell consumer boycotts in Germany, the Netherlands and the UK. While the British Commonwealth expelled Nigeria, and the USA and other nations imposed diplomatic sanctions, more meaningful actions, such as governmental boycotts of Nigerian oil exports, never occurred (Bob, 2005), and Shell continued to operate in Nigeria.

Ethos analysis

In examining ethos strategies utilised across the two risk issues, this chapter will first look at persuasion through stance – namely the wider attitudinal framework adopted by persuaders, and the tone taken towards the topic of interaction and its context. It will then look at persuasion through moral character, involving credibility and legitimacy claims; and persuasion through personality, central to which is the ability to identify with audiences (Aristotle, 1965).

Persuasion through stance

Historically, one of Greenpeace's strong scientific stances is the need for the precautionary principle, which gives the benefit of scientific doubt to planetary welfare rather than to potentially hazardous human activities (Morris, 2000). Indeed, Greenpeace was instrumental in getting the precautionary principle adopted by key international regulatory bodies (Brown and May, 1991). Despite this historically strong stance, during Greenpeace's seven-week direct action campaign (30 April–20 June 1995) over deep-sea disposal, Greenpeace's press releases never directly referred to the precautionary principle, but promoted it indirectly through the cloak of pathos, using emotive and vilificatory language. For instance, Greenpeace stated that deep-sea disposal was '*short-sighted* and the latest example of governments allowing industry to treat the seas as a *toxic dump*' (Greenpeace-UK, 1995, author's emphasis).[3] Such stark accusations were married with Greenpeace's Video News Releases (VNRs) of dramatic, visually appealing and accessible direct action (like activists boarding the Spar via dangerous helicopter drops through high-pressure water sprays from Shell's surrounding vessels) (Bakir, 2005). These activities caught journalists' attention – initially in Northern Europe: 'the Germans and Dutch had ships and helicopters with multiple crews covering the events' (Lambon, personal communication).[4] As UK media attention gradually increased, Greenpeace was interviewed – allowing it to elaborate its risk stance directly to the UK public:

[deep water disposal] is obviously a very much cheaper option. But it is not the most desirable option. Quite simply, because we have no idea of what the long or indeed the short-term impact of dumping on the deep-sea floor. (Dr Paul Johnston, Greenpeace, Exeter University, Channel 4 News, 1995)[5]

Thus, although Greenpeace's '"positions" are essentially moral ones, intervening on the moral boundary of an "issue"' (Rose, 1993, p. 291), Greenpeace initiated media attention with pathos-laden direct action and emotive claims regarding the Spar's toxicity. This accords with Dale's (1996, p. 115) observation that Greenpeace International are a filtering mechanism so that morally inspired, zealous campaigners do not put off news editors, who: 'search for the "gotcha" value, not moral lessons'.

Shell's stance regarding the precautionary principle was selective and self-serving. It used precautionary principle language in only one press release and only in relation to onshore disposal (the more expensive disposal option that Shell had rejected): 'Of onshore disposal, McDermott[6] said: "The evaluation has highlighted ... areas of uncertainty that may have a substantial impact on the feasibility, safety and financial aspects"' (Shell-UK, 1995).[7] Thus, Shell used the precautionary principle only where it suited its agenda, urging caution regarding technical, occupational safety and financial, but not environmental, risks. Such selective usage of principled stances does not build long-term trust. When projecting stances, maintaining continuity is important, otherwise exposing persuaders to damaging criticisms of distortion or hypocrisy (Cockroft and Cockroft, 1992). Understanding this, Greenpeace maintained its risk stance throughout both issues. As over deep-sea disposal, Greenpeace condemned Shell for its short-sightedness in the Ogoniland issue: 'If Shell had really cared about the effect of the gas flaring on the local population they would never have let it go ahead in the first place' (Greenpeace-UK, 1995).[8]

Throughout the Ogoniland issue, Shell's main projected stance was that commercial organisations should not interfere with politics – a stance particularly suited to Shell-Nigeria's operations, where in order to attract foreign investments, the Nigerian Government has allowed lower environmental standards (Fryas, 1998). Shell reiterated this stance when it was urged to appeal to the Nigerian regime to commute Saro-Wiwa's death sentence. However, sending a mixed message through its actions, Shell appealed for clemency at the last minute. This inconsistency between stance and action was focused upon in a live interview with Group Managing Director of Shell-International, Mark Moody-Stewart – an inconsistency the viewing public would take note of given that TV presenters are highly trusted by the UK public partly *because of* their preparedness to press power holders to explain and justify their actions (Petts, Horlick-Jones and Murdock, 2001, p. 86). Here the presenter aggressively attacked Shell's stance, accusing Shell six times of having had 'political conversations' with the Nigerian Government in London. On receiving repeatedly evasive responses like 'I have no idea which meeting you're talking about'

(BBC2, *Newsnight*, 1995),[9] the presenter rearticulated his question (see below) and the interview concluded with what looked like an admission from Shell of its inconsistent stance:

> *Presenter*: Did you or did you not engage in discussions with the Nigerian High Commissioner – your own colleagues – engage in discussions with the Nigerian High Commissioner about how Nigeria should publicise the trial, should deal with the Ogoni problem?
> *Mark Moody-Stewart*: My colleagues would certainly have discussed with the High Commissioner the impact of the outcome of the trial and so on, on, on Nigeria – that is quite possible. In discussion ...
> *Presenter* (interrupting): Isn't that political involvement?
> *Mark Moody-Stewart*: In discussions [talking over presenter], in discussions we may well, be called upon and asked for advice on various things which we will give. We did, in fact, give advice. (BBC2, *Newsnight*, 1995)[10]

Greenpeace's and Shell's varying ability to maintain continuity in their stances is likely to have influenced not just news audiences' trust in them, but also journalists' future assessment of their trustworthiness as sources. Indeed, journalists and editors questioned for this study observed that among the routes by which sources became established, 'consistency' (BBC, personal communication)[11] and 'proven reliability' (ITN, personal communication)[12] were important.

Persuasion through moral character

Legitimacy claims

In terms of projecting its legitimacy to campaign on the environment's behalf, Greenpeace has a strong ethical capital base accumulated over years of campaigning. Aristotle argued that the ability to persuade required individual virtue and integrity to be anchored in place (Cooper, 1932). Indeed, in the deep-sea disposal issue, Greenpeace's ethical capital was augmented as it promoted its oneness with nature (its virtue) and its integrity (and hence its legitimacy to criticise Shell).

Greenpeace is adept at promoting imagery of itself as at one with nature. For instance, the phrase 'The sea itself has granted us a stay of execution today' (Greenpeace-UK, 1995),[13] in reference to storms preventing Shell from boarding the Spar and ejecting Greenpeace activists, evokes the order of natural justice. A visual 'sight-bite' as Greenpeace's victory over Shell was reported again suggested nature's bond with Greenpeace: a rainbow appeared over the Spar as it was being hosed by Shell's surrounding ships (BBC1 Regional News, 1995).[14]

Greenpeace is also adept at promoting its integrity. Several months after Shell's U-turn, an independent audit of the Spar found that Greenpeace's high toxicity estimates were wrong, with the true figure closer to Shell's estimate (Shell-UK, 1995).[15] Greenpeace quickly admitted its error: 'Greenpeace relies on the trust of the public. Because of this we were happy to make it known that we had made a minor mistake' (Greenpeace-UK, 1995).[16] While Greenpeace's mistake was highlighted by UK news broadsheets, there was minimal damage to public perception of Greenpeace's integrity, since deep-sea disposal was out of the spotlight of TV news (Bakir, 2006). Indeed, in 1996 Bob Worcester, Chairman of polling firm MORI, argued that Greenpeace won the battle by ten to one in the eyes of the British public, and that although its scientific methods were flawed its recovery was open, direct and immediate (Worcester, 1996). More damaging were journalists' and editors' perceptions of Greenpeace's integrity. MORI's survey of editors in October–November 1996, found that Greenpeace generated significantly more 'unfavourable' impressions than other environmental NGOs measured, with 23 per cent having a very, or mainly, unfavourable impression (C.Rose, 1998). Similarly, one broadcast journalist questioned for this study stated that 'truthfulness' was a characteristic of a good source, rating Greenpeace as 'not very credible' (BBC, personal communication).[17] However, Greenpeace's admission of its mistake appeased some journalistic gatekeepers: as one editor observed, 'openness' and 'transparency of motive' were amongst the characteristics of a good source, rating Greenpeace as '8/10' in terms of source credibility (ITN, personal communication).[18]

Shell attempted to project its legitimacy and licence to operate mainly through portraying itself as concerned with corporate social responsibility:

> The Government has endorsed the plan after several months' careful consideration of the options and three years of painstaking analysis by Shell. Both Shell and independent assessments have concluded that the impact on the marine environment will be very localised, and negligible. Fishing and environmental organisations consulted have agreed with this analysis. (Shell-UK, 1995)[19]

Here, lexical choice like 'careful consideration' and 'painstaking analysis' emphasises Shell's arduous care. Shell notes the independence, and hence legitimacy, of supporting environmental impact assessments. Only the most obvious stakeholders are mentioned in general terms. This vagueness projects an impression of widespread consultation, whereas in fact Shell had consulted only those explicitly required by the British Petroleum Act (UK Parliament, 1987; Tsoukas, 1999). However, Shell's attempts at projecting its legitimacy were stymied by Greenpeace's ability to make the Spar an international symbol of corporate social irresponsibility through sight-bites of the Spar's rusting, abandoned hulk framing all direct action VNRs, and soundbites: 'The lesson of the Brent Spar for the oil industry must be that they can't go on behaving like unaccountable spoilt children who think they can do exactly what they like' (Rose, 1995).[20]

Similar strategies were used in the Ogoniland issue to project legitimacy. Greenpeace accused Shell of ignoring its corporate social responsibility: 'Due to Shell's oil operations in the Niger Delta, the Ogoni people have lost their farmlands, fisheries and livelihood' (Greenpeace-UK, 1995).[21] However, Greenpeace's double target – both Shell and the Nigerian regime – diluted Greenpeace's message: in the fortnight between the announcement of the death sentence and executions, TV news framed the issue as a human rights rather than an environmental issue twice as often.[22] Shell promoted its high corporate social responsibility, this time by highlighting its good intentions – its search for 'solutions' to 'complex issues' with anonymous groups (see Table 11.1, sentence 16). While Shell gives the impression of social concern bolstered by a list of its 'contribution to improving the communities' quality of life' (Table 11.1, sentences 17–8), it does not detail whether it is making good its past damage.

Through such 'impression management' techniques (Allen and Caillouet, 1994, p. 44) Shell attempted to promote its legitimacy. Unfortunately for Shell, these details did not filter through to news broadcasts. Rather, by drawing attention to its corporate social responsibility, Shell gave the news a hook on which to attack it. Numerous broadcasts aired calls for Shell to operate to the same environmental standards as in Europe or to withdraw from Nigeria. As Saro-Wiwa's son, Ken Wiwa, complained: 'Less than a week after Ogoni activists had been executed, they're planning to go ahead with the biggest em – venture they've ever had in Nigeria. It's just – it's absolutely astonishing and it's in line with the insensitivity of this – of that company' (BBC News, 1995).[23] Arguably, Shell's statements on corporate social responsibility further negatively associated it with an oppressive regime.

Credibility claims

In addition to legitimacy, a key aspect to the projection of moral character is credibility. In the final days of its direct action campaign over deep-sea

Table 11.1 Shell's projection of its legitimacy

Sentence	Data
... 16	... Shell sympathises with many of the grievances felt by the communities in the oil producing regions of the Niger Delta, and while it will not intervene in Nigeria's domestic politics, it is involved in discussions with a wide range of groups who are interested in finding solutions to these complex issues.
17	In addition, Shell makes its own contribution to improving the communities' quality of life, funding roads, clinics, schools, water schemes, scholarships and agricultural support projects.
18	Spending on these community projects will reach more than US$25 million this year alone.

Source: Shell press release, 31 October 1995.

disposal, Greenpeace utilised the rhetorical structuring principal of logos to augment the credibility of its toxicity claims for the public, and also to maintain its high position in the news agenda by generating fresh angles. Thus, in eyewitness mode, Greenpeace publicised its own scientific analysis of samples taken by activists on the Spar (Greenpeace-UK, 1995;[24] Channel 4 News, 1995[25]) and garnered independent scientific testimony by publicising an old leaked document from the Ministry of Agriculture, Food and Fisheries (MAFF) to the Department of Trade and Industry (DTI) stating that 'the zinc and copper aboard the Spar should be "treated as hazardous waste" ... and very stringent controls should be applied' (Greenpeace-UK, 1995).[26] No independent scientific opinion was published on the disposal issue during the direct action campaign (Bakir, 2006) because of the relatively long time it takes to get published in scientific journals.[27] Since scientific journals and magazines are important sources in mass media coverage of environmental stories (Pearce, personal communication),[28] Greenpeace's scientific allegations were not subjected to tougher credibility tests.

Credibility is greatly influenced by appearances on camera – particularly when pressurised by difficult questions in live interviews (Fearn-Banks, 1996) where close-up shots capture all changing expressions and tones of voice – both intentional and unintentional – and where changes in stance can be scrutinised. Unfortunately for Shell, news space for live interviews tends to be created only when there is a particularly dramatic crisis point that the news wishes to elaborate.[29] Indeed, in the deep-sea disposal and Ogoniland issues, the only live interviews were on the days of Shell's U-turn and the execution of the Ogoni activists. In both issues, Shell was accused of changing stance – in the Ogoniland issue over commercial involvement in politics, and in the deep-sea disposal issue, over its risk stance (a fragment of which is presented in Table 11.2). Here the presenter leads with a loaded and inaccurate statement (row 1) which Shell-UK's Chairman, Chris Fay, tries to correct (row 2) only to be cut off by the presenter who accuses Shell of changing stance (row 3). Fay corrects this damaging accusation but is left with the awkward task of explaining its U-turn (rows 4–5). In both live interviews, Shell's representative tries to bolster Shell's credibility by appearing calm, courteous, responsive, direct, positive and truthful, so conforming to Fearn-Banks's (1996) suggestions for interviewees. However, whereas Shell managed to maintain this projection in the deep-sea disposal live interview, its ability to project directness and truthfulness was minimised in the Ogoniland live interview, as demonstrated by Mark Moody-Stewart's evasiveness over Shell's 'political conversations' (detailed earlier).

Persuasion through personality

Greenpeace is practiced at orienting itself towards its audiences. For instance, in the deep-sea disposal issue, Greenpeace promoted the precautionary principle while avoiding technical language, so catering for the

Table 11.2 Attacks on Shell's credibility in the deep-sea disposal issue

Row	Visuals	Audio
1	Studio mode: Cut to close-up (CU) of Fay who looks impassive. Cut to CU of presenter, reading. He looks up with consternation at 'environmentally-unfriendly'.	We have got this straight, haven't we? You are now going to dispose of this construction in the most environmentally unfriendly way available to you.
2	Cut to CU of Fay. He shifts in his seat. Caption: 'Chris Fay, Shell-UK'.	Fay: Well – it's not the most environmentally unfriendly way. What has been said tonight ....
3	Presenter voice-over with Fay remaining in shot.	Presenter: Well it's what you've been saying up 'til now.
4	Fay engages in direct gaze with presenter, using his hands for emphasis.	Fay: No, no. I think you're already mixing your words. What the Ministry has said is totally and utterly true.
5	Cut to CU of Tim Eggar (Industry Minister) (live link-up). Cut to CU of Fay. He leans forward at the words 'not the worst' for emphasis.	The deep-water disposal option is the best environmental option when you take everything into account. We do not deny that at all. The second-best option – not the worst – is indeed to bring the rig onshore. Now, I do not have a license to bring that onshore and I have to secure that license from the British Government.

Source: BBC2, Newsnight, (London, BBC2, 20 June 1995, VHS recording).

wider public (who are not scientifically aware) and journalists (who need to present a clear message in a small time frame).[30] In this sense, Greenpeace is better than scientists in presenting risk issues: 'scientists tend to be academics and as such are seldom good for TV as their answers are inevitably too intricate and lengthy' (Lambon, personal communication).[31] Greenpeace projected its deep-sea disposal messages across the three European nations where its public support was the strongest, receiving much media attention and stimulating consumer boycotts.

In contrast, Shell-UK did not anticipate a campaign extending across Northern Europe; nor did it identify the strength of its audiences' principled stance on dumping. Rather than taking moral stances on the environment, Shell utilised logos strategies, maintaining that deep-sea disposal was 'based on sound science, reason, and careful balance' (Shell-UK, 1995). In line with Shell's historically technocentric thinking (Boele, Fabig and Wheeler, 2001), Fran Morrison, Shell-UK's Media Relations Manager, stated that Shell's strategy was 'to explain the technical, regulatory and scientific case to all who would listen' (Shell-UK, 1995, p. 8). Typical press releases read 'Deepwater disposal of the Spar has been independently assessed as the best option from an environmental point of view, and in terms of several other considerations including health, safety and economic efficiency' (Shell-UK, 1995).[32] This stance, frequently broadcasted on TV news, utilises a cost-benefit tool called the Best Practicable Environmental Option (BPEO) that claims to look rationally at multiple factors when planning actions (Rudall Blanchard Associates, 1994). Unfortunately for Shell, its explication of BPEO failed to convince large sections of north European consumers.

By the time of the Ogoni activists' death sentence in autumn 1995, Shell had learned lessons. Rather than trying to explain its actions in technocratic terms, Shell avoided this altogether, opting to categorically reject Saro-Wiwa's accusations of pollution: 'we do not believe we have polluted it and rendered it infertile. It is simply not true'.[33] However, these stark rebuttals, while making TV news, were belied by frequently broadcast and equally stark images of open gas flaring in Ogoni farmlands (broadcast in 9 out of 21 Ogoniland TV news broadcasts). Appreciating the high emotive charge connected to the human rights aspect of the Ogoniland issue, as the death sentences on Ogoni activists were announced, Shell released a press release crafted to appease its many critics (see Table 11.3).

Here Shell refers to organisations calling for the corporation's involvement as 'respected' (sentence 5), so orienting itself towards those who support these organisations' causes (most people are against death penalties for free speech). Later, however, Shell reminds us that these organisations have agendas (sentence 10). Shell minimises its own power, referring to 'its perceived "influence"' (sentence 6), then suggests Saro-Wiwa is a 'criminal' (sentence 8), so reinforcing that it would be wrong to intervene. These statements augment Shell's stance of commercial non-interference in nations'

Table 11.3 Shell's orientation towards its audience

Sentence	Data
5	Throughout the trial a number of respected organisations and campaigners raised questions over the fairness of the trial procedure.
6	There are now demands that Shell should intervene, and use its perceived 'influence' to have the judgement overturned.
7	This would be dangerous and wrong.
8	Ken Saro-Wiwa and his co-defendants were accused of a criminal offence.
9	A commercial organisation like Shell cannot and must never interfere with the legal processes of any sovereign state.
10	Those who call on us to do so might well be the first to criticise in any situation where that intervention did not suit their agenda.

Source: Shell press release, 31 October 1995.

politics (sentence 9). Shell's attempts to engage with its western audiences' perspective had some success in making TV news. For instance, in the live interview with Group Managing Director for Shell-International, Mark Moody-Stewart expounds Shell's stance with an example that the British audience would relate to:

> We generate for example in the North Sea huge amounts of revenue for the government. We do not tell the government how to spend its money – a hospital here, a hospital there, more money for the people of Aberdeen. That's not our business and if we did it, we would be rightly, strongly criticised for it. (BBC2, *Newsnight*, 1995)[34]

The use and utility of ethos?

While no persuasive discourse stands alone, the rhetorical structuring principle of ethos is demonstrably important in generating trust through TV news-oriented rhetorical strategies in risk issues. The following points in using ethos can be made, with insights for those seeking to use TV news to generate trust presented in italics.

Stances, once projected, should be maintained both in words and actions, otherwise one risks alienating or provoking journalists and wider audiences. Greenpeace's historical risk stance was maintained throughout the deep-sea disposal issue whereas Shell selectively used the precautionary principle. Shell's stances on the BPEO and non-interference in politics, while projected consistently in press releases, were undermined by its actions in U-turning and in appealing for clemency. These changes in stance were scrutinised by in-depth TV news broadcasts where Shell appeared inconsistent at best and evasive at worst.

In terms of moral character and legitimacy, Greenpeace metonymically projected its oneness with nature, so augmenting its legitimacy to criticise Shell. *Legitimacy should be augmented through plausible, recognisable and memorable soundbites and sight-bites.* Shell projected its own corporate social responsibility consistently throughout both risk issues. However, in the deep-sea disposal issue, this projection was scuttled by Greenpeace's ability to make the Spar a symbol of Shell's corporate social irresponsibility across Northern Europe. *Projection of one's own legitimacy should consider the nature and extent of attacks from legitimate opponents in international media from countries where one operates.* Shell's projection of its corporate social responsibility in the Ogoniland issue was undone by TV news frames that exposed the disparity between Shell's rhetoric and actions, and further negatively associated Shell with an oppressive regime. *Projection of one's legitimacy should identify likely journalistic framings and consider whether the strength of one's legitimacy will bear the weight of these framings.* In the deep-sea disposal issue, Greenpeace displayed its integrity through immediate and open admission of its toxicity mistake. *Challenges to legitimacy should be pro-actively addressed quickly and publicly*. In the Ogoniland issue, Greenpeace was unable to construct a simple symbol of corporate social irresponsibility, as the issues involved a military dictatorship as well as an oil giant. TV news correspondingly focused on human rights to the detriment of the environment. *Attacks on opponents' legitimacy should be as targeted and simple as possible.*

In terms of moral character and credibility, Greenpeace strengthened the credibility of its scientific risk claims for the public by referring to endorsements from its own and government scientists. *Cultivate credibility through endorsements from credible third parties*. Greenpeace's mistake over the Spar's toxicity damaged its trustworthiness in the eyes of some broadcast news editors, but not in the public's eyes, as TV news attention was minimal when the mistake came to light – a predictable occurrence given that the direct action campaign had long since ended. *Decide whether it is more important to maintain credibility in the eyes of journalistic gatekeepers or the public*. Shell's credibility was severely questioned through extensive and pointed live interviews of its representatives as it U-turned in the deep-sea disposal issue and appealed for clemency in the Ogoniland issue. *Only attempt to project credibility through live TV interviews (that are created to explore the crisis from an oppositional viewpoint) if you have a defensible stance that is commensurate with your actions and that you can articulate simply and consistently.*

Personality, and orientation towards audiences, is important. Greenpeace broadcast its stance on the precautionary principle across Northern Europe through awareness of what appeals to journalists and editors, initially attracting their attention through pathos (such as emotive direct action), bolstering its claims through logos (presenting scientific endorsements of its stance in non-technical language), and only directly articulating its stance on the precautionary principle on gaining access to the public through TV news interviews. *Attract journalistic attention through appropriate use of pathos and logos, then use the media platform generated to project the main moral stance*. Shell's stance that deep-sea disposal was the BPEO was presented in technical language that downplayed the environment's importance: thus, while gaining access to TV news, Shell failed to connect with the public. In the Ogoniland issue, this time mindful of its western audience, Shell carefully crafted its stance on non-interference in politics while conveying its sympathy for the Ogoni. This gained access to TV news, but within a frame of human rights abuses that minimised Shell's legitimacy. *Ensure that your stance is understandable to, and understanding of, your various audiences – both journalistic and public*. In the Ogoniland issue, Shell minimised its technocratic language with its stance on pollution projected through clear and simple refutations of Saro-Wiwa's claims. However, TV pictures of gas flaring in farmland publicly undermined Shell's stance. *Ensure simplified verbal statements are evidenced by appropriate visuals.*

Ultimately, however, mass-mediated rhetoric only goes so far in building trust. While between the intensive media coverage of the deep-sea disposal issue (April–June 1995) and the Ogoniland issue (October–November 1995), Shell became more aware of the importance of ethos and more practiced in orienting itself towards its audience, Shell also recognised the disparities between its rhetoric and action, so initiating its 'Transformation'[35] (Knight, 1998, p. 2). Although Shell continued to operate in Nigeria, its relationships with opinion formers and stakeholders (like local communities and consumers) were given greater importance in its strategy-making post-1995, with explicit recognition of the importance of sustainable development and human rights (Knight, 1998; Boele et al., 2001; Bob, 2005). Such actions work to bolster Shell's stance on corporate social responsibility and its moral character not just for wider audiences, but perhaps more importantly for journalists and editors who act as gatekeepers and framers for wider audiences. If Shell maintains its ability to orientate its message towards its audiences, including journalists, when the next crisis hits, Shell may have a stronger basis from which to project its ethos.

Notes

1. *The Economist*, June (1995) 80.
2. Systematic qualitative analysis of all Greenpeace-UK's and Shell-UK's press releases and all UK national terrestrial TV evening news broadcasts (BBC1, BBC2, ITN, Channel 4) related to the two risk issues during 1995 when media coverage was most intense, allowed identification of Greenpeace's and Shell's ethos strategies. National evening news broadcasts were chosen because of their credibility and their large UK national audiences – making them important channels for those seeking to influence public opinion. Some Scottish regional news broadcasts were chosen to generate a wider range of televisual reportage: it was expected that the Spar, being towed around the tip of Scotland, would generate specific regional interest. Semi-structured postal and e-mail questionnaires conducted in 2000 with UK journalists and editors who had covered each risk issue facilitated understanding of their perceptions of Greenpeace and Shell.
3. Greenpeace-UK press release, 30 April 1995.
4. T. Lambon, Freelance Producer/Cameraman/Editor to US and UK news networks, questionnaire response, March 2000.
5. Channel 4, *7.00pm News*, (London, Channel 4, 23 May 1995, VHS video).
6. McDermott Engineering (Europe) Ltd. is a world leader in offshore engineering.
7. Shell-UK press release, 15 June 1995.
8. Greenpeace-UK press release, 15 November 1995.
9. BBC2, *Newsnight*, (London, BBC, 14 November 1995, VHS video).
10. BBC2, *Newsnight*, (London, BBC, 14 November 1995, VHS video).
11. Anonymous questionnaire response, *BBC*, April 2000.
12. Anonymous questionnaire response, *ITN*, March 2000.
13. Greenpeace-UK press release, 22 May 1995.
14. BBC1, *Reporting Scotland*, (London, BBC, 21 June 1995, VHS video).
15. Shell-UK press release, 18 October 1995.

16. Greenpeace-UK press release, 5 September 1995.
17. Anonymous questionnaire response, *BBC*, April 2000.
18. Anonymous questionnaire response, *ITN*, March 2000.
19. Shell-UK press release, 16 May 1995.
20. Channel 4, *7.00pm News*, (London, Channel 4, 16 June 1995, VHS video).
21. Greenpeace-UK press release, 31 October 1995.
22. Predominantly, the Ogoni activists were referred to as 'human rights' and 'pro-democracy' rather than 'environmental' campaigners/activists, and there was extensive reference to the flawed trial, international pleas for clemency and interviews with human rights campaigners.
23. BBC1, *6.00 News*, (London, BBC, 15 November 1995, VHS video).
24. Greenpeace-UK press release, 16 June 1995.
25. Channel 4, *7.00 pm News*, (London, ITN, 21 June 1995, VHS recording).
26. Greenpeace-UK press release, 20 June 1995.
27. *Nature*'s policy is not to offer unpublished evidence to the media (Anderson, 1997).
28. F. Pearce, Environment Consultant, *New Scientist*, questionnaire response, March 2000.
29. For instance, the modal length of time for Spar national TV evening news broadcasts was 2–3 minutes (supporting the findings of Heinderyckx [1993]).
30. Research shows that scientific and technical risk aspects are often ignored within environmental reporting (Dunwoody and Peters, 1992; Sachsman, 1993).
31. T. Lambon, Freelance Producer/Cameraman/Editor to US and UK news networks, questionnaire response, March 2000.
32. Shell-UK press release, 16 May 1995.
33. BBC2, *Newsnight*, (London, BBC, 14 November 1995, VHS video).
34. BBC2, *Newsnight*, (London, BBC, 14 November 1995, VHS video).
35. One element of the transformation involved an international programme of conversations with people to understand society's expectations of MNCs (1996) and another to explore the reputation, image and overall standing of Royal-Dutch Shell.

12
The Media's Role in a Transition Society: From Public Lies to Public Trust?

Kaja Tampere

Historical context

The end of the 1980s was a significant turning point for a large part of Europe. The liberal political winds blowing from Moscow brought about several unprecedented developments – the fall of the Berlin Wall, the breakdown of the socialist/communist regime in many European countries, the development of completely new economic-political communities and changing societies. All this also triggered the appearance of new values, the rethinking of former principles and rules, and the development of new meanings and views.

Societies changing from totalitarian to democratic are called transition societies. Transition constitutes a complex reworking of old social relations in the light of processes distinctive of one of the boldest projects in contemporary history – the attempt to construct a form of capitalism on and with the ruins of the communist system (Stark, 1996; Smith, 1997). After the revolutionary changes in the eastern part of Europe in 1989, the concept 'societies in transition' has become a common phrase referring to the countries of Eastern Europe and the former Soviet Union. In each of them, one may speak of systemic changes at all levels of society as a whole, which would result in the emergence of a new kind of society. Societal, social and individual levels of change in every post-communist country are integrated into the systemic whole by common cultural characteristics, partly rooted in national culture, but at the same time strongly influenced by the all-European cultural environment and by global processes (Lauristin, Vihalemm, Rosengren and Weibull, 1997, p. 26). The year 1989 did not mark a political shift from autocratic, mono-party regimes towards parliamentary, multi-party systems – the ultimate victory of democracy; nor was it an economic break from a socialist, planned, command economy, to a basically free, capitalist market – the second birth of capitalism. It did not see radical transformation of institutions, or the restitution of some earlier social order – 'the return'to Europe, to the West, to 'normality'. Rather, it started the reconstruction of a new social order from a strange mixture of components of varied origin. It was a major cultural and civilisational break a beginning of the reconstruction of the deepest cultural tissue as well as the civilised surface of society, the slow emergence of a new post-communist culture and civilisation (Sztompka, 1996, p. 120).

Trust and society

Trust, truth and lies had a special meaning in complicated post-communist environment.[1] Trust operates entirely differently in autocratic regimes. Whereas democracy institutionalises distrust and only as a paradoxical consequence, through the establishment of accountability and pre-commitment, begets trust, autocracy attempts directly to institutionalise trust, and turn it into a strongly sanctioned formal demand (Sztompka, 1999, p. 148). The institutionalisation of trust proceeds through political socialisation, indoctrination, censorship of the media, closing the flow of information from the outside and through rigid political control, harshly punishing all breaches of trust, like dissidence, contestation and opposition, and even milder doubt and criticism (Sztompka, 1999, p. 148). We have moved from societies based on fate to those moved by human agency. In order to face the future actively and constructively, we need to deploy trust (Sztompka, 1999, p. 11). Our world has become extremely interdependent. As our dependence on the cooperation of others grows, so does the importance of trust in their reliability. The ongoing process of global interdependency will only increase the demand for trust as an essential condition for cooperation (Misztal, 1996, p. 269). The idea of trust has had a centuries-long intellectual career (Silver, 1985, p.52). Trust is produced by democracy, and helps to sustain democracy (Sztompka, 1999, p. 139). A system – economic, legal or political – requires trust as an input condition. Without trust it cannot stimulate supportive activities in situations of uncertainty and risk (Luhmann, 1988, p. 103).

Arguably, trust is produced by democracy, and helps to sustain democracy. Democracy provides a rich context of accountability. Democracy, through its emphasis on a binding and stable constitution, creates the context of pre-commitment. The emphasis on accountability and pre-commitment means that trust in a democratic regime is due precisely to the institutionalisation of distrust in the architecture of democracy (Sztompka, 1999, pp. 139–40). Countries and societies that have come from communist regimes are in a special situation, because on the one hand, they dream of a democratic order of life and thus they are more ready to trust and their expectations of finding the truth are higher. But usually, in the author's opinion, such high expectations are accompanied also with disappointments, because such ideals are difficult to fulfil. The experience of the Communist society, however, is based on experiences and memories, it is an attitude that has been created with upbringing and it is difficult to relinquish.

Media and totalitarian society

Soviet society and media were characterised by control and ideological canonisation. In the censored and ideologically edited version of reality described by the official Soviet media, people did not recognise their own experiences. I contend that this was a period of deep and serious 'public lies'.

Journalism served the functions of public relations (PR) and communication management in the Soviet Union: there was no free media in the communist society, and also no professional PR function (Vihalemm and Lauristin, 2001, pp. 134–42). The treatment of communism based on Lenin's doctrine looked upon journalism as a major part of the political system. To quote a well-known saying by Lenin, journalism had to be and, in fact, was 'not only a collective propagandist and a collective agitator, but also a collective organiser' (Lenin, cited in Brezhnev, 1977, p. 560). Lenin drew a parallel between journalism and the scaffolding around a building; journalism should serve as a means of communication between the different groups of the Party and the people, thus fostering joint construction of the edifice of communism. The Russian Bolshevik Party under Lenin's guidance, and dozens of other communist parties, viewed culture and communication pragmatically, discerning in them Machiavellian means of gaining power. In its treatment of journalism, Leninist-Communist doctrine rested upon the following logic: history is the struggle between classes; every person must inevitably take sides with one or the other class in society; spontaneous movement and the natural evolution of events can only lead to the domination of bourgeois ideology; in order to defeat bourgeois ideology, it is necessary to arouse the workers' class-consciousness, to organise and discipline them, thus changing them from a class in itself to a class for itself (Høyer, Lauk and Vihalemm, 1993, p. 177). These goals can be realised by the Party that uses journalism for this purpose. The party principle governing journalism was absolute. The party principle was also acknowledged as the underlying principle of activity for all cultural and social institutions (Høyer et al., 1993, p. 177):

> Journalism must serve as an instrument of socialist construction, giving detailed reviews of model communist achievements, disclosing the reasons why they are successful and what economic methods they use. But at the same time, journalism must pillory those communists who obstinately continue maintaining 'capitalist traditions', such as anarchy, idleness, disorder and speculation.
>
> (Lenin cited in Brezhnev, 1977, p. 560)

Media and transition society

Since 1989, economic and political changes have liberalised and commercialised the media. Estonia may seem more special among other post-Communist countries because the changes in society have been very rapid and radical, and the liberalisation of the media far-reaching.

The Estonian political climate in the 1990s was shaped by expectations of successful economic reforms, and even the growing disappointment and dissatisfaction with the outcomes of reforms among sizeable portions of the population (like farmers, pensioners, tenants of de-nationalised houses, Russian-speakers and the unemployed) could not deflate the general atmosphere of optimism (Rose, 2000a).

During the first periods of transition (the political breakthrough period of 1987–91 and the radical political and economic reforms period of 1991–4) the media played an important, even decisive role in the formation of the national mass movements. This was a result of political choices made by journalists who felt themselves responsible for the future of the nation. The Estonian media deliberately distanced themselves from active participation in politics after the restoration of independence (the so called stabilisation period after 1995) (Lauristin and Vihalemm, 2002, pp. 17–63). The Estonian media in general helped to create a climate of opinion that supported the politics of shock therapy[2] in society launched by the first reformist governments (1990–7). Without this supportive climate of opinion, the reforms could not have been managed. The extremely liberal economic policy of the first governments also opened the way to foreign capital investment for the media itself, and the media supported this policy for obvious reasons (Lauristin and Vihalemm, 2002, pp. 17–63). Another strong factor emerged which made the media an ally of the reformists in government even if the journalists did not support one or another concrete decision: the policy of the government elected in 1992 was strongly favourable to the younger generation. The 'clean the place' slogan of the *Isamaa* (Pro Patria) Party, the winner of the 1992 elections, did not call for repression but for the generational replacement and abolition of the 'old guard' of the Communist bureaucracy. After 1991, the old establishment left office without an overt struggle, and almost overnight new and often very young people become the decision-makers in various fields (Lauristin and Vihalemm, 2002, pp. 17–63). Similarly to the quiet disappearance of the Estonian Communist Party from the political scene, the older generation of journalists retired after the privatisation of their outlet, or left to work in other areas. The majority of the journalists' jobs were soon filled with young people who represented the generation of 'winners'[3] (Lauk, 1997). Many of these old journalists found a new job in the PR departments of organisations, PR being a new field in post-communist Estonia that needed people. As the media in the Soviet society had had a similar role to PR, the former journalists felt confident and professional in that situation. Such a situation was also encouraged by organisations, who viewed PR as a process for releasing positive news to the media and who still remembered how during the Soviet times positive labour victories were reported. The new generation of Estonian journalists overwhelmingly supported radical reforms. Sometimes this support was the result of a good PR job, or lobbying and manipulation by right-wing politicians, but mostly this liberal policy corresponded to their own interests and convictions, too.

Commercialisation of the media created a high interest in scandals. The news criteria changed rapidly after 1991: politics lost its appeal, and journalists tried to find any conflicts and 'skeletons in the closet' of politicians in order to catch the audiences' attention. In a paradoxical way, commercialisation supported the 'watchdog' position of the media, even if journalists themselves politically sympathised with the new political elite. This 'watchdog' attitude helped to keep the political balance in news coverage. When, in 1998 and during subsequent years, Estonia was listed among the least corrupt of post-Communist countries, this achievement is clearly connected with the effects of the 'watchdog media' (Lauristin and Vihalemm, 2002, pp. 17–63). During the second half of the 1990s, the position of the media became generally more critical towards the political system and politicians. High political expectations of the first years of transition were replaced by more pragmatic attitudes, and politics was represented by the press as a game where elites pursued their group interests. The election campaign of 1999 was greatly influenced by professional PR and advertising companies. Political debate between the parties was designed according to the principles of political marketing. The personalisation of the elections, using 'image selling strategies', contradicted the principles of proportional representation built into the election law. The election law was meant to support the consolidation of the party system with clear, politically defined content, but the logic of political marketing pushed the parties to hunt for popular names in their lists from outside the political field, like sportsmen, TV stars or millionaires. As a result, public attitude towards politics became even more alienated and cynical (Lauristin and Vihalemm, 2002, pp. 17–63). Towards the end of 1999, the Estonian media landscape stabilised. Even if some further mergers or bankruptcies occur, the appearance of new dailies or national TV channels is hardly imaginable (Lauristin and Vihalemm, 2002, pp. 17–63).

After the initial confusion created by the liberalisation and marketisation of the media, Estonian society became more familiar with the new media environment and expressed critical demands concerning the quality of media content. While the media observed politicians, the politicians themselves became concerned that the media would favour some political parties over others. Tensions between the media and politicians stimulated the media to draw grim pictures of politics in general. Growing disillusionment created fruitful soil for the negative representation of the government, of political parties and of politicians. Complaints about alienation between politicians and 'ordinary people' expressed by the media deepened the feelings of disappointment and contributed to creating a vicious circle of public mistrust. Almost all successfully reformed countries have gone through such kind of backlashes. Surveys recently conducted in Central European countries demonstrate a growing dissatisfaction of the population (Munro, 2001, pp. 18–23).

Trust in political institutions is lower in many other post-Communist countries than in Estonia (Rose, Mishler and Haerpfer, 1998; Mishler and Rose, 2001). Alienation and distrust characterises the relationship between people and political institutions. In many successfully reformed countries, elections had brought back to power former Communist functionaries. This tendency is nostalgia for the past on the part of ordinary people who were disappointed after quick and radical reforms and whose living standards had regressed. The most striking example is that of the Polish elections of 2001, where half the population did not participate at all (turnout dropped to 46 per cent), remnants of previously glorious Solidarity did not even pass the threshold, and the former Communists won a clear victory (Rose and Haerpfer, 1998; Mishler and Rose, 2001). Investigating the reasons for such a backlash, Jacobs (2001) found that two sets of causes are relevant. First, in all countries investigated (the Czech Republic, Hungary, Poland and the former East Germany), structural reforms in the economy had led to serious social problems; a notable part of population suffered from poverty and lack of everyday security; and the gap between the rich and poor was growing. The second were the cultural factors, especially socialisation in times of the Socialist regime. The revolutions of 1989 created high expectations of a coming 'free and fair society', different from the miserable existence inside the closed and repressive socialist camp. Ironically, the content of those expectations of a 'bright future' was deeply influenced by socialist and communist ideology including: hostility towards the market, equity in the distribution of goods and a leading role for the state in providing for the welfare and employment of everyone. These ideas are still widespread among people who were socialised under Communist regimes, but people themselves often fail to recognise traces of Socialism in their expectations and assessments. Even if there is a similar pattern of social and political developments in almost all post-Communist countries of Europe, the processes in each country differ in the details and in the timetable of events. In each country, questions can also be asked about possible alternative choices.

Trust and the media

In July 2002, the Chancellery of the Parliament of Estonia ordered a big national survey to be conducted on Estonian society (Estonian Parliament,

Research Report, 2002). The survey produced 'a ranking list of trust' of government and public institutions (Figure 12.1) and showed that journalism and the media only occupy the last but one place in the list in terms of their trustworthiness. Political parties are the least trusted. But what is interesting is the fact that the president was top of the rank. These results can be interpreted to draw the speculative conclusion that the period of Communism has, on the one hand, retained in people a strong respect for the highest leader but, on the other hand, politics, politicians and parties are not very trustworthy in the eyes of the people. The institution of President in Estonia is not – from a theoretical viewpoint – directly connected with the concrete party. In practice, from elections in 2001, the post of president has been held by a person with a Communist past and he is strongly supported also by *Rahvaliit* (National Union). But the phenomenon of public opinion is hard to understand – in the author's opinion the current president's popularity stems from a mixture of his pleasant, peaceful image and nostalgia for the communist past.

The media's unpopularity probably has many causes. The media are seen as unreliable according to Estonian Parliament survey research, due to many different factors. It is clear that the media as a propagandist from the era of Communism has not yet fully established and promoted its new role under the new conditions. People do not see the media as the 'watchdog' or the fourth estate yet as it is viewed in democratic societies, but more as the propagandist remembered from the past. Another reason for the media's low popularity is the fact that during the new transition society, the media have become a battleground for numerous scandals, especially for the purpose of commercialisation – as scandals sell. Although people claim to be sceptical about the intrigues portrayed in the media and clearly disapprove of such an orientation to commerce and scandal, the economic success of the media is still directly dependant on specific sales figures: people still consume the media, despite the fact that they increasingly do not really trust the media. Arguably, a third reason for the media's unpopularity concerns past experience of media ethics and journalistic ethics. Both in the communist past and in the post-communist society, it is quite normal that journalists are influenced, manipulated and sometimes paid by different interest groups in society: this is called corruption in democratic societies but is a traditional part of life culture in communist society. This is illustrated by interviews I conducted with journalists in November 2005,[4] that show that attempts to influence journalists persist:

> I was doing a health programme. The press representatives of pharmaceutical companies were quick to react and began pressing me quite forcefully about what they should do to get an interview in the programme, where should they turn to in order to get this interview on the air. They are used to the attitude that if you pay, you get everything. It was very difficult to

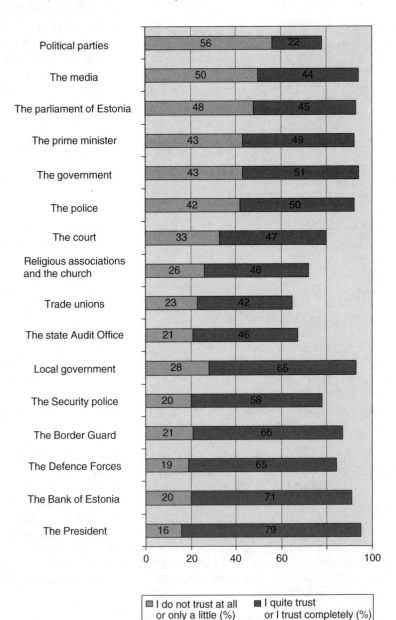

Figure 12.1   Trust in government and public institutions 2002
Source: Estonian Parliament, Research Report, 2002.

explain to them that this is a public radio and no turning or paying will help, because we do not buy or sell advertising time. There was a case when they actually asked how much they have to pay. After such things I end all relationships with them. (Radio, Editor, 2005)

Before the 1995 elections for the parliament, a PR manager of a party leaked a popularity poll of the parties to me. The poll had been falsified for the benefit of this party. Today, such a thing would destroy the party. There was also a case when the entire PR of a company was targeted at me. (...) two transit companies shared the port. The public relations of one of the companies was targeted at me for a week and a half, they kept calling me, took me to tours around the port, and offered a special lunch at the port's restaurant. (TV, Editor, 2005)

A few weeks before the elections, some politician would come and ask us to publish or not to publish things that concerned them. (Newspaper, Editor-in-Chief, 2005)

Recent research on Estonian Society[5] shows that general confidence has somewhat increased from 2003 to 2005 (Figure 12.2). The number of people with high and very high confidence has increased by 6 per cent, the number of people with average confidence has increased by 1 per cent, and the number of people with very low and low confidence has decreased. But only 34 per cent of the participants in 2003 and 40 per cent of the participants in 2005 in the survey express high or very high confidence in what is going on in Estonia, which suggests that the effects of the communist society are still quite strong and that distrust, scepticism and doubt remain in people's attitudes.

Research results of trust towards to media were more critical than results towards Estonian society in general (see Figure 12.2 and Figure 12.3). However, while 3 per cent fewer people considered their confidence towards media to be very high in 2005 compared to 2003, the confidence of those people who in 2003 had high, average or low confidence has increased by 1 per cent each, and the number of people with very low confidence has slightly decreased – by 1 per cent (Figure 12.3).

The reason for the decline in very high confidence in the media from 2003 to 2005 can be explained by factors contributing to the media's unpopularity, discussed earlier – namely, the commercialisation of the media and its desire for scandals (people have clearly expressed their disapproving attitude towards 'yellow journalism'[6] and intrigues in the media). Another reason could be people's conviction that, despite the current social regime, the media can be manipulated by interest groups (a belief based on the experiences of the Soviet society, together with a certain disappointment in the political decisions taken after regaining independence). Yet, Figure 12.3 also shows that most people trust the media (although not excessively) – and this figure has risen from 2003 to 2005

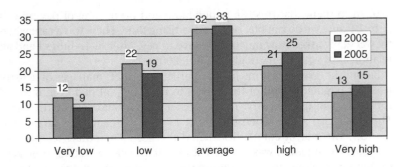

Figure 12.2 The change from 2003 to 2005 in general confidence in Estonia (%)
Source: MEEMA project 2003 and 2005.

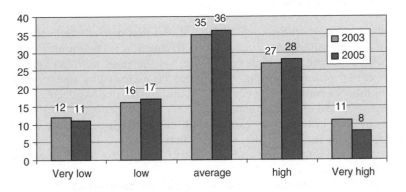

Figure 12.3 Confidence towards media in Estonia from 2003 to 2005 (%)
Source: MEEMA project 2003 and 2005.

(with 62 per cent expressing average or high confidence in the media in 2003, and 64 per cent doing so in 2005). Perhaps this indicates the establishment of a more critical trust (rather than blind faith or idealism) from the public, in Sztompka's words, the start of the institutionalisation of distrust.

Conclusion

Post-communist transition societies have a very special relationship with public trust. Historical experience from Soviet society has made people believe that media and other public institutions tell nothing but lies. These are 'public lies'– when the entire society knows about the lies, and the truth can be discerned on the basis of the evidence of the life world.

This was typical for Soviet society. When the official channels stated something very categorically, it was usually a lie and people found out the truth through direct experience of, and evidence of, the lie. An example is all the news reports on the good health of Brezhnev, when at the same time it was clear from the aspect of the leader talking on TV that he was very ill. The same category also includes news about social labour victories and continuous fast economic growth under the leadership of the Communist Party – when everyday practice demonstrated completely the opposite. The same category also includes all cases of *'pakazuha'*;[7] ethical views were casual and interpreted as convenient, and also cases of 'deep language' or 'double speech'– a communication style created by communist ideology and initiated by Lenin during the revolution. The whole process was clandestine and people were called to violent resistance with sentences such as 'We hope that it will be a peaceful demonstration'– in fact an appeal for a very bloody demonstration. 'Deep language' was systematically developed by Stalin. For example, Stalin's statement announcing the promotion of a comrade in reality was his/her death sentence (Radzhinski, 2000). 'Deep language' was preserved in the language use of subsequent state leaders in different forms, depending on the activity of the Party and the personality of the leader. Over time it was ingrained in the whole society because people understood that it was safer and more beneficial to use the same style as the leaders.[8]

While people in post-communist societies today are sceptical and critical in their attitude[9] because of their experience with public lies, this tendency is likely to change. Although it is unwise to trust the media, people have expectations and desire information – which media channels supply. However, the media also offer the possibility for self-promotion by people (such as politicians and businesspeople). As a result, PR, especially media relations, is relatively dominant in post-communist society. When painting a public picture through the media and with the help of PR, the priority in post-communist societies is often not the truth but so called *'pakazuhha'*– fictitious illusion and image building. Resulting from this paradox, trust is a controversial issue in a post-communist society. On the one hand there is a historical memory and experience from Soviet society but on the other hand there is a strong will to become a democratic state with different values, morality and ethics. As Sztompka says: 'We have moved from societies based on fate to those moved by human agency. In order to face the future actively and constructively, we need to deploy trust' (1999, p.11).

For post-communist societies, in contrast to 'public lies', 'public truth' holds a special interpretation – that of complete truth, transparent, clear and idealistic. Sztompka (1999) believes that trust is produced by democracy, and helps to sustain democracy. Democracy provides a rich context of accountability. Democracy through the emphasis on a binding and stable constitution, creates the context of pre-commitment. The emphasis on accountability and pre-commitment means that trust in a democratic regime is due precisely to the institutionalisation of distrust in the architecture of democracy (Sztompka, 1999, pp. 139–40). This can be seen as a dream of post-communist societies and the media could help the dream come true. In practice, however, this ideal will not be realised that simply – as indicated by the growth tendencies in different post-communist states (discussed previously in this chapter). People's confidence and positive attitude are probably affected by economic, cultural and social aspects. The general deterioration of living standards run contrary to expectations (that by changing society, everything will get better). This, together with media-publicised scandals, intrigues and conflicts, fatigue people and the effects are psychologically deleterious. This is augmented by political developments – Soviet culture, Soviet style corruption, *'pakazuha'* and propaganda being replaced by political culture. Altogether, this presents a depressing situation for citizens.

In summary, it cannot be said that the public lie that was present in Soviet Union, has been replaced strongly with public truth in the transition society and the affairs and attitudes based on trust. The transition society, shocked by its radical and fast changes, needs comprehensive social dialogue. Here, a leading role could be held by the media accompanied by the growth and professionalisation of PR. Given the problems in trusting the media, explored in this chapter, PR is fast 'developing into a complementary form of public communication characterised by strong appeal to the positive values – success, competitiveness, openness and optimism' (Vihalemm and Lauristin, 2001, pp. 134–42). Interestingly, these authors point out that the PR professionals are opposing the 'watchdog' role of journalism and creating a more balanced picture of reality.

Furthermore, given today's information-overload, lack of time and experience of complexity, people desire more packaged information. As such, information packaging and communication management that are oriented towards dialogue with an informed public, are becoming one of the most rapidly expanding areas. In the new communication environment the role of PR as a part of social management is growing. New information and discussion channels are emerging and organisations are establishing direct contacts with their target groups, thus bypassing the media as a mediator. 'Symmetric PR is promoting plurality and reflexivity in society and has good possibilities for co-operation with public journalism' (Vihalemm and Lauristin, 2001, pp. 134–42). PR and journalism complement each other in promoting a common basis of information and understanding in the framework of a dominant liberal normative model and fast-developing interactive electronic communication environment.

Notes

1. In 2001, I analysed two cases of lying – the first was the 'picture scandal' of the Prime Minister of Estonia, where the main issue was lying to the public, and the other was the doping scandal of the Finnish skiing team during the Lahti Championships, where the main problem consisted again of lying to the public (Tampere, unpublished work, 2001). My study showed that the Estonian society was much more permissive of lying than the Finnish. This was a clear sign of the fact that in Estonia people are willing to be more flexible about morality and ethics. They have probably become like this historically, as a result of the constant public lies that the Soviet society produced and that the people finally became immune to. In Finland, however, thanks to the continuous and long-term democratic worldview, the attitude to lying was much more intolerant – a clear sign of the attitude towards the questions of truth and lies in a totally different type of society.

2. 'Shock therapy' means that reforms to change society from communism to democracy were very radical in character and also rapid.

3. The generation of 'winners' were the young journalists, and also specialists from other fields, who had not held key positions in communist period, and were now more accepted in the labour market. For example, in the Estonian context, it was and is normal that the prime minister is about 30 years old (for example Mart Laar was about 30 when he was a prime minister for the first time), and managers of biggest companies are usually younger than 30 years old.

4. The target population for the study was Estonian journalists working for written and audiovisual media. Interview respondents were selected by non-random theoretical sampling. In-depth interviews were conducted with 21 Estonian journalists and editors, eight from newspapers; three from weeklies; four from radio and six from television. Nine respondents were from public broadcasting media and 12 were from privately owned media. Interview results were analysed using discourse analysis. Discourse analysis helps to discover, through the analysis of language use, the ideas a certain group, or interpreting community thinks and talks about an issue (McQuail, 2000). In the current study the interpreting community was journalists and the issue they were asked to describe was PR. Interview questions were divided into three larger blocks to analyse their responses: personal experience; influential external factors and the relationship between the PR sphere and journalistic sphere.

5. The survey *Me. The World. The Media.* (MEEMA, 2003, 2005) conducted by the Department of Journalism and Communication of the University of Tartu, Estonia in 2003 and 2005 tried to create a sociological picture of the social changes that have taken place in Estonian society through a specific media perspective. The idea of the survey was that coping with changes in society and self-positioning under new social circumstances (institutional, technological, social, ideological and cultural environment) does not happen only through objective factors but also depends on how the media has helped to create a collective perception of what is going on (Lauristin and Vihalemm, 2004, p.23). The empirical material was collected by order of the University of Tartu, Estonia (MEEMA, 2003, 2005), in 2003 (Kalmus, Lauristin and Pruulmann-Vengerfeldt, 2004) and 2005, also analysing confidence in general in society and confidence towards media. More than 1000 persons, aged between 15 and 74, participated in the interviews and filled in the questionnaires.

6. 'Yellow journalism' is the term for more scandal and entertainment-oriented newspapers, where facts and truth are not important.

7. *Pakazuha* (in Russian) is a highly positive presentation of a thing, situation or event, which was not necessarily based on truth; an example which was more like fiction – as the success of Soviet economy, which in reality was farce.

8. This communication style was characterised by a 'syndrome of lies', that meant that in order to understand the actual content of information one had to read 'between the lines' and have a critical attitude towards texts. This style was one of the instruments of the Communist Party for controlling and influencing people. Organisations in communist society used 'deep language' mixed with very specific technical language that obstructed their communication with the public and gave birth to a lot of the communication problems even today, in the transition society.

9. The young generation, who does not have Soviet experience – who were born after 1985 – has different attitudes from older and middle aged people. This young generation is linked also to the 'generation of winners'.

13
Trust in a Time of Crisis: The Mass Media as a Guardian of Trust

Amisha Mehta

Trust is a critical element in all principal–agent relationships, where an agent acts on behalf of principals in political, social and financial exchanges. Within these relationships, Shapiro (1987) suggests that in order to proceed, both parties require impersonal trust, that is, trust built without personal history and with the potential for vulnerability. To overcome issues associated with vulnerability, Shapiro (1987) introduced the concept of guardians of trust, who act to preserve trust on behalf of both parties. Set within principal–agency theory, traditional guardians of trust are government or professional associations, or the law (Zucker, 1986).

Although recent studies in principal–agency theory have been undertaken in non-traditional settings, studies of guardians of trust are limited. This paper sets out to define and place trust in principal–agency relationships and examine the role of mass media as a guardian of trust. A model is built around mass mediated exchanges between the Australian Federal Minister for Health and the Australian Medical Association President who were involved in the resolution of a medical indemnity policy crisis at a time when both agents were new to their role and thus brought very little historical information to their exchanges. The findings show how mass media acted as a guardian of trust and also set expectations for an agent among principals. To conclude, this chapter poses a set of research initiatives based on the model to refine our understanding of the guardianship of trust in social systems.

Defining trust

Trust has been defined in many ways by authors from many disciplines. According to Mayer, Davis and Schoorman (1995, p. 712), trust is the 'willingness of a party to be vulnerable to the actions of another party based on the expectation that the other will perform a particular action important to the trustor, irrespective of the ability to monitor or control that other party'. In this definition, Mayer et al. (1995) set trust apart from other constructs

155

including cooperation, confidence and distrust. Rosseau, Sitkin, Burt and Camerer's (1998, p. 123) definition of trust as a 'psychological state comprising the intention to accept vulnerability based upon positive expectations of the intentions or behaviour of another' is commonly accepted in management literature. However, Mayer et al.'s (1995) emphasis on monitoring and control are significant to this study of impersonal trust.

Trust is both personal and impersonal. According to Lane (1998, p. 12), impersonal trust exists when organisational actors cannot 'rely on commonality of personal characteristics or a past history or guaranteed future of exchange'. This view is supported by Zucker's (1986) treatment of institutional-based trust, which suggests that socially produced and legitimated structures guarantee trust, and Luhmann's (1988) claim that impersonal trust underwrites interpersonal trust. Common mechanisms for impersonal trust are political legitimacy and technical and professional knowledge systems that guarantee individual expectations (Lane, 1998). When personal information is scarce, it is common to enter into relationships and draw conclusions using impersonal cues. This chapter is motivated to understand how principals manage agency relationships through impersonal trust mechanisms.

Trust in principal–agent relationships

Traditionally, principal–agent relationships focus on exchange and incorporate hierarchy (Olson, 2000), delegation (Castelfranchi and Falcone, 1998; Beccera and Gupta, 1999; Schulze, Lubatkin, Dino and Buchholtz, 2001) and contracts (Schulze et al., 2001). Recent studies have been undertaken in non-traditional settings such as religious institutions (Zech, 2001) and family businesses (Schulze et al., 2001). Trust is a critical element in all types of principal–agent relationships. According to Shapiro (1987, p. 626) 'principals – for whatever reason or state of mind – invest resources, authority, or responsibility in another (agent) to act on their behalf for some uncertain future return'. In so trusting their agent, principals bear risks.

Primarily, principals assume risks associated with an inability to observe how and when agents complete assigned tasks (Shapiro, 1987; Zech, 2001; Miller and Whitford, 2002). Instead, principals trust 'agents to bridge the barriers of direct physical access to information and property' (Shapiro, 1987, p. 627). Singh and Sirdeshmukh (2000) suggest that principals use market signals to overcome information asymmetry. For example, principals can use reputation indices, corporate rankings or accreditation as surrogate indicators for agent actions. Although market signals do not allow principals to measure exactly their agent's efforts, they can make inferences based on the outcome, which is a combination of both the agent's actions and external factors (Miller and Whitford, 2002).

To preserve and maximise outcomes, Eisenhardt (1989, cited in Creed and Miles, 1996, p. 23) suggests that organisations adopt controls and provide incentives to avoid agents acting in their own self-interest. To protect themselves, principals must encourage agents to achieve positive outcomes even without monitoring (Miller and Whitford, 2002).

Trust is one mechanism of organisational control that responds to the opportunism bias in agency theory (Creed and Miles, 1996). Beccerra and Gupta (1999) suggest that agency theory is a useful vehicle to study and understand the production of impersonal trust, particularly in situations where lack of trust is relatively high and information is relatively low. While trust bridges uncertainty in situations of imperfect information (Lane, 1998), Singh and Sirdeshmukh (2000) suggest that as access to personal information increases, principals' reliance on agency devices is replaced by personal trust expectations.

Trust between agents and principals promotes exchange (Mishra, 1996; Tyler and Degoey, 1996), and produces beneficial outcomes for both parties (Singh and Sirdeshmukh, 2000). Given this importance for trust, principals must also look to insure trust in their relationships with agents.

Examining guardians of trust

Acknowledging its many benefits, several authors have studied the insurance or protection of trust (see Zucker, 1986; Shapiro, 1987; Gambetta, 1988b; Tyler and Kramer, 1996; Bachmann, 1998; Lane, 1998). The vulnerability of principals in situations of impersonal trust led Shapiro (1987, p. 635) to introduce guardians of trust, 'a supporting social-control framework of procedural norms, organisational forms, and social-control specialists, which institutionalise distrust'. Guardians of trust assume the role of principals, acting on their behalf, to monitor agents (Shapiro, 1987).

Traditional guardians of trust are institutions such as government or professional associations (Zucker, 1986; Shapiro, 1987). Professional bodies use membership or accreditation to monitor the performance and hold accountable the actions of its members who operate in positions of trust (Shapiro, 1987). From an economic perspective, Williamson (1994, cited in Aldrich, 1999) identified several substitutes for trust including bonds, hostages, disclosure rules and agreements on dispute resolution. However, there is no substitute equal to real trust. Even if formal contracts exist, effective relations depend on trust (Mishra, 1996).

Although recent research on guardians of trust is limited, Ayios (2003) examined the monitoring of trust in new international business relationships. Monitoring is defined as the preference of one party 'to closely regulate and monitor the relationship through reliance on formal processes, contracting, assumptions and behaviours' (Ayios, 2003, p. 193). This cross-cultural study showed that monitoring, when undertaken at the expense of interpersonal processes, produces conflict and distrust (Ayios, 2003). Similarly, Barney and Hansen (1994, cited in Lane, 1998) argue that if a variety of governance mechanisms are adopted to deter opportunism, only weak trust may develop. Guardians of trust, like the principals they represent, require information from agents. The task of information collection and dissemination is entrusted to agents (Shapiro, 1987). All parties rely on news media or research to build knowledge relevant to their relationship.

The mass media as a guardian of trust in a time of crisis

In non-traditional principal–agency relationships and without related guardians of trust, such as regulatory bodies, contracts and escrows (where a third-party holds in trust an asset until a legal contract is met), this chapter proposes that mass media act as guardians of trust. This proposal is based on three criteria for guardians of trust. Guardians of trust are grounded in institutional norms (Zucker, 1986; Shapiro, 1987), able to access information (Zucker, 1986; Shapiro, 1987; Ayios, 2003) and actively monitor agents on behalf of principals (Shapiro, 1987). The mass media meet the first two of these criteria. Firstly, in social systems, the media have long been established and taken for granted as a reporting and news-sharing institution in social systems. Secondly, based on this institutional legitimacy, the mass media gain access to information through the reporting process and are recognised as a traditional source of information for agents, principals and even traditional guardians of trust (Shapiro, 1987). Answering mass media's contribution to the third criterion of guardians of trust, monitoring agents on behalf of principals, is the focus of this chapter. This third criterion has a direct relationship to impersonal trust.

Figure 13.1 illustrates the role of mass media as a guardian or monitor of trust in relationships between principals and an agent. Overseeing these relationships and protecting for trust is the role of the guardian of trust, which in this case is the mass media. Mass media are posited to have an impersonal connection to the principal–agent relationship. That is, the mass media, although not connected directly to an agent or principals, can be an indirect source of information pertaining to the relationship between agents and principals.

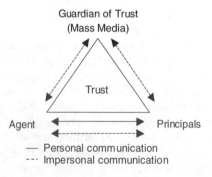

Figure 13.1   The mass media as a guardian of trust.

This model gains legitimacy when set within a crisis and when an agent is new to his/her role. A crisis is an organisational issue that has reached a critical stage and can threaten organisational performance (Cutlip, Center and Broom, 2006). During a crisis, mass media are a common communication tool between organisations and publics (Grunig and Hunt, 1984), thus meeting a guardian of trust criterion of providing access to information. Mass media framing of crises can affect stakeholder perceptions of organisations, and, as such, principal–agent relationships benefit when information is communicated clearly (Mishra, 1996).

In a time of crisis, principal–agent relationships can maintain trust through role stability (Thomas, 1998). Role reorganisations increase opportunities for actual violations of trust which often results in lower levels of trust (Thomas, 1998). Roles, and the expectations and violations associated with them and reported in the mass media will be used to orient this study and answer these research questions.

1. How does the mass media report established roles of agents during a crisis?
2. How does the mass media act as a guardian of trust in principal–agent relationships during a crisis?
3. Do mass media's actions as a guardian of trust change after the crisis?

Studying the mass media as a guardian of trust

This chapter proposes that the framing of mass mediated exchanges is the basis of mass media's role as a guardian of trust. Given its relationship to crises, the study has operationalised mass media's framing of roles as indicators of its guardianship of trust. Framing is a technique used to arrange disparate pieces of information into a meaningful structure. Framing has been applied to understand the role of journalists and analyse political communication.

Framing impacts both content and structure. Nelson, Clawson and Oxley (1997, p. 1) argue that framing examines the 'effects of media content rather than mere coverage of a problem'. From a structural perspective, Entman (1993, cited in Nelson and Kinder, 1996) defines framing as a process where a source defines and constructs an issue for a receiver. According to Shen (2004), frames emphasise particular messages and influence public knowledge. Framing also influences public opinion (Nelson and Kinder, 1996). Such definitions support this chapter's proposal that the mass media acts as an information source to connect principals and agents.

This chapter's claims are examined through a case study of mass media coverage of the medical indemnity crisis in Australia. Medical indemnity is a significant issue for medical practitioners and affects their relationships with the federal government, patients and other stakeholders. In April 2003, Australia's largest medical indemnity organisation, United Medical Protection, filed for provisional liquidation, affecting the legal protection of more than 60 per cent of doctors. The Australian Medical Association (AMA) called for government assistance to protect its members against existing and future medical claims and threatened strike action. In response, the federal government agreed to protect doctors against existing claims, and some state governments changed personal liability and legal services advertising legislation in an attempt to reduce future claims. This debate was waged between the federal Health Minister and AMA president. In late 2003, new agents were appointed to these roles. A federal government cabinet review saw Mr Tony Abbott[1] move from the workplace relations portfolio to become the federal Health Minister and Dr William Glasson was elected AMA president. These appointments saw both men become agents for the principals of voters and medical practitioners, respectively. This study selects the agent–principal relationship represented by federal Health Minister Tony Abbott and the general public. In representing the public interest, the federal Health Minister is securing effective and efficient access to doctors.

This study was conducted using newspaper articles, which were limited to national and capital city newspapers including *The Australian*, *The Weekend Australian*, *The Courier-Mail*, *The Canberra Times*, *The Sydney Morning Herald*, and *The Age*.[2] A search of major Australian newspapers using *Lexis-Nexis* and *Factiva* identified 102 articles containing the words 'medical indemnity', and 'Glasson' and 'Abbott'. These search keys were selected to examine an exchange relationship restricted to the medical indemnity issue. The analysis itself focuses on one agent, federal Health Minister Tony Abbott. Articles were clipped from 29 September 2003 to 11 May 2005 inclusive. The start date identified the role changes associated with one agent's appointment to a new federal government portfolio with resolution to the issue achieved on 31 October 2003. The end date was selected to capture the most recent mass media reports of the agents' interactions.

The data were analysed in three steps. Firstly, following Simon and Xenos's (2000) framing methodology, an initial analysis of media coverage identified broad content themes that reflected the consecutive development of the issue. Secondly, a content analysis identified role frames or sites where the mass media identified the roles of actors. Thirdly, these role frames became a platform for the interpretation of trust guardianship, which was examined through mass media's identification of roles and treatment of role violation and reification. These role frames were used to signify cases where mass media monitored an agent on behalf of principals and therefore acted as a guardian of trust. This approach to mass media framing supports the proposed model's assertion of mass media as having an impersonal connection between principals and agents.

Although similar to other news framing studies, the study is limited to explore the agent using the single issue of medical indemnity. Further, investigation of mass media's role in trust guardianship is limited only to those principal–agent cases deemed newsworthy by the mass media.

Case study: Australian medical indemnity policy crisis

Mass media reporting of established agent roles during a crisis

From 29 September to 31 October 2003, the mass media acted as an impersonal information source for principals. Within this first working frame, 30 articles reported changes to the federal government cabinet. Of these 30 articles, 10 used role frames to describe to principals the characteristics of their agent, the new federal Health Minister. The mass media's framing of Abbott's reputation was based on his previous role as workplace relations and employment minister (see Table 13.1).

These role frames captured and communicated both professional and personal characteristics of the agent, Abbott, to his principals.

Mass media as a guardian of trust

The mass media acted as a guardian of trust during this first time frame but under a different content frame. After reporting the historical roles of Abbott, the media projected roles for Abbott in negotiations with key health stakeholders. These role projections saw the mass media establish expectations with principals for change within their newly appointed agent (see Table 13.2). Reports of role projections were established by journalists as well as other health stakeholders including the AMA.

The role discussion reported in Table 13.2 occurred soon after the announcement of Abbott's appointment as federal Health Minister. Within a few days of this announcement, doctors threatened strike action and resignation over the medical indemnity levies. As an agent for voters and healthcare consumers, Abbott entered negotiations with the AMA president. Within this content frame, 60 articles were printed and 23 employed role framing. In

Table 13.1   The mass media establishes agent's roles

Role frames	Case examples
Established roles for agent	Renowned political bruiser Tony Abbott (Frenkel, 2003).[3] Former boxer Tony Abbott will jump into the ring to tackle Labor head-on ... he is the government's hard man and one of their toughest players (AAP, 2003).[4］ He's a head-kicker ... notorious bruising debating style (Schubert, 2003).[5] Mr Abbott's tough approach to workplace reform meant union leaders were happy to see the back of him (Jones, Edmistone and Odgers, 2003).[6] Trusted confidant of the Prime Minster and certainly a spear carrier (Pavey, 2003).[7]

Source: Various Australian newspapers, 2003.

12 articles, mass media framed roles in conflict with those established in the first working frame (Table 13.1) but in support of role projections established by journalists and other healthcare stakeholders (Table 13.2). The role reification for the agent is described in Table 13.3.

In reporting the actions of Abbott, the mass media questioned both his decisions and skills against his established reputation. It is through the mass media's identification of the inconsistent role traits displayed by the agent that the media act as a guardian of trust on behalf of principals or patients. Although the reified role traits displayed in Table 13.3 conflict with the historical roles of the agent, it is interesting to note that they hold consistent with the role projections reported in Table 13.2.

Table 13.2   The mass media projects agent's roles

Role frames	Case examples
Projected roles for agent	His conciliatory approach was immediately reciprocated by the doctors and did not surprise one of the Howard Government's most successful health ministers, the now-retired Michael Wooldridge (Gordon, 2003).[8]
	Abbott … is compelling, thoughtful, and many hope, controversial enough to provoke some good debate about health policy (Schubert, 2003).[9]
	… Mr Abbott's fighting instinct would win a better deal for patients (Farr, 2003).[10]

Source: Various Australian Newspapers, 2003.

Table 13.3   The mass media reports agent's role reification

Role frames	Case examples
Role reification	A conciliatory Tony Abbott … moved to defuse the crisis (Gordon, 2003).[11]
	Tony Abbott's transformation from political head-kicker to a caring, listening Mr Fixit started yesterday (Dunlevy, 2003).[12]
	Mr Abbott was close to conceding the doctors' two key demands after twice meeting with AMA president (Frenkel, 2003).[13]
	Almost as important as the reprieve from an immediate doctor walkout is the goodwill that Abbott has cultivated with doctor advocates …. Abbott … has gone to the other extreme, shamelessly sucking up to doctors (Schubert, 2003).[14]

Source: Various Australian Newspapers, 2003.

Table 13.4 The mass media reports agent's return to original roles

Role frames	Case examples
Reversal of role reification	... Abbott was heading for a showdown with Sydney's 200 rebelling public hospital doctors last night, insisting he would make no concessions 'under duress' on the escalating medical indemnity dispute (Metherell and Pollard, 2003).[15] Abbott describes as 'facile' any comparison of his restrained posture with the doctors to his aggression as workplace relations minister towards the building unions .... By Thursday night, after three sessions of inconclusive talks, his language was firming. The government would not bow to 'duress' or 'ultimatums' (Metherell, 2003).[16]

Source: Various Australian Newspapers, 2003.

Shortly after reporting these roles and actions, the media commented on a second role reification, which saw the agent return to role traits consistent with roles established in Table 13.1. In six articles, the mass media framed roles in symmetry with those established in the first working frame, calling on Abbott to not concede to doctors' requests (see Table 13.4).

Mass media as a guardian of trust after a crisis

While medical indemnity negotiations in October 2003 between Abbott and Glasson avoided mass resignations from doctors and a health crisis for principals, two months later, the situation had changed. In December 2003, federal cabinet declined to meet Abbott's proposal to provide a $480 million guarantee to prevent the collapse of the indemnity organisation at the centre of the crisis, United Medical Protection, Australia's largest medical defence organisation. Instead, cabinet proposed a new package that also required contributions from doctors and taxpayers or principals.

During this timeframe, only five articles were published in the mass media. Three articles contained mass media reports of Abbott's roles, which were in contrast to his original roles (see Table 13.5).

During this final content frame, it is important to note that while Abbott remained the agent for study, his exchange partners included both the AMA president and the federal government cabinet.

Discussion and conclusions

This study extended mass media's traditional role as an information source in principal–agent relationships to establish it as a guardian of trust. Focusing on the need to overcome vulnerability and risk in principal–agent relationships, the findings showed that through the reporting and questioning of an

Table 13.5   The mass media reports agent's negotiation outcomes

Role frames	Case examples
Roles in contrast to original role	*Abbott*: I think the government has gone a long way to react to every reasonable concern. What I wanted was a package that was fair to doctors, fair to patients, and fair to taxpayers, and that's what we've got (Jones and Edmistone, 2003).[17] Abbott had delivered on his promise to take the crisis out of medical indemnity (Anon, 2004).[18]

Source: Various Australian Newspapers, 2003, 2004

agent's roles and subsequent changes to these roles, the mass media acted as a guardian of trust to meet the needs of principals.

Principal–agency theory identifies three criteria for guardians of trust. The first two criteria, grounding in institutional norms and access to information, have long been met by media. This study confirmed support for these criteria. The mass media established that personal and professional information about an agent, in this case the federal Health Minister, can be communicated to a number of principals through impersonal media at very little cost. This finding supports the study's model and recognises Zucker's (1986) argument that exchange partners must recognise the time and effort costs associated with direct measures of and signals for trust. Although external sources of information, including the media, are also used to shed light on the actions of agents, access to such information in a time of crisis and when an agent is new to their role becomes difficult. This situation increases the reliance of principals on guardians of trust and offers further justification for the mass media's role as a guardian of trust.

The third criterion of a guardian of trust, monitoring an agent on behalf of principals, remained a largely unexplored role for the mass media. After establishing role expectations for the agent, the data revealed two points. Firstly, the mass media reported actions of the agent against established traits. In cases where the mass media's role frames disagreed with these established traits, the mass media acted as a guardian of trust on behalf of principals, that is patients. In its role as a guardian, the mass media not only reported these role changes but actively commented on the inconsistencies displayed by the agent. In essence, the mass media championed the cause of principals, and attempted to secure a better outcome by questioning the actions of the agent.

Secondly, the data revealed that the mass media projected role expectations for the agent. The change in the agent's roles and actions were consistent with mass media role projections. The influence of media in setting an agenda for the agent or influencing the expectations of principals for their agent, requires further investigation. Such influence must also be considered with other sources of change such as the nature of the health portfolio, relationships among health stakeholders and proximity to a federal election.

While the mass media acted as both a provider of information and a guardian of trust during the medical indemnity crisis, its role as a guardian was not evident after the crisis subsided. In the period after the crisis, the mass media reported the changes in the agent's role but unlike its actions during the crisis, the media did not actively comment on inconsistencies between the agent's established and reified roles. In part, this change in the role of the mass media may be attributed to a reduced level of newsworthiness of the medical indemnity issue over time. Further studies should broaden the investigation of the agent beyond the medical indemnity debate.

This research has implications for both principal–agency theory as well as media studies involving trust. Research also indicates that as principal–agent relationships evolve and access to information improves the relative influence of trust changes (Singh and Sirdeshmukh, 2000). As such, further research that investigates the evolution of trust in these relationships over longer periods of time would be useful. Such studies should also use alternative and more direct methodologies to explore principals' understanding of these issues and influences of guardians of trust. The mass media's role as a guardian of trust should also be considered in relation to existing and commonly accepted guardians of trust. The news framing of information from traditional guardians of trust would provide an interesting location for such a study. Most principal–agency studies focus on the relationship between principals and their agent alone. However, the mass media often report exchanges between two agents who act on behalf of their opposing principals. The mass media offer an interesting platform from which to view and compare its guardian of trust role across two agent–principal relationships.

This research should also be considered in light of mass media studies relating to public trust in media and extended to examine the influence of intercultural differences in principals' use of media. A recent study by Botan and Taylor (2005) showed that in a developing country, principals' political affiliations affected their trust in media. Further studies that explore the role of media as a guardian of trust should also consider the perspectives of principals. Beside these limitations, this study has identified a useful alternative or addition to traditional guardians of trust such as contracts and regulatory bodies in principal–agent relationships. In principal–agency relationships, this study has shown how the mass media indirectly guards trust in times of crisis. Ayios (2003) identified that direct monitoring can produce conflict and distrust in some cultures. Providing the mass media can gain access to the relationship or exchange situation, it can act on behalf of principals and avoid direct interference by acting at an impersonal level to guard for trust in times of crisis.

Notes

1. After joining parliament in 1994, Mr Tony Abbott was promoted to cabinet in 2001 as the Minister for Employment, Workplace Relations and Small Business. In October 2003, following a cabinet reshuffle, Mr Abbott was appointed Minister for Health and Ageing.
2. The mass media in Australia is both publicly and privately owned by the following major corporations: News Limited, Publishing and Broadcasting Limited, John Fairfax Holdings Limited and the Australian Broadcasting Corporation. News Limited produces a range of newspapers including *The Australian* and *The Weekend Australian*, which are national newspapers, *The Courier-Mail*, which is based in Brisbane. John Fairfax Holdings Limited also produces a range of newspapers including *The Sydney Morning Herald* and Melbourne-based *The Age*. Rural Press Limited publishes specialist agricultural and regional press including *The Canberra Times*.
3. J. Frenkel, 'Dumping Welcomed,' *Herald-Sun*, 30 September (2003) p. 7.
4. AAP, 'Liberal Hardman Takes on Health,' *Hobart Mercury*, 30 September (2003) pp. 1–4.
5. M. Schubert, 'Radical Surgery,' *The Australian*, 4 October (2003) p. 1.
6. C. Jones, L. Edmistone and R. Odgers, 'Patterson Rejects Claims of Frontbench Demotion,' *The Courier-Mail*, 30 September (2003) p. 1.
7. A. Pavey, 'Fed–AMA says Don't Kick our Heads,' *AAP*, 30 September (2003).
8. M. Gordon, 'Howard's Team Healthy, But Not Home,' *The Age*, 4 October (2003) p. 7.
9. M. Schubert, 'Unstable Prognosis,' *The Australian*, 11 October (2003) p. 24.
10. M. Farr, 'Shaping Up for Election–Abbott Scores in Ministry Shuffle,' *The Daily Telegraph*, 30 September (2003) p. 2.
11. M. Gordon, 'Abbott Moves To Mend Fences With Angry Doctors,' *The Age*, 4 October (2003) p. 8.
12. S. Dunlevy, 'Tony Changes Hats to Nut out a Deal,' *The Daily Telegraph*, 4 October (2003), p. 7.
13. J. Frenkel, 'PM Rolls Abbott,' *The Herald-Sun*, 10 October (2003) p. 2.
14. M. Schubert, 'Unstable Prognosis,' *The Australian*, 11 October (2003) p. 24.
15. M. Metherell and R. Pollard, 'Doctors' Dispute at Flashpoint,' *The Sydney Morning Herald*, 10 October (2003) p. 13.
16. M. Metherell, 'Under The Knife,' *The Sydney Morning Herald*, 11 October (2003) p. 53.
17. C. Jones and L. Edmistone, 'Medical Bailout to Halt Exodus,' *The Courier-Mail*, 18 December (2003) p. 1.
18. Anon, 'Games reclassified: Computer Games will Fall Under the Same Classification as ...,' *The Canberra Times*, 14 May (2004) p. 8.

14
'It Was a Mascara Runnin' Kinda Day': Oprah Winfrey, Confession, Celebrity and the Formation of Trust

Sherryl Wilson

In his book *Dude, Where's My Country?* (2003), Michael Moore posits that should Oprah Winfrey stand against George W. Bush in the 2004 election she would win by a landslide. He claims that she would succeed because Oprah is a real person. This is an interesting claim to make about an individual who is only really known through her screen persona. And yet Moore claims that he is perfectly serious. He argues that Winfrey would beat Bush 'hands down' because 'America loves her and her enormous personal wealth means that she can't be bought' (Moore, 2003, p. 27).[1]

Moore is pointing to a real problem: the zeitgeist in which trust in politicians is low, who are seen to be acting out of self-interest rather than that of the public. Nonetheless, his identification of Winfrey as a viable alternative to the existing choices for political leadership presents a paradox. On the one hand, a symbol of individualism and success, celebrity does present a position of distinction imbued with a certain discursive power. As Marshall (1997) says, 'Within society, the celebrity is a voice above all others, a voice that is channeled into the media systems as being legitimately significant' (pp. 48–9). On the other hand, the sign of celebrity is also 'ridiculed and derided because it represents the centre of false value'. Celebrity, then, is an articulation of 'the individual as commodity' (pp. x–xi).

There is a further paradox in Moore's formulation of Winfrey as an ideal presidential candidate. Her celebrity persona has developed through her long time performance as a talk show host. *The Oprah Winfrey Show* is predominant within a much-derided genre which attracts vilification largely on the grounds that individual distress is exploited for public spectacle and commercial gain. Talk shows emphasis on the emotional rather than rational, along with their lack of substantive political content, has engendered not a small degree of concern for the cultural pollution that the programmes are believed to generate (Himmelstein, 1984; Keller, 1993; Abt and Seesholtz, 1994, 1998; Collins, 1998;[2] Fraser, 1998[3]).

However, within the context of contemporary media culture, Moore's eulogy of the Oprah persona is not surprising. The Oprah phenomenon indicates a popular appetite for the authentic that appears to be located at the level of individual response to situations and systems beyond personal control. Oprah[4] is a charismatic individual whose specific attributes are particularly effective in the contemporary cultural context that is marked by instability, uncertainty and anxiety. Some of the messages posted on fan web-sites support this claim. One such example comes from Dixie Lady: 'Because you have touched my heart so many times and in so many ways, I offer a part of my heart to you'. Another comes from Laura who writes 'Oprah, thank you for many years of growing and learning ... Oprah is the one hour of serenity I can count on every day where I can regain my balance' (Gifts from the Heart, 2004).

Whether or not we see her through the same lens, it can be of no doubt that Winfrey is a media cultural icon of some considerable stature. In 2005, *Time* magazine voted her one of the 100 most important people of the 20th century, the National Civil Rights Museum granted the National Freedom Award and she was admitted to the National Association for the Advancement of Colored People's Hall of Fame. She has won seven Emmies for 'Outstanding Talk Show Host' and nine Emmy Awards for Outstanding Talk Show. Winfrey is the highest earning black woman in America, wields considerable power in owning not just her own TV production company, *Harpo*, but also the magazine, *O, The Oprah Magazine* and *Oxygen Media* which comprises the *Oxygen.com* web-site (http://www.oxygen.com) and the *Oxygen TV* network.[5] One of the most interesting aspects of this catalogue of success is that it is predicated on a persona whose trademark is the 'ordinary' and the 'everyday'. While Oprah is not unique in her ability to convey a sense of ordinariness, the longevity of her popularity, the intense attachments and degree of trust she appears to engender suggests a particularity to her performance that is worth examining in detail.[6]

Oprah-as-celebrity has been created through her daily interactions with the 'ordinary people' who appear as guests on her show in which the subject material is the ordinary – sometimes extraordinary – real life experiences of the everyday. Crucially, Oprah's practice of revealing aspects of herself and her life experiences as a means of empathising with her guests and/or presenting the rationale for that day's subject, is the means through which she represents herself as ordinary and, therefore, authentic. Clearly, Oprah Winfrey is anything *but* ordinary and everyday, but I would argue that her show's emphasis on the emotional life of herself and her guests fosters a particular kind of relationship which, although mediated by commercial television, is grounded in a representation of the 'real' that has a powerful cultural resonance. The figure of Oprah offers the possibility of thinking through the fragility of self-formation within contemporary culture when trust in political and legal systems appears to be low.

This chapter explores the interactions between Oprah, her guests and viewers as a means to understanding the ways in which she negotiates her celebrity status and works to produce the levels of trust within her viewers that is expressed by Moore and the fans cited above.[7]

It should be pointed out at this stage that there is a wealth of material that addresses a range of issues in relation to TV talk shows in general and to Oprah Winfrey in particular. Many of them consider the shows from a feminist or gender perspective (Squire, 1994; Epstein and Steinberg, 1995, 1996; Gamson, 1995, 1998a, 1998b; Shattuc, 1997); the public sphere (Carpignano, Anderson, Aronowitz and Diafazio, 1990; McLaughlin, 1993; Livingstone and Lunt, 1994; Alcott and Gray-Rosendale, 1996); class (Grindstaff, 1997) and 'race' (Masciarotte, 1991; Peck, 1994). Many of these categories overlap producing a debate that is as rich as it is complex. While the Oprah persona cannot be separated from the larger political concerns that speak to class, gender and 'race' my approach here is to focus very specifically on the dynamic between Oprah's highly mediated celebrity persona and her audience as a means to understanding the particularity of this relationship. This, I argue, enables us to understand not only the Oprah persona but also the relationship between the nature of celebrity and the formation of trust within TV audiences more generally. To do this, I look how Oprah manages her celebrity status through the foregrounding of her 'ordinariness' that is facilitated through her adoption of a confessional mode of address.

The ritual of confession which, according to Foucault (1978, p. 58), operates as an 'agency of truth and power in Western society' and its link with emotional talk lies at the heart of *Oprah*. As Eva Illouz (1999) argues for TV talk shows, emotional talk is a way of framing embattled relations that threaten the integrity of the self. A structure for understanding the relationship between self and others, emotion in talk shows offers ways of talking about 'a broken (or longed for) social solidarity' (Illouz, 1999, p. 119). Further, emotion becomes the only reliable currency once moral prescriptions can no longer be relied on; it offers the framework with which to make sense of everyday life. This is akin to Ien Ang's (1985) findings in her frequently cited work *Watching Dallas* in which she identifies an emotional realism which, despite the non-realistic representation of life portrayed on the screen, enables viewers to relate to the characters' experiences and dilemmas. So, in fiction and non-fiction TV, emotion-as-truth forms a recognisable point of reference for, and offers a connection with, the viewers.

The attachment to Oprah expressed online by Laura and Dixie Lady is a result of the para-social relationship that exists between celebrity and fan. This fosters what Schickel (2000, p. 311) calls 'the illusion of intimacy' but is premised on a gap between the famous personality and the unknown audience. However, at the heart of *Oprah* is the foregrounding of subjective experience that operates as a means of breaching the gap between private individual and public media celebrity.

In a culture characterised by consumption, by the endless play of images divorced from any inherent meaning, and by depthlessness, celebrity also indicates a compulsive search for the 'real' (Moran, 2000, pp. 137–52). Of course, the terms 'truth', 'real' and 'authentic' have to be properly placed within qualifying apostrophes because all of these images are highly mediated and stage managed (see Grindstaff, 1997). However, Oprah conflates notions of the 'authentic' with a highly mediated construction that is the celebrity persona so that they become inextricably linked.

Celebrity and the ordinary

Oprah manages to contain the contradiction of being simultaneously ordinary *and* extraordinary through her knowledge and experience of the everyday. This is tricky enough. But the construct that is the Oprah persona is made more complex by the fact of being an African American woman, an aspect of her identity that she frequently foregrounds and which forms a significant feature of her life experiences recounted on her show.

Winfrey's 'racial' identity is further underpinned by her film roles in Alice Walker's *The Color Purple* (1984), Toni Morrison's *Beloved* (1987) and in the TV film of Gloria Naylor's *Women of Brewster Place* (1989). This not only works to confer star status, but explicitly indicates a connection with a body of black feminist writers whose work posits the possibility of self-recovery and self-realisation through the excavation of a personal and collective history and through the articulation of one's own story (Walker, 1983; Collins, 1991; hooks, 1990a, 1990b). What emerges from this is the empowering possibilities inherent in claiming one's own experiences as valid rather than seeking validation through the bourgeois expertise articulated by the various therapists that appear on the program. On her show Winfrey's relationship with this black feminist tradition is signalled by references to, and admiration of, prominent writers such as Maya Angelou (1970, 1974, 1981), Walker (1983) and Morrison (1987, 1999).

Winfrey's identification with a culturally and historically marginalised group is ever present and represents a key aspect of the Oprah persona. However, she is addressing a mass and mixed audience. The financial viability of her programmes therefore necessitates that her mode of address works towards inclusion. This is facilitated by and through Oprah's confessional practice that not only signals intimacy, but also mirrors the position of many of her guests.

Oprah's particular form of celebrity arises from more than one medium, however, she is both a TV celebrity and a film star. The two are qualitatively different but are, in her case, also mutually reinforcing. As Marshall

(1997, p. 119) points out, 'the film celebrity plays with aura through distance [whereas] the television celebrity is configured around conceptions of familiarity ... [and] embodies the characteristics of ... mass acceptability'. The mass acceptability of Oprah derives from her TV persona which is predicated on ordinariness while her star status is shored up through her various film performances for which she has received acclaim.[8]

Drawing on the work of Max Weber, Dyer argues that the charismatic quality of a personality exists within a cultural or historical specificity that, in turn, determines his/her relationship with society. Of particular interest here is Dyer's (1979, p. 35) further assertions that the charismatic personality is particularly effective 'when the social order is uncertain, unstable, and ambiguous and when the charismatic figure or group offers a value, order or stability to counterpoise this'.

The idea of a promise of stability held out by a charismatic figure is useful in thinking about the cultural significance of *Oprah* in the age of late capitalism, but further qualifications need to be made before we can apply it to Oprah. So far, I have been using the terms 'star' and 'celebrity' interchangeably. Dyer's work looks at film stars whereas Marshall explores the specific ways in which celebrity is constructed through the various media of film, TV and popular music. Marshall (1997, pp. 14–5) argues that the concept of a film star holds a different construction of power from that of celebrity. Where the star is a 'publicly organised identity that arises from fictional film', the celebrity 'is specifically an engagement with the external world ... the celebrity element of the star is its transcendence of the text in whatever form'.

This notion of a transcendent quality that arises from an engagement with the material world is most useful in the consideration of the Oprah persona which is predicated on her 'down homeness' and is shored up by Oprah-as-film-star which emphasises the ambiguity of star-as-ordinary/ star-as-exceptional discussed by Dyer. The suggestion of the presence of an aura that is created through the star's engagement with the ordinary most profitably describes the power inherent in the Oprah persona which has evolved more through her position as talk show host than as a film star – although she is that also. For this reason Oprah is more accurately described as a celebrity than as a star.

All of the voices heard on the program, and the form that their articulations take, are facilitated by and filtered through Oprah whose own authority resides in her struggles to overcome difficulties. This discursive structure is underpinned by the ways in which Oprah works to apparently close the gap between her celebrity self, the guests and audience. An intimate and empathic relationship with her guests – who are more often 'ordinary' people than famous individuals – is constructed through confessional discourse. This constitutes the show's narrative glue, lending coherence to the disparate narratives supplied by her guests. Oprah's adoption of the confessional position reduces the otherness of others despite the acknowledged fact of her power, wealth and extraordinary success.

Oprah as confessing subject

An old *Oprah* show broadcast in Britain in December 1995 ('Lose Weight, Lose Friends') reveals in close-up how Oprah works to engender an intimacy with her guests and audience. This particular program examines the repercussions of losing weight. Here we have a number of women guests who are invited to speak about their weight loss and how this has affected their self-image. The show's emphasis is on the way in which the move from a negative to a positive sense of self – signified by and through weight reduction – has adversely affected these women's relationships with those family and friends closest to them. During the course of the show Oprah places herself in a variety of positions, locating herself as host and star of *Oprah*, interlocutor, friend, interpreter and fellow confessor. As each guest discloses her own experience relating to weight gain and/or loss and self perception, Oprah frequently interjects with examples of her own experience in this area; as regular viewers will know, Winfrey's fluctuating body weight is a recurring theme of the show. Apart from being the source of much of her own distress, the issue of weight works as one of the more powerful ways in which Oprah fosters an apparent intimacy and parity with guests and audience. This particular program not only deals with problems experienced by the invited guests, but also articulates a shift, evidenced by some viewers, in their relationship with the Oprah persona. The issues explored on this particular program act as a frame for Oprah/Winfrey to explore her own relationship with her audience, a relationship that is defined through and by the fluctuations in her own weight. Large bodies constitute a range of issues too complex to explore here, but it should at least be noted. As Ellman states:

> The fat woman, particularly if she is non-white and working class, has come to embody everything the prosperous must disavow: imperialism, exploitation, surplus value, maternity, mortality, abjection and unloveliness ... [S]he siphons off this guilt, desire, and denial, leaving her idolized counterpart behind: the kind of woman one sees on billboards, sleek and streamlined like the cars she is often used to advertise. (Cited in Russo, 1995, p. 24)

Introducing a number of letters 'from people who think I have, quote, changed [after weight loss]', Oprah seeks to demonstrate that she too has known the troubles faced by the guests appearing on this show. A sequence of letters is shown on the screen with sections highlighted and accompanied by images of the authors. All correspondents are female, and all are white. A Judy Marcum writes 'I'm sick of hearing about your wonderful weight loss [aided by a specialist diet chef and a weight trainer] .... You do not live our lives, so quit pretending that you are just ordinary folk'. This is the final letter to be shown and is followed by Oprah announcing 'And this is Judy who wrote that letter friends!' The word 'friends' immediately places the audience on an intimate footing with the show's host, but at the same time emphasises the fact that this is what Oprah actually is, celebrity and host. None of the correspondence is from personal friends, and the fact that viewers have been sufficiently moved to write to her in such familiar terms supports her status rather than detracts from it.

Foucault (1978) characterises confession as a process through which relations of power are formed. The speaking subject confesses in the presence of an authority who judges, punishes, consoles, forgives and reconciles, who offers salvation and liberation. Through the exchange between Oprah and the correspondents, it becomes evident that while she is the authority to whom confession is made, she also performs as confessional subject herself. This has the effect of effacing her own extraordinariness as she, in turn, confers authority on the guests – and by extension, the audience – to whom the confession is made, so that the locus of power *apparently* migrates.

Judy is positioned in the front row of the audience; Oprah joins her in order to discuss further the intention and meaning behind the letter. Judy and Oprah are now a part of and apart from the rest of the studio audience. Judy explains 'I just don't feel comfortable with you any more. You don't come across as the same person. When you were on TV you were just like down home folks to me before'. Judy continues to evaluate the difference in Oprah by locating an inner change which is attributed to a greater self confidence; before this shift, Oprah was someone that Judy would have invited into her home 'and offered a doughnut' to. Now she 'doesn't come across as that same person'. Oprah replies that she *feels* like the same person but 'lighter'. Judy refuses this evaluation: 'You're a different person, not like us any more'. Pertinently, it is the *way* in which Oprah has achieved her goals that has alienated these viewers: the paid help and support of a chef and trainer. These are props that are beyond the scope of ordinary viewers, whereas the numerous diets that had been used in the past were those that all had access to. That Winfrey is a (very rich) black woman does not figure in the dialogue at any point in this show.[9] The Oprah who is met now is a usurper. Judy explains her reasons for coming onto the show:

Judy: I wanted to come here and see if you were the same person.
Oprah: But you didn't know me before.
Judy: But I saw you on TV all the time and I felt like you could come to my home. Like you were my cousin. Now I think 'she's forgot about us'. I feel this in my heart, like you forgot about all us people.

As Judy confesses her discomfort with Oprah, Oprah seeks to reassure that she still feels 'like down home folks. If anything I feel even more downer homer [sic]'. She is the authority to whom the confession is made, but she does not punish, judge or exclude. Rather, she uses Judy's confession as the platform from which to make her own disclosure. Oprah states that she used the weight gain/loss as a 'metaphor for all the other stuff that I was carrying ... pain, non-confrontation, not dealing with fears'. The specificity of this pain and fear is not referred to but has been disclosed in other shows and will be well known to regular viewers of *Oprah*. They include sexual abuse, teenage sexual promiscuity, poor self-image enabling Oprah to reiterate her claim that 'I feel like I'm Every Woman; I've had almost every problem!'

What is particularly noteworthy is the fact that although Oprah, through her own confessions, signals intimacy with Judy, she (Judy) disavows this by insisting on her preference for the down home Oprah of the past who she has come to know through TV. The irony of the flesh and blood version of Oprah being insufficient to seduce Judy from her preference for the earlier TV version is left unexplored.

Interestingly, from this exchange and the others that follow, the issue of wealth is declared not to be of concern to the women who had written letters similar to that of Judy's. This is somewhat contradictory as wealth is the means through which Winfrey achieved weight loss this time, and that has worked to alienate these particular viewers. What this implies is that so long as wealth is not foregrounded, the myth that Oprah is like 'down home folks' can be sustained. Once this appearance is violated viewers' perception of the screen persona, and their relation to it, changes.

The boundaries between notions of friendship and family ties are continually blurred. The earlier guests – Lisa and Sheila – who are cousins, relate to each other as friends, while Judy regards Oprah as a friend who might also be a cousin. Oprah further seeks to efface differences between herself and audience by using the address 'friends'. This raises questions about what the word 'friend' signifies here. From the dialogues of Judy and the other guests, it would seem to refer to a person who is not likely to judge negatively, and a person who might be another family member. More importantly, 'friend' signifies a relationship premised on trust.

However, these relationships are problematised by and through their construction in an economic production: we know that Judy and the other letter writers/readers are viewers who represent ratings and the commercial viability of the *Oprah* show. The presence of these women – and their relationship with the show's host – represents the commodification of familial networks and bonds of friendship that is articulated through confessional discourse and mediated by the means of commercial TV.

Oprah's exemplification of individualism and success along with the trust that she subsequently engenders does indeed mark her as exceptional. But her authority resides in experiencing the same problems articulated by her guests. This enables her to make such declarations as 'I feel like I am every woman'. However, paradoxically, the more Oprah insists that she is 'down home', the more her celebrity position is confirmed. On the one hand, the confessional nature of her speech intimates a reconfiguration of the power relations produced through confessional discourse. On the other, her practice of frequent interjection signals her license to assert control over what is spoken, when and by whom. The gap between herself as celebrity and the audience is thus reinforced while acts of confession imply an equality of relations.

There are occasions when this contradiction is flagged however. In 'Oprah's Diets' the entire first segment is devoted to a reading of Oprah's journal entries written over a period of two and a half years; what we hear is a catalogue of the food eaten and not eaten, expressions of anguish and self-loathing as the lost weight returns: 'Control ... Trying to regain the control God gave me ... Sometimes I can feel the connection between my own fears and my weight. So what are my fears?' We are also shown a series of images that have appeared (and been derided) in the press along with footage of Oprah at TV award ceremonies. The contradiction that exists within the person and the persona is made manifest through the visual images of a successful woman collecting an award juxtaposed with a contemporaneous diary extract proclaiming shame and self-hatred for becoming so large. Her decision to display extracts from her journals works towards creating a sense of authenticity through which we develop a sense of knowing who she is; trust in Oprah is engendered through the act of self-revelation. It is this quality that Moore identifies when he states that 'I have been on *Oprah* three times. I saw grown adults break down and sob after shaking her hand. Why? I think it's because Oprah is a real person ... She's one of us who somehow made it' (2003, p. 27).

Celebrity and the engendering of trust

The voices that speak on *The Oprah Winfrey Show* are mobilised through the system of celebrity – embodied by Oprah – that itself acts as an avowal of the cultural ideals of individualism and success that are in turn enmeshed with notions of commodity and consumption. And the show itself would not exist without them. However, the process of commodification is undercut through the sharing and rehearsal of everyday problems and experiences. The African American model of selfhood referred to earlier that informs the Oprah persona also infuses the narratives of self that are presented on the show. This is a self that is tied to community, familial and social networks and which is capable of overcoming oppressive forces. In this way, Oprah manages to appeal to a mass and mixed audience. Trust is produced through the charismatic persona that offers the possibility of thinking through the fragility of self-formation within the post-modern context with its attendant uncertainty, social fragmentation and mass mediation, and accounts for her popularity *at this particular moment in time.*

Notes

1. M. Moore, 'How to Talk to your Conservative Brother-in-Law', *Guardian Weekend*, 4 October (2003) pp. 22–30.
2. M. Collins, 'Tears 'R' Us', *The Guardian*, 15 January (1998) pp. 4–5.
3. N. Fraser, 'The Cheap Triumph of Trash TV', *The Guardian*, 31 January (1998) pp. 1–2.
4. I use the name 'Oprah' to signal the screen persona as distinct from the person who is Oprah Winfrey.
5. *O, The Oprah Magazine* was launched in May/June 2000 as a personal growth guide with a target audience of women between the ages of 25 and 49. Winfrey is a co-founder of *Oxygen Media*, which operates a 24-hour cable TV network for women and launched in 1998 (see http://www.oxygen.com/).
6. This 'ordinariness' is not a phenomenon peculiar to, or invented by, Oprah. As Murray (2001, p. 187) points out, in the 1940s and early 50s it was recognised that TV stars had to 'exude an honesty or naturalness that would engender trust in the audience' – especially when endorsing a product. Holmes (2004) also explores the apparent contradiction between stardom and an authenticity that is premised on ordinariness in relation to the reality TV program *Pop Idol* (broadcast in the UK on ITV1, from 2001).
7. While the popularity of TV talk shows is in decline – at least, they occupy less space within British TV schedules and generate far fewer column inches in newspapers – I would argue that they have left an indelible trace made manifest through the plethora of reality TV programming that can be characterised through their placement of subjectivity at the core of the shows' narratives and which is often accessed through the process of confession.
8. The examples used to support the arguments presented in this paper come from a number of *Oprah Winfrey Shows* that precede Winfrey's acquisition of *O* and *Oxygen*. However, the tone and content of her current work mirrors that of her earlier TV talk shows in which her celebrity persona was formed. The mode of address, range of concerns and the emphasis on the everyday remain consistent. See Illouz (2003) for a discussion of the ways in which Oprah performs across the full range of media platforms.
9. Winfrey has been criticised for her accommodation of white normative codes in the pursuit of her celebrity status (Peck, 1994; Ferguson, 1998).

15
Branding Trust: The Ideology of Making Truth Claims through Interactive Media

Janet Jones

The promise of technological transcendence

This chapter analyses how the Internet and Interactive TV might encourage a new culture of communications. Specifically, it investigates whether audiences are predisposed to trust the content of media that depend on participatory user relationships, and how important user interactivity is in the perceived authenticity of the end product. Based on empirical data collected between 2001 and 2006,[1] this study seeks to better define the fluid boundaries between users and producers of new media products through an analysis of the specific contexts within which interactive technologies are taken up. It investigates two disparate, international media brands: firstly, *Big Brother*, a constructed reality game show with audience interaction and secondly, *Indymedia*, self-defined as the largest, global, public, democratic media news network in existence.

In theory, the technology underpinning digitally based media products is well placed to support the democratisation of broadcasting, with unprecedented opportunities for enhanced levels of interactivity pushing the locus of control from the centre to the periphery. Both *Big Brother* and *Indymedia* exploit these convergent technologies by fostering a sense of audience agency and mobility. They variously advance the notion that the role of producer can be supplanted by the power of the user, *Big Brother* through voting, and *Indymedia* through open publishing, which channels new technology into a broadening of public access, or 'citizen journalism' by eroding the role of the gatekeeper whereas *Big Brother* employs the powerful combination of telephone, TV and computer to create enhanced levels of interactivity.

I suggest that maintaining trust through the management of strong, hyper-mediated relationships is core to the success of both *Indymedia* and *Big Brother*. Yet, I conclude that despite the potential of new media technologies to change the nature of production, and create more equal relationships between users and producers, the ecology of access to content buckles under the constraints of technical, commercial and social realities.

Truth claims

The ideology of making truth claims through the media has been at the centre of two critical debates over the last ten years. In the UK, the documentary form received a battering in the 1990s when the public's trust in the media's ability to reproduce authentically the 'world out there' was eroded through a series of high-profile fakery scandals (Winston, 2000; Jones, 2003). In addition, the proliferation of hybrid forms such as the docu-soap, which relied heavily on contrived and often fictional premises, forced audiences to question the media's ability to deliver a reliable image of the real. The hybridisation of the factual form, the fluidity of borders between entertainment, factual and fiction, heralded what John Corner (2002) describes as the era of post-documentary culture, and what Kilborn (2003, p. 178) refers to as the dawn of a more media literate age where audiences have 'developed a generally more sceptical attitude to what they see and hear on their TV screens'. This suggests, in a sceptical, post-documentary climate, that it might be advantageous for new media products to forge innovative relations with users by removing the pervasive suspicion of mediation.

A second high-profile media debate that continues to beleaguer both Europe and North America is the public's trust in broadcast news output. In 2005, 2000 journalism educators and industry leaders gathered in San Antonio, in the USA for a conference (Conference on Restoring the Trust in Journalism, 2005) conceived partly in response to a Gallup poll showing that only 44 per cent of Americans expressed confidence in the media's ability to report the news accurately and fairly, the lowest level since Gallup first posed the question in 1972. As the public trust in the news media waned amid revelations of misdeeds and ethical lapses, the debate naturally focused on how to reverse this trend. The talk at this conference was of content 'coming from the people' and 'bottom-up' news replacing the editor-in-chief challenging the normative hierarchical operations of conventional newsrooms. Industry leaders were beginning to ask difficult questions about the future of conventional news in a world where the Internet is redefining the relationship between the producers and consumers of news heralding a transformative change in the way news might be delivered and consumed.

Exploiting the teleology of young media users

To help place this analysis of *Indymedia* and *Big Brother* in a broader audience context, I conducted a general study of young people's Web-based, information-seeking behaviour with the data amassed through a Web-questionnaire.[2] Although conventional Web news services such as *Guardian On-line*, *Reuters* and the *BBC* were common destinations for the over 35s, they had less allure for the younger citizen. Instead, this young group (16–34) showed a tendency to seek out unconventional sources that appealed to their interactive tastes.

The sites preferred by these informants were disparate such as centres of online communities and chat groups based around special interest groups of a political or social nature. The study revealed that there were no clear lines of separation between political and non-political networking, consumerism, entertainment and chat. I was able to distinguish three specific categories of usage highlighting the attractiveness of low-mediated, user-instigated, interactively based content. Each one of these approaches represents a specific aspect of the Internet communication culture. First, there is the *social network approach*, which is illustrative of what has been dubbed the horizontal communication of civic interaction whereby users want to discuss and exchange information on a level, non-hierarchical basis (Dahlgren, 2005). It also represents an aspect of what Baym calls 'epistemaphilia' in her discussion of online soap opera fans. This is not simply a pleasure of knowing, but a pleasure of exchanging knowledge (Baym, 1998, p. 127).

Secondly, indicative of this group of respondents, is the '*infotainment approach*'. In this category, information sourced through entertainment-based channels has a similar stature to information sourced through more conventional news sites. Historically, news cultures have promoted a strong separation of the two, but more recently there has been an acceptance of generic breakdown triggered in part through the convergence of media and also by the hope that ludic, information-seeking behaviour might better engage young audiences in the political arena. Blumler and Gurevitch (2000) list the blurring and hybridisation of genres, and the erosion of the distinction between journalism and non-journalism as a notable online trend, and Curran stresses that entertainment, 'should be recognised as a positive part of the media's contribution to the democratic process' (Curran, 2002, p. 238).

The final category emerging from this study, and critical to the argument I am making here, is the '*seeking reality approach*'. This is where the main themes of authenticity, trust and the perceived absence of mediation (the strong hand of the editor) are best articulated. Here we see a strong connection between trust and Internet usage. The results indicate that Web-based media are perceived as low-mediation and high-trust with a strong degree of 'pull' or user-instigated and user-controlled activity, elements vital to the establishment of any truth claim and central to the two media brands under discussion.

These findings are supported by data from a UK, Independent Television Commission research study highlighting the importance of trust to Internet users, reporting that the Internet is trusted to tell the truth by 71 per cent of users, and that young people trust the Internet more than any other age group (ITC, 2002).

Indymedia – The case for trust

In the world of conventional news, there exists a core consensus about which individuals have the right to be heard, who should be trusted to speak and who should not. But, sites such as *OhmyNews* in Korea and *iTalkNews* in the USA and the *Global Indymedia News Network* are on the vanguard of a shift in journalistic practices.

Indymedia defines itself as the largest, global, public, democratic media news network in existence today (Covell, 2003). Its first major outing was the streamed Web video coverage of the anti World Trade Organisation (WTO) protests in Seattle. Since then it claims that over 27 million people have visited its sites around the world and during significant events it can reach up to 3.5 million hits on a single day. It is a 'technologically-inspired', interactive and open-sourced news platform that abandons traditional notions of gatekeepers where mediation is either transparent or ideally non-existent. It aims to be a non-hierarchical network of information exchange, part of the fulfilment of the Habermasian vision of an idealised, democratic public sphere achieved through a system of open, equal and fluid interconnectivity (Habermas, 1987, 1989, 1996).

It is part of the resurgence of 'citizen journalism' based on a philosophy of open publishing. Open publishing is a process of creating news that is transparent to the reader. Anyone can contribute a story and see it appear instantly in the pool of stories available publicly. Ideally, readers can see editorial decisions being made by others. They can see how to get involved and help create content. It is a prime example of what Platon and Deuze (2003) define as an open journalistic culture with a concentration of public connectivity. Advocates of open-source journalism believe that it is well paced to cure the malaise of mistrust through its transparent delivery mechanisms. Its central philosophy derives from a deep frustration at the mainstream media's perceived failure to cover certain issues fairly. This frustration found an outlet in the organisation's principle slogan, 'don't hate the media, be the media'. It claims that it has no hierarchy, no single person in charge, and that all important decisions are made by consensus.

Low mediation solution

Platon and Deuze suggest that authority at *Indymedia* is not derived, as in conventional news culture, through the use of experts and elite commentators, but rather from the collective. 'Truth is not seen as an absolute but an infinite sampling of perspectives of a given situation' (Platon and Deuze, 2003, p. 34):

> This is one of the main advantages of open publishing. You get direct accounts. They do not have to be true per se. This is a little bit beside the point. I believe it is the truthfulness of the person saying it that matters. It is the very image of that person, reporting what he/she really believes. And that strikes some chord inside most people. (Interview with an unnamed senior staff journalist, cited in Platon and Deuze, 2003, p. 345)

Thus, the 'direct account' neutralises the fear of the gatekeeper. The following comments, taken from a discussion group held online between a British Broadcasting Corporation (BBC) staff journalist, Bill Hayton, and regular *Indymedia* users in 2003, are further indicative of this cultural philosophy.

1. It's all about the commodification of information. To me it's not just about good reporting, that is not what is so f****** amazing about *Indymedia*, it's the creation of an open space that does not mediate and does not make money off the information.
2. The dividing line (between corporate media and *Indymedia*) is that you (Corporate Journalists) take a pay packet home. The issue is, is truth free or does it cost?
3. *Indymedia* doesn't talk to people, people talk to *Indymedia*.
4. The mainstream media is being viewed as untrustworthy by ever larger numbers of people as awareness of its failings spread via the Web. My mother trusts my impression of a protest far more than the nightly news. Corporate media started dying the day the Internet was invented.

Direct testimony without producer intervention or editorialising has an attractive indexical quality. The communicative grammar of the Internet lends itself to the approach taken by *Indymedia*. Integral to this relationship with its users is a decentralised organisational structure, empowering individual users/contributors through autonomy and interactivity. Kim and Sawhney (2002, p. 227) suggest that interactivity is best defined by 'spontaneous, open, communicative human behaviours where people have control and can exchange roles in the communication process'. Thus, essentially the distinction between audiences and producers becomes irrelevant and trust is built through a process whereby editorial decisions are transparent, visible and verifiable. Covell (2003, p.2) asserts that 'control of quality and truth stays in the hands of the reader since every news item can be commented upon and argued about.'

Indymedia – The case against trust

Ideally, what defines *Indymedia*'s relationship with its users is its decentralised organisational structure, aimed at empowering individuals through the interactive nature of open publishing. However, practical restraints mean that there are significant limits to its open-access editorial policy. When everyone is empowered to have their say in an unrestrained and anonymous environment, the output is potentially chaotic. There are those who would take advantage by using the service to spread hate and extreme views. A lack of accountability produces opinion-based content and 'fact checking is often met with cries of censorship'. In addition, the content is often badly written and presented, lacking basic journalistic skills (Whitney, 2005).

All international *Indymedia* sites have had to tackle these problems. Editorial guidelines are specific to each culture. Typically, these involve instructing volunteer 'wire-cleaners' to hide illegal posts. These can be repeated, non-news (comment or opinion); discriminatory (sexist, racist and so on); inaccurate or misleading; advertising; hierarchical; disruptive or those copied and pasted from other sites. Naturally, censorship of illegal posts is a sensitive issue within the collective. 'In many IMC[3] collectives, the editing vs. free speech dichotomy is argued as hotly as abortion is debated by members of congregations and Congress' (Whitney, 2005). There is an ongoing tension between protecting the news wire from lawsuits and upholding the philosophy of openness. The editorial function is carried out by groups of volunteers who monitor the sites to keep them current and free of racist postings in particular, but also a back office team to ensure the smooth running of the elaborate computing systems. This effectively creates an elite team in a position of power.

Arguably, the list cleaners or 'admins' act very much like the silent, invisible hand of the 'corporate' news editor. The true test for each collective is how they manage this elite and how they make them accountable. The ongoing challenge is to prevent the benevolent dictatorship structure from becoming corrupt with the normative values of one select group defining the content for all. *Indymedia UK* has an open access process site where opinions can be voiced and issues of editorial policy discussed. One vocal dissenter from the Bristol UK branch of *Indymedia UK* launched this attack on the working practices of the central London administrators: 'What laughable lengths you appear prepared to go to – to censor stories you don't approve of with neither discussion nor explanation' (27 September, 2004, IMC-UK process). This comment reflects an important aspect associated with the act of censorship. How can accountability be built into the hiding process? One significant debate focused around a proposal to change the current editorial policy. The suggestion was that the list cleaners use a 'watermark', which would leave a vague imprint where a hidden story was originally launched, less conspicuous than the present policy that uses black text on a black background. Both systems would act to leave a trace of the editorial decision to kill a story but the new proposal would be more subtle. However, the new system would allow only the 'admins' to read the censored stories. This was ostensibly to protect *Indymedia* from legal threats connected with hate literature and libellous statements, but, also had the added benefit of keeping control in the hands of a few and arguably lowering accountability. One watermark proposer argued:

> Accessibility is not about making the rubbis-sorry, the hidden posts ;-) easier to smel-sorry to read. :-p ... In my opinion making hidden posts harder to read is a form of respecting and appreciating the work that the very dedicated 'hiders' do. Remember that it is a very ungrateful task and one which also makes the site "more accessible", yes, and less frustrating for people

who do not have much time...and given that we are giving those (hidden) posts Web space even though we ALL do not approve of them, at least let's provide that Web space with a difference. (2 February, IMC-UK process)

Several similar disputes posted between 2004 and 2005 were monitored and the following case was symptomatic of the problems facing the collective. An article appeared, and was immediately 'cleaned', as it contravened *Indymedia*'s rigid anti-advertising policy because it mentioned where readers might purchase a particular book that exposed a 'right wing conspiracy'. The censored individual wrote: 'So who hid it? The BNP,[4] The World Bank, NATO[5] ... or was it Mr. Smith's mate that hid it – another anonymous player of "pass the password".... lying/ditching editorial guidelines to cover his tracks' (3 April, 2005, IMC-UK process).

The row that ensued involved vitriol, libelous statements and ended with the call for the censored individual's expulsion. There didn't appear to be any organised 'appeal' procedure against hidden posts, leaving the system open to the criticism of unfair practice.

Chris Atton conducted a parallel analysis of the journalistic sources used in a local UK activist newspaper, *SchNEWS*. He concluded that, 'the UK experience suggests that the primary definers in the radical community press remain as an elite, as hierarchically structured as those for the mainstream media' (Atton, 2005, p. 26). Atton describes these dominant sources as a 'counter-elite' and suggests that the deployment of these sources is just as reliant on expertise, authority and legitimacy as are mainstream corporate press' sourcing routines. He suggests that the primary reason for this was most likely to be, 'low capital funding, poorly-paid or voluntary staff and organisational pressures' (Atton, 2005, p. 13). These limits, he suggests, 'might lead to a structural determinism as powerful and predictable as that of the mainstream media. To ignore these limits and their outcomes is to idealise alternative media as 'free spaces', mysteriously liberated from the everyday, structural considerations of the practice of journalism' (Atton, 2002, pp. 154–6).

The very existence of *Indymedia* and its equivalents challenge all news organisations to find a way of integrating public discourse into the thriving Internet culture of interaction without losing the user's trust and respect. Yet, if trust is related to mediation then the real challenge for all news providers is not to remove mediation but to create an authentic and authoritative environment that makes mediations transparent.

Big Brother – The case for trust

The mainstream entertainment market is not blind to the marketing power and financial potential of the hyper-mediated environments of the Internet and Interactive TV. Innovative media products like the internationally franchised *Big Brother* series have been very successful in engaging audiences with a combination of liveness, interactivity and immersion. It trades under the label of 'Reality TV' and intimates a democratisation of the airwaves through the casting of 'ordinary people' and the empowerment of audiences through shared editorial control. 'Trust us' is the implied message; what other programme broadcasts its rushes 24 hours a day, seven days a week?

The *Big Brother* format, despite its quite limited and ritualised degree of audience participation in the narrative, has been able to create a strong interactive bond with its user base. The franchise has exploited interactivity and user control in a ritualistic way, yet, my research indicates, in a manner sufficient to win the trust of its fans (Jones, 2003, 2004). *Big Brother's* 'reality' is constructed in a hyper-mediated environment by foregrounding the terms and conditions of the artificial gaming world. The producer is acknowledged in the form of 'Big Brother', and the audience is recognised through its interactive status. Despite the obvious synthetic basis of the programme's construction, the viewer perceives the images to have a found authenticity – an antidote to the contrivances of the docu-soap and the lost credibility of the factual television form. This new fashion governing mediated factuality is enabled through convergence. *Endemol* Executive, Gary Carter, describes the product as a multi-platform, multi-technology, pull entertainment series that gives its audience a sense of control over reality:

> This is the first generation to grow up with television as only one of several technologically advanced entertainment media – and certainly the first for whom television offers a frustratingly limited lack of control, given their experience of interactive new media. This is a generation for whom pull is replacing push. It's as if the experience of control over the outcome is a contemporary edge we demand of entertainment. Interactivity in media means control .... And this is one of the things which is interesting about BB and other reality projects. (Carter, 2002)

The user is thus promised an unmediated experience evoking an immediate and therefore authentic emotional response. The interactive image appears to bypass its relationship to the displaced TV image whose grammar is traditionally associated with heavily mediatised accounts (Corner, 2002; Jones 2003, 2004).

Fear of mediation

I started this chapter by suggesting that the UK's experience in the 1990s of a high number of documentary fakery cases jarred relations between producers and consumers of factually based media. As filming techniques were exposed as synthetic, viewers lost faith in TV's ability to present more than just the illusion of reality (Jones, 2003). When confronted with challenges to the authenticity of the footage, a format was needed that would rebuild the viewer's trust in the screened reality.

A solution was found in the new model of factuality that started in Europe in 1999 and was reproduced around the globe into over 40 local versions by 2005. I was able to question viewers of *Big Brother UK* through their official Channel 4 website over a period of three years. My research suggests that the *Big Brother* format buys the audience's confidence and trust by positioning viewers as editors, judges and jurors. In the UK, the illusion of found authenticity is primarily supported by the 24-hour access to the programme's rushes on both the Web and E4 (Channel 4's interactive channel) along with the useful and ritualised use of voting, selecting tasks for housemates and allowing customers to control the webcams. The game is enhanced by the expectation of ownership over the narrative.

In order to gain a degree of pleasure or satisfaction from the viewing, these fans need the confidence to be able to do two important things. They need the tools to gauge the apparent authenticity of each contributor and at the same time they need the ability to vet the producer's cut. This enables viewers to develop strategies that allow them to sit in judgement of the actuality, despite the format's obvious constructedness (Jones, 2003, 2004).

Mediation anxiety is significantly lowered because users have access to the rushes via the Internet and Interactive TV. They take pleasure from the power to accept or question the dominant mediated frame broadcast in a packaged version each evening. In theory, they are able to police the veracity of the broadcast version as the following quotes[6] suggest, answering the question, 'why do you watch the live feeds?'

1. 'Much more intense and naturalistic, enclosed. You get to see far more of BB. Because you can watch it live you don't have to rely on good/bad editing and it makes it easier to get closer to the core of people.'
2. 'I'm interested in the Big Brother production team's presentation of participants.'
3. 'Watching unedited sources i.e. without any production bias.'
4. 'See what's going on during the day/night, as in to catch whole conversations rather than being shown which ones they want me to see. It's a real-life soap opera, it has all the intensity of say *Friends*, but these are real people and real relationships.'
5. 'I am fascinated by how the producers edit the footage to manipulate the audience into thinking certain characters are nasty.'

The comments suggested that viewers are comforted by the presence of the webcams and E4 live feeds. Although a small minority of viewers actually view the 'live' feeds, the significant majority still only use the producer's cut, they are greatly reassured by the offer of access to the live, and ostensibly unedited, rushes.

In this way user trust is built through:

1. A 'direct' dialogue between users and producers.
2. The viewer at the centre of activity with multiple opportunities for them to engage with the narrative (through voting, suggesting tasks, controlling webcams etc).
3. A sense of control – with viewer placed as judge and juror.
4. Reassurance that the housemates or producers cannot elude the reality net.

Thus, the *Big Brother* format created a natural antidote to previous perceived mediation frauds. The perception that 'the real' can be experienced through the artifice is strong. The viewer feels in control.

Big Brother – The case against trust

Despite the fact that the series does allow for limited interaction, there is no significant power shift from producer to user. *Big Brother* enjoys the highest shooting ratio in TV history; that is the number of minutes shot compared to number of minutes used. Narratives are carefully controlled and even the live footage is subject to a 15 minute delay to allow for heavy editing and contextualising. Despite, innovative methods of securing the viewer's trust, 'Don't be fooled', said Mel, one of the first UK contestants to leave the house, 'that wasn't me you saw, it was just a caricature of me' (BBC One, 2001).

In addition, there is an irreconcilable contradiction between the economic model of TV and true interactivity. The balance of power cannot strictly shift from the centre to the periphery because the producer cannot relinquish the locus of control. In a commercial environment, interactivity is inevitably artificially grafted onto commercial media products that depend on an inherently 'hierarchical, centralised and closed network system' (Kim and Sawhney, 2002, p. 226).

In her article, *Jamming Big Brother*, Pam Wilson (2004) describes what happened in the first US season when, for a short time, a real threat existed to the power of the producer. The first season was hi-jacked by activist online fans, and these 'media-jammers' almost succeeded in taking over the narrative by using a variety of stunts to persuade the housemates to abandon their game and leave the house in a mass walkout. This was not the form of empowerment and interactivity that the producers wanted. The networks would have lost a great deal of money had the show ended abruptly at its mid point. The producers eventually won by persuading the housemates to stay and continue to play the game by the book. Wilson concludes that the

American *Big Brother* audience was merely 'throwing small rocks with their sling-shots against the culture of the corporate giant' (Wilson, 2004, p. 206). It is clear that *Big Brother's* use of interactivity is primarily channelled for the commercial benefit of the producer and leaves little room for a true anarchic response on behalf of the users.

Talk back!

I have argued here that the source of legitimacy for both *Indymedia* and *Big Brother* users is the attraction of the apparently unmediated. Both case studies reveal how critical user interactivity and the perceived (yet illusory) lack of mediation are in defining and maintaining trust and building strong and profitable hyper-mediated relationships. Young people are especially drawn to 'unofficial' accounts driven by a distrust of the mainstream or producer's cut.

The activity surrounding the Web and Interactive TV is often ludic in nature. There is a playfulness that drives user-instigated news seeking behaviour and a perceived privilege in producing and vetting the edited version. Both activities are based on the confidence of control over the content; trust derived from the (apparent) removal of formal barriers between users and producers.

Schultz concludes that the challenge of the future is for the corporate news media to integrate public discourse into its culture of interaction (Schultz, 2000, p. 217). Implicit here, is that interactivity should be the focus of any redesigned democratic mediation, but, there are few successful large-scale models to draw upon. In spite of the many discourses surrounding new media and interactivity suggesting that news information should be two-way and not top down, most regular and online news sources still only pay lip service to the notion of two-way communication. *Indymedia*, at least, tries to be different.

Thus, the 'narrative of hope', which was the focus of much intellectual work in this arena five years ago (Castells, 2000; Ludlow, 2001; Mitra and Watts, 2002), has been more recently replaced by sober reflections. James Carey terms this Internet euphoria the 'rhetoric of the technological sublime' (Carey, 2005, p. 443). This ambivalence is also reflected in Lee Salter's analysis. He describes the potential of the Internet to be a decentred, textual communications system providing 'non-hierarchical, open protocols, open communication and self generating information and identities' helping to restore forums of rationale, critical debate and remedy the 'communicative deficit' in society (Salter, 2003, p. 122). But he also warns of the potential for Internet social relations to be steered by instrumental relations of efficiency and what he calls a pathological effect of technological structures (Salter, 2005, p. 306).

This study serves as a reminder that these 'pathological effects' are undoubtedly at play and new media products that bank on their interactivity, transparency and lack of mediation cannot easily sustain their idealistic philosophies under very real commercial, financial, legal and technical constraints.

Notes

1. The research is based, in part, on an Internet questionnaire posted on the *Big Brother* website in July 2002, which received 19,000 responses, and, in part, on an ongoing field study of *Indymedia UK*, which began in December, 2003.
2. This study was conducted in July 2002 through the UK Channel 4, *Big Brother* website and received over 19,000 responses. It was designed to reflect the young 'wired generation' with over 90 per cent of these young informants regularly accessing the Internet. Only 2 per cent claimed to be new users and only 0.5 per cent labelled themselves as 'incompetent' users. A self-reporting questionnaire (linked to the *Big Brother* website for 24 hours) was used to generate both quantitative and qualitative data through open questions encouraging one sentence or short paragraph answers and closed-ended questions. This produced a large data pool that could then be easily interrogated providing statistically meaningful quantitative data. I also had thousands of short written statements from the respondents, varying in length from 20 to 300 words that provided the core of the quantitative data. Self-reporting questionnaires alone are a blunt tool and perhaps not an entirely satisfactory method of detailed audience interrogation (only those who had access to the Web could complete this questionnaire), however, in support of the data I found that the Web-based demographic profile was largely consistent with Channel 4's broadcast audience profile although the skew that a Web-based questionnaire would normally generate was quite evident with fewer older respondents and a greater concentration of younger viewers. Also, the fact that this audience questionnaire reached only those interested enough in the programme to surf the Channel 4 website and spend 20 minutes answering a questionnaire, allowed us to study specific fan attitudes towards the multi-platform viewing experience. At the very least it enabled a clear focus on *regular* and *repeated* viewing attitudes, thus making it possible to get data on how viewers actually *dealt with* (rather than glanced at) the show.
3. IMC is the umbrella name for *Indymedia* USA
4. BNP is the British National Party.
5. NATO stands for North Atlantic Treaty Organisation.
6. To generate both quantitative and qualitative data both open questions encouraging one sentence or short paragraph answers and closed (tick box) questions were used. Over 30,000 responses were received over the three years, 2000–2.

16
The Technology of Distrust

Gary Gumpert and Susan J. Drucker

Probe #1: The truth is what you create

When President Bush laid out the potential threat that unconventional weapons posed in Saddam Hussein's hands in his 2003 State of the Union address, he became tongue-tied at an inopportune moment.

The line read, 'It would take one vial, one canister, one crate, slipped into this country to bring a day of horror like none we have ever known.' But Mr. Bush stumbled between the words 'one' and 'vial.' And when at the word vial, he pronounced the 'v' as if it were a 'w.'

Yet in a new Republican commercial that borrows excerpts from that speech, Mr. Bush delivers that line as smoothly as any other in the address, without a pause between 'one' and 'vial,' and the v in 'vial' sounds strong and sure.

Republican officials acknowledged yesterday that the change was a product of technology. The line, they said, was digitally enhanced in editing 'to ensure the best clarity'. (Rutenberg, 2003)[1]

Social contract

Much has been written about social contract theory; the justification for political authority that claims that government arises out of an agreement among free individuals who surrender some degree of freedom in exchange for security provided by the state. Distinct versions of the social contract have been proposed by John Locke (Laslett, 1988), Thomas Hobbes (1982), Jean-Jacques Rousseau (1968), and in more recent years, John Rawls (1999 [1971]) and David Gauthier (1977).[2] Rather than a specific set of negotiated conditions, social contract theory is generally considered a metaphor for the relationship between the individual and the state (Baldwin, 2003). The very existence of the state is morally justified by an agreement between the residents of a geographical area and the state, a theory sometimes called *contractarianism*. Modern versions of social contract theory assert that basic rights and liberties originate in mutually beneficial agreements made between members of society. Contract implies a binding agreement between parties raising undeniable issues of trust and suspicion.[3] The agreement creates a relationship of rights and duties that inherently contain a measure of distrust that is addressed by legal remedies (*West Legal Dictionary*, 2004). Social contract theory is vague and leaves unanswered many questions 'related to its scope and credibility, among them: Is there a real contract, or is the social contract merely a helpful framework for thinking about what our obligations and rights ought to be? ... Are the terms of the contract static or evolving?' (Baldwin, 2003, p. 1).[4] Has the contract been breached?[5] In considering the concept of the social contract, the specific contract creates a fiduciary relationship (in which the trustee acts in the best interests or in trust for the *beneficiary*). A violation of that obligation results in what is known as a breach of trust. In such a relationship, the trustee uses their discretion or expertise to benefit the other party in the relationship.[6] Law forbids the fiduciary from acting in a way that is adverse to the interests of the beneficiary or from acting for the trustee's own benefit. The trustee is required 'to make truthful and complete disclosures to those placing trust in him' (Lectric Law Library, 2004). If the government is viewed as a trustee of the people, do misleading intelligence reports justifying war, suspension of civil rights, damaging international coalitions, jeopardizing international commerce or spying on citizens, breach the fiduciary duty?

The social contract requires a system of checks in which a citizen has the ability and the instrumentation to assure that the contract is functioning. Imagine a transparent curtain separating the activity of the governing and the governed. Theoretically, it was once pulled aside when potential face-to-face interaction between government and the governed was possible. With the increasing size of government and population the degree of transparency became less translucent and the press became the primary means relied upon to check the nature and operation of government.

Probe #2: The ceremonial bugler

It looks like a bugle. It sounds like a bugle – hauntingly enough to move a funeral mourner to compliment Glenn Hasheider on his rendition of taps last week at Jefferson Barracks National Cemetery near St. Louis.

But what Mr. Hasheider did not have the heart to tell the mourner was this:

It's not a bugle, exactly.

It is a bugle discreetly fitted with a battery-operated conical insert that plays the
24 notes of taps at the flick of a switch. It is all digital, with no human talent
or breath required. All you do is hold it up, turn it on and try to look like a
bugler ....

After a six-month trial involving more than 1000 funerals in Missouri, the
Pentagon announced this month that the device, known as the ceremonial
bugler, could be used across the world at military funerals for which a human
bugler is not available. (Dao, 2003)[7]

Media and the social contract

This essay seeks to articulate a dilemma. The naturally adversarial relationship between the governed and government, inherently shrouded in some
necessary degree of wariness and misgiving, was augmented with increased
responsibility and reliance placed on a vital and independent press. By definition, a governing gap exists as the public (for example, voter, subject) was
separated from the seat of government by time, place and medium. The
question then becomes not simply questioning government, but also, it follows, questioning the press and any form of communication that connects
the public and the governing sector.

It has become fashionable to question '*the media*', to question and doubt
the editorial and factual positions of a multitude of press associations' services. However '*the media*' are not synonymous with the press. The singular
term refers to a means of transmission. A medium of communication is
required by any form of the press, be it newspaper, magazine, radio or TV
station, but a medium of communication does not have to serve a news and
information function. A medium does not have to be a mass medium, nor
is it limited to one sense modality. The distinction is important because
while the concept and execution of the press have a moral and responsible
dimension to it, a medium (a technology) has no intrinsic moral character.
It is not judged or evaluated from an editorial or critical standard, but
generally by the standard of accuracy and precision. For our purposes, a
medium is a specific communication technology. However, a medium (often
in combination with a group of other media) always has characteristics that
shape and alter one's understanding and perception of that which is transmitted. It is not neutral. The dilemma alluded to involves the power of a
medium generally, seen by most people, as neutral and non-invasive, as having defining characteristics that allow for manipulation, alteration, and
changes by artistic and/or editorial forces.

There is an illusion of transparency, a sense of permeability of function and
medium, obliterating traces of production which construct mediated connection or message. The differences between mediated and direct experiences

have become less distinct. Analogue media made it difficult to *mask* alterations but with the shift to digital media it becomes increasingly difficult, if not impossible, to *detect* alterations. With analogue media there are continuity errors, evidence of edits or jump cuts, inherent noise and distortion that reveal the creation/manipulation process at work (Tucker, 2004).[8] Analogue media capture the actual sound or image while digital media are representations of sound. This is important because studies suggest that the less apparent or obtrusive the medium is to the audience, the less evident is the *influence* of the medium. The degree to which an image or message is perceived to be trustworthy is associated with the perception of the neutrality in transmission.[9]

With the bureaucratic growth and expansion of government, the responsibility of transparency has shifted, been relegated or relocated to communication technology that allows for surveillance of one body by another. We have moved from public governing to mediated governing. The public process has been replaced by technological connection.[10]

The press and social contract

The illusion of transparency is fostered by an ever-growing environment of press coverage of the governors and institutions of government. This is coupled with more sophisticated use of media technologies to make the government appear more accessible and open to the governed. Each branch of government, from national to local is located a mouse click away. E-government and digital cities offer 'one-stop' public access for local information. From news channels broadcasting 24/7 to the proliferation of online publications, the illusion is apparent increased coverage and information about government. Yet, Lee Bollinger, president of Columbia University, argued 'the quantity and quality of coverage of public issues and concerns seems to be in decline' (Edlund, 2000). The global pattern of increased concentration in media ownership does not result in increased coverage or diversity in coverage (Bagdikian, 2004; McChesney, 2004).

Probe #3: Verifying the improbable – From Lumière to Armstrong to Mars

In 1902 George Melies created a film version of Jules Verne's Trip to the Moon. In 1969 Neil Armstrong landed on the moon and said 'One small step for man, one giant leap for mankind.' The first was clearly a fictional fantasy. The second illustrated to an audience of millions that man could actually travel and land on the moon although some individuals continue to question the authenticity of the event. (Milne, 2000). The apparent exploration of Mars by the two NASA rover vehicles is a spectacular conquest of space, but requires the tacit trust with a governmental bureaucracy that the event is actually taking place.

Rebecca Solnit (2003, p. 114) has defined technology, as 'a practice, a technique, or a device for altering the world'. Communication technology facilitates the social contract by apparently providing a potential solution to the problem of the loss of transparency by extending the connection of locations in time and/or place. The trouble is that increasing technological complexity and sophistication does not provide equal advantage of transparency to both the governing and the governed.

The metaphor of the translucent or transparent curtain has outgrown its usefulness and has had to be replaced by a new and more realistic notion of that of a controllable 'one way mirror' permitting one side to watch the other by controlling light. Two-way checks and balances remain a philosophical imperative but have been replaced by one-sided surveillance. It is theoretically possible for the governed to support or refute those in power through the process of the vote. Contemporary government has an extraordinary and surreptitious advantage over the governed in checking and controlling sentiment and action through a highly sophisticated means of communication technology – through eavesdropping and recording the communication actions and patterns of the governed (Steinhardt, 2004; McCullagh and Broache, 2006; Monaghan, 2006).

The media contract

Every medium rests upon a conditional degree of authenticity. Each extends thought over time and place. The transmission of information is either delayed or immediate. There is, however, a relationship between the renderings of thought to medium and the subsequent interpretation or perception of that original rendering: that relationship is either isomorphic or representative; either a one-to-one connection between two points in time or space or a symbolic connection with a prior point in time or space. An *isomorphic assumption* rests upon the capability of a medium to reproduce an image or sound that is, to some degree, faithful to the original. We are not referring to the capacity of a medium to duplicate itself – that is to produce exact multiple reproductions of itself (Gumpert, 1987). We attribute to a medium both the notion of replication and the issue of authenticity upon which it is judged. Keeping that distinction in mind, photography, and later the reproduction of sound, is unique because it was technologically assumed that the product observed corresponded exactly to that which was preserved or transmitted or recorded and replayed.

When watching TV, viewers are engaged in a relationship with a variety of texts that create meaning. There has been a great deal written about how individuals perceive the real world, how the real is distinguished from the imagined, (Merleau-Ponty, 1962; Casey, 1976) and how language shapes perceptions of reality (Chase, 1956; Whorf, 1956; Cronkhite, 1976).[11] With the appearance of the technologies of photography, motion pictures and TV, new languages were introduced which called into question the process by which individuals decode iconic messages (Barthes, 1979). Although much has been written about the encoding and decoding of media messages,[12] (Fiske and Hartley, 1978), little has been done to explain the composite construction of media messages. Today the TV image is more than the product of a camera pointed at an image but consists of a series of assembled parts. The producers of Digital Versatile Discs (DVD) assemble discrete items known as assets – any medium used in the creation of the product – like video, audio, graphics and subtitles.

The camera eye

In the 1860s, Eadward Muybridge enhanced his photographs of clouds through darkroom chemistry and artistry. In her account of Muybridge's pioneering work, Rebecca Solnit states

> What truth meant in photography was not yet settled-retouching was almost a universal practice, and some of the more respected photographers made composite images. No one minded clouds that had been added later. Was the white sky that came from technical limitations truer than a sky full of realistic-looking clouds that just happened to be from another time and place? The clouds were, in a way, the lie that tells the truth, the manipulation that made Muybridge's photographs look more convincing and more 'artistic,' as art was then imagined. (2003, p. 48)

Perhaps contemporary audiences have learned to question the facsimilic quality of photographs, but there remains an intrinsic propensity to process photographs without taking manipulation for granted because of this 'isomorphic assumption' that the camera replicates that which is revealed before the 'camera's eye'.

The realisation that the mirroring capability could be manipulated never fully altered the basic aesthetic capability of replicating and transmitting an image or sound from one site to another. Despite this obvious capability, manipulation of the image still remained in the realm of the unethical and alien. We are not suggesting that people do not know this but wonder who actively questions when the TV screen is filled with images of weapons inspectors testifying on Capitol Hill about mistaken intelligence reports and a picture of the captured and disheveled Saddam Hussein is inserted in the corner of the screen while an identifying graphic is placed below the speaker and the continuous scrawl of temperatures around the country continues.

Is it real?

With digital processing, all data are at least once removed from their original source. Computerised data can be reconstructed, rebuilt, altered and distorted. There are no exceptions. With the increasing trend for computer convergence, with the Internet serving as a platform for other media, the computer becomes a multi-media technology with the ultimate capacity to restructure data. This is no simple way to detect tampering or the reconstruction of information.

Performers have been *lip-synching* for a long time – lips move but what the audience hears is a recording. But a new variation has now been perfected. During the Super Bowl half-time performances, singer's vocal attempts have been electronically altered, in real time, to correct off-key notes just as they were coming out of the singer's mouth (Nelson, 2004).[13]

The grammar that defines one medium from the other is also built into the expectations and attitudes of a public that uses a medium. The individual TV viewer accepts the convention of multiple points of view and the relocation of self in relationship to place. Every medium of communication imposes a set of such conventions. Every individual is expected to be literate in film, radio, TV and the Internet although this may not always be the case. *Medium theory*, particularly helpful in considering the large-scale impact of media, examines:

> such variables as the senses that are required to attend to the medium, whether the communication is bi-directional or uni-directional, how quickly messages can be disseminated, whether learning to encode and decode in the medium is difficult or simple, how many people can attend to the same message at the same moment, and so forth. (Meyrowitz, 1994, p. 50)[14]

From restructuring to control

The producer–consumer contract

There is an implicit editorial/artistic contract that exists between producer and consumer. That contract is based upon an implicit contract of trust and intention. The existence of manipulation, alteration and editing has always been recognised as being apparent and necessary in some forms of communication. The painter renders and the writer uses words to interpret. The editor assembles. Their artistic, or controlling, editorial presence is understood. The hand of construction is more or less apparent. The degree of their foreground and background presence is determined by the technological complexity of the medium. But the creative and foreground presence of such editorial or artistic control gives way to the grammar or components of a technology that automatically imposes liberties, restrictions and directions. The camera imposes angle and magnification. Multiple cameras add modes of transition and insertion. The addition of sound necessitates synchronicity or non-synchronicity. The point is that all information requires decision and direction, but the scale to which the presence of the artist or creator is at hand varies according to the dense complexity and technology of the chosen medium.

The artist of a work, the communicator of information, may be simply seeking to enhance, augment or enlarge upon editorial need or impulse. The hand at work is evaluated by the *isomorphic assumption*, a tacit agreement between the recipient of a message, the perceived nature of the medium and the degree to which the grammar of the medium is used and manipulated.

Thus live in-performance editing (such as deleting an expletive during a time delay in a live broadcast) is assumed to be part of the TV process, but impossible editing, the juxtaposition of impossibility such as a shift in time and place, indicates greater manipulation – a post production editing process facilitated by the emergence of videotape. There is an inherent logic to editing that provides information to the viewer of a TV programme. There is also an inherent possibility of manipulation, not simply construction, in the presence of recording capability. A 'live' programme may have been recorded and not 'live at all'. A dense minute of TV news may consist of live and recorded video plus live or recorded audio – a small part of a newscast actually recorded a half hour earlier – for the convenience of time zones in countries such as the USA. Every medium involves some degree of *disconnection* between person and actual event or location.

These technological developments firmly establish that all data are to be judged and evaluated on the basis of isomorphism. That is to say, has a composition of sound and/or images been transferred in which the structure and identity of form or shape is essentially duplicated – in other words, a one-to-one correspondence between the elements of two or more sets? That an item is perceived to be non-isomorphic simply introduces the realisation that information and/or data has been altered, changed, transformed and that the transfer of form or shape has not been duplicated. This is not to be seen as a value judgment of that which is transmitted, but merely an awareness of change.

When an image is perceived to be isomorphic but is the result of electronic implanting, the question of the isomorphic fallacy becomes more complex. Today entire electronic sets provide the environment seen by TV viewers. Chroma-key, once the domain of Hollywood special effects artists, has expanded to include video and computers. The chroma-key effect combines two sources allowing the second source to 'show through' the first in those places where the first source is the given colour: thus the newscaster sitting in front of a location is not really there but in front of a blue or green screen. Increasingly entire newscasts are set in such environments. Likewise, product placements and billboards are electronically injected. Team logos, field markers and advertisements are increasingly injected into the coverage of sporting events. A famous example of this technology was seen in the coverage of the Super Bowl XXXV in 2001 in which a first down line (an additional four downs is awarded upon gaining ten yards)[15] was inserted, only visible to TV viewers (Hey, 2002). Virtual product placement has been used to tailor advertising to specific markets. Columbia *Broadcasting News* (CBS) replaced a *National Broadcasting Company* (NBC) logo with its own on NBC's *Jumbotron* screen during its live broadcast of New Year's Eve in New York's Times Square. Virtual advertisements have appeared on billboards during baseball and motor racing telecasts, and TV dramas and sitcoms. The insertion of items into series TV was evidenced by the drama 'Seven Days' in which product images for Evian water, Wells Fargo bank, Coca-Cola and fashion retailer Kenneth Cole were all digitally placed into an episode through a process developed by Princeton Video Image Inc., which seeks to create images 'indistinguishable from actual objects' (Elliot, 2000).[16] While some TV production companies have stringent policies that would prohibit virtual product placement, others see this as a technology that can go far beyond product placement to create an opportunity for diverse background locations and high end special effects at low cost and high quality. The isomorphic fallacy may have great market value.

Controlling the governed and reading the governing

Probe #4: The USA Patriot Act

> The USA PATRIOT Act, passed by Congress shortly after September 11, 2001, increased government surveillance, detention and other law enforcement powers while reducing basic checks and balances on such powers. The Department of Justice is currently drafting legislation designed as a sequel to the USA PATRIOT Act. 1 ... The draft legislation, which has been dubbed 'Patriot Act 2,' would grant sweeping powers to the government, eliminating or weakening many of the checks and balances that remained on government surveillance, wiretapping, detention and criminal prosecution even after passage of the USA PATRIOT Act. (American Civil Liberties Union, 2003).

We now need to return to the matter of the 'social contract', a concept only viable if there is some degree or range of equity in the relationship of those that govern and those that are governed. There are two aspects of thought that need to be considered in that regard. The present condition is that the governing have increased their surveillance of the governed by imperceptible

means and techniques. The inability of the citizen to detect government surveillance results in the state of awareness in which we assume and ultimately accept that surveillance as cultural and technological norm. Twenty-four
hour surveillance of all communication activity is not only possible, but
probable – video surveillance, satellite inspection, telephone wiretapping,
the recording of Internet activities (e-mail and web transactions), the docu-
mentation of library activities, the recording of any and all electronic transactions (Steinhardt, 2004; Monaghan, 2006). It must be assumed that some
form of surveillance is embedded into the very fabric of daily life. Yet, while
government powers of unobtrusive citizen surveillance have increased, the
citizens' powers of surveillance of mediated government have decreased. This
violates the social contract, which requires a system of checks in which the
citizen has the ability and the instrumentation to assure that the contract is
functioning.

Conclusion

The American Dialect Society voted word *truthiness* the word of the year in
2005. *Truthiness* has come to mean 'the quality of stating concepts one wishes or believes to be true rather than facts' (Truthiness voted 2005 word of the
year, 2006). The word caught on after it was reintroduced on the *Colbert
Report*, a satirical news show on the Comedy Central television channel. The
concept has received much attention, some have said because 'we live in the
age of truthiness' (Rich, 2006, p. 16).[17] We have tried to intertwine several
strands that tie together a complex situation leading to this age of truthiness
and a deficiency of suspicion:

1. That the social contract between government and the governed has been
   severely tested if not violated.
2. That changes in communication technology, the shift from analogue to
   digital, should lead to a greater awareness of manipulation and suspicion
   and therefore less trust in mediated interaction and information. The
   paradox however is that by erasing traces of manipulation, digital media
   foster more trust and less suspicion.
3. That the citizen's trust of communication technology and the press as a
   means of checking on government is flawed and based upon unwarranted
   assumptions of social and technological trust.
4. That the press, particularly radio and TV news organisations, have
   imposed an often unrecognised narrative structure in their coverage and
   reporting.
5. That the citizen with increasing media access has less and less ability to
   check on the contractual obligations of government.

6. That communication technology has been transformed into an instrument of surveillance potentially and probably violating the civil rights of each citizen.

That leaves us somewhere, between a rock and a hard place with conclusions that are depressing and lack substantive remedy. So what can be done? Several concrete, perhaps extreme suggestions come to mind. We recommend a mandatory media literacy-training program in elementary and secondary education. Each citizen could be provided the moral and legal right to protection from the violation and invasion of privacy by unapproved governmental institutions. A news rating system could be introduced by regulators, requiring broadcasters to identify the degree to which information and data have been manipulated.

Notes

1. J. Rutenberg, 'Technological Dub Erases a Bush Flub for a Republican Ad', *New York Times*, 24 November (2003) p. A 19.
2. There are distinct versions of social contract theory that have evolved over time. The classical theorists represent important modern traditions in political thought. Hobbes (1982 [1651]) thought the state of nature, that of no government, would be one of war, lacking in type of higher justice since without law and institutions for law enforcement, there could be no justice. The state of nature is so dangerous that we agree to exchange some freedom for the promise of protection by others. Government represents the interests of the people rather than the interests of government itself. Locke argued that the state of nature is not as dangerous as Hobbes (1982 [1651]) thought but a pre-political society where humans are bound by natural law in a moral society. A social contract, an actual binding agreement, is made between citizens who institute a government to prevent people from violating natural law and showing partiality.
In *A Theory of Justice* (1971), revised in 1999, John Rawls posits a slightly different form of social contract that he calls Justice as Fairness. Rawls (1971, p. 11) sets forth the proposition that 'Each person possesses an inviolability founded on justice that even the welfare of society as a whole cannot override. Therefore, in a just society the rights secured by justice are not subject to political bargaining or to the calculus of social interests'. To Rawls, each person has a right to basic liberties, and inequalities in the distribution of wealth and power are just only when they can be expected to benefit those who are poorest. For Rawls, justice does not require equality in social position, but requires that people share one another's fate. David Gauthier (1977) criticised Hobbes's version of social contract in his work 'The Social Contract as Ideology'. Gauthier disagreed with the Hobbesian notion that obligations needed to be supported with the threat of punishment in order to be effective. He argued that in some cases self-interest can drive people to meet obligations. To Gauthier, it is a rational choice to honour certain obligations. Individuals can see it is in their own long-term self-interest to meet obligations to the community even if in the short-term meeting these obligations does not appear to be in one's self interest.

3. In law, a contract is an agreement that creates a legal relationship of rights and duties. There are three factors necessary to create a contract: an offer, acceptance, and consideration. One party makes an offer, the second party must accept the offer and there must be consideration exchanged. Consideration has to be something of value (http://www.legal-definitions.com/contract.htm). Although debate has raged over whether an individual must consent to the provisions of a social contract, it is easily argued that the social contract is actually a *quasi contract* – a contract created by law for reasons of justice without any expression of assent.

4. A fiduciary contract is defined to be an agreement by which a person delivers a thing to another on the condition that he will restore it to him.

5. The social contract requires a degree of confidence that the duties are met. What constitutes a breach of the social contract? When dealing with the social contract between individual and the state what is a *material breach* – a breach serious enough to destroy the value of the contract rather than merely a *partial breach*, a breach that does not destroy the value of the contract? Does failure to provide a security amount to a material breach?

6. A fiduciary duty implies an obligation to act in the best interest of another and exists when one person places a special trust and confidence in another person and relies upon that person to exercise his discretion or expertise in acting in their behalf using the fiduciary's own discretion and expertise.

7. J. Dao, 'Live or Digital? The Bugler's Lips are Sealed', *The New York Times*, 16 September (2003) p. A 12.

8. A. Tucker, President Foothills Digital (2004).

9. In studies involving media and stereotyping in a multination study of stereotypes conducted in 1985 and 1999, a difference was found between those dependent on mass media for knowledge and those who had direct knowledge (Gumpert and Cathcart, 1989; Drucker, 1999). A significant difference was found between subjects reporting high media use and those with direct knowledge and low media use. While it might seem counter-intuitive to think the mediated experience is more trusted than direct experience, these studies indicate great trust and reliance placed upon the indirect mediated experience: the qualities of the digital media foster confidence in the mediated message.

10. Technological developments have facilitated a change in the psychological landscape, making practicable unrestricted private life for those seeking safety and security. Communication media, in particular, significantly impact our perceptions, expectations and relationships to people, places and institutions. Communication technology has elevated connection and availability to a new level, while simultaneously serving to control a potential hostile environment (McLuhan, 1962).

11. For a discussion of language and perception see Benjamin Lee Whorf and Edward Sapir's hypothesis on 'The Theory of Linguistic Relativity' (Whorf, 1956). For an examination of the conventions of audience perception regarding literature, see Todorov (1973).

12. Semioticians, functionalists and structuralists have provided insights into how humans interpret the content of TV (Fry and Fry, 1986) Additionally, for interesting examples of early efforts to articulate the relationship between TV text and the process of decoding, see Birmingham School of Cultural Studies (Hall, Hobson, Lowe and Willis, 1981).

13. C. Nelson, 'Music; Lip-Synching Gets Real', *The New York Times*, 1 February (2004) Section 2, p. 1.

14. Media theorists taking this approach ask the question: What are the relatively fixed features of each means of communicating and how do these features make the medium physically, psychologically and socially different from other media and face-to-face interaction? According to Joshua Meyrowitz (1994), medium theory represents a perspective through which to understand how a medium is appropriated by a culture and tries to account for its social, psychological and political impact. It is not only media content but also the form of the medium that must be considered. While the focus is on the medium, this is not to suggest that medium theory looks at the technology alone. Rather, it is the interaction between the media technology and humans that is significant. Taken together, these two media theory perspectives provide an approach through which to examine the individual, interpersonal and societal impact of media. It is the paradox of communication technology that 'The more communication choice offered, the less we trust the information we receive' (Gumpert, 1996, p. 41).

15. In American football the playing field is 100 yards long. The offence has four chances to advance the football either far enough to score a touchdown or far enough to gain another four opportunities to score. Upon advancing the ball 10 or more yards the team is awarded an additional set of downs (plays) in an effort to score.

16. S. Elliot, 'A Video Process Allows the Insertion of Brand-name Products in TV Shows Already on Film', *The New York Times*, 29 March (2000) p. C 11.

17. F.Rich, 'Truthiness 101: From Frey to Alito', *The New York Times*, 22 January (2006) Section 4, p. 16.

Part IV Conclusions: Trust and the Media

17
The End of Trust?

Vian Bakir and David M. Barlow

In considering the relationship between trust and a range of media genres and forms, the fourteen contributions in this volume reflect events in a number of continents and span a period from the first decades of the 20th century to the early years of the 21st century. The contemporary mediated public communications environment is far removed from the idealised public sphere (presented in Chapter 2) in which participation was open to all and where status and private concerns were set aside in order to provide the conditions for citizens to engage in civil and wide ranging rational debate about matters of general public interest. In this idealised setting communicants were trusted to abide by four truth claims. Communication was expected to be logical and understandable, true, appropriate and sincere, with non-adherence implying a sense of distorted communication. These matters are at the heart of the majority of contributions in this volume.

This final chapter is organised in two sections. The first focuses specifically on the matter of trust, or distrust, as it relates to the media, and addresses three emergent themes. Continuity, as much as change, is a feature here. The second and final section draws out implications for media communication in the 'Age of Suspicion' and suggests future research directions.

Trust matters

In Chapter 1, we noted that key political, economic and media institutions are distrusted in the UK, the USA, Australia and Central and Eastern Europe. We asked what role the media have played in bringing about this pattern of distrust – this Age of Suspicion. From our contributory chapters, three related, overlapping and interconnected themes are apparent, that together answer this question. The first theme focuses on the management of communication and the growth of communications professionals. The second concerns the extent to which the views and opinions of the wider public are represented in mediated communication. The third relates to both the transparency and non-transparency of 'new' media. Each theme is discussed below.

Professionalising communication

In the contemporary public sphere governments and business tend to be the dominant communicators and communication is more strategic. Governments are keen to both promote their own views and policies and persuade the electorate of their success, while business relies on effective public communication to promote their commercial interests and project the image they seek as corporate citizens. With institutions reliant for their survival, at least to some extent, on the successful management of public communication, it follows that the risk of leaving publics to reach their own views on matters of public interest is too great, requiring that 'public conversation' be administered both for local and global audiences. To varying degrees, these and related issues are addressed in a number of the contributions in this volume. Increasingly, the responsibility for organising and managing public communication has been designated to public relations (PR) professionals or, in recent parlance, 'spin doctors', and in order to ensure effective and wide ranging dissemination, the media, 'old' and 'new', become key players operating, as they do, as 'agenda setters', 'gatekeepers' and 'framers'.

In an extremely competitive, commercialised and fragmented media market, media organisations are hungry for copy and content. In such a context, governments and corporations, with the resources to do so, are in a position to co-opt – and subsidise – the media by producing press releases and carefully controlled interviews which, with minimal amendment and challenge, may become 'news', while simultaneously ensuring the dissemination of a particularly favoured perspective.[1] While in very different eras and in sharply varying media environments – but with war the continuing thread – contributions to this volume (Redley, Chapter 3; Archer, Chapter 4) illustrate the ploys used by governments in the UK, Australia and the USA to manage – or manipulate – public communication. Similarly, another contribution (Bakir, Chapter 11) examines the ways in which a major global corporation set about constructing and disseminating its truth claims. The potential for co-opting media also occurs because of their dependence on the advertising revenues available to governments and business[2] as well as income generated by other means. Examples include the increasing use of 'product placement' in films and the commercial broadcast media, and the growing inclination of governments around the world to ensure that selected policy campaigns on, for example, literacy, AIDS and drug use, appear as integral elements in the scripts of popular soap operas (see, for example, Franklin, 2004, pp. 90–5). It is the extent to which such practices are transparent that exercises concern about trust.

While business, media and governments have very different roles and functions, they all require employees with similar skills, and there are advantages to both organisation and employee if previous work includes experience in each of these three settings. Writers, journalists and political strategists are recruited by governments to manage communications and, on occasions, to generate overt propaganda. Once their term of office is over, employment awaits in the media or in the PR departments of large corporations.[3] The refinement of communication for commercial gain in the broadcast media is also evident in the work of our contributors. Here, there is evidence that training has become much more sophisticated in order to ensure that presenters are better equipped to attract and retain the audience demographic that is most attractive to advertisers and sponsors (Barlow, Chapter 5). Another example centres on the confessional television genre, which has become commercially successful because, at least in part, it is judged by viewers to be trustworthy due to a perceived authenticity (Wilson, Chapter 14). It is, therefore, noteworthy, that elements of confessional language can be detected in the formal speeches and media presentations of key politicians, some of whom also choose to make guest appearances on daytime TV, where audiences would be expected to have an affinity with such language. Such strategies are designed by people who make communication their business. The prevalence of PR may reflect back to the public an accurate representation of consumer society (Tampere, Chapter 12), but publicity alone does not equate to public opinion and neither does it breed trust.[4]

Forming or informing publics?

One of the media's key roles is to provide a forum for information and debate, and to act as a check on the state by representing the public's views back to power. By providing information and facilitating debates that encompass a wide diversity of views and opinions, the media assist towards the achievement of full citizenship. However, public opinion, or something approaching it, only becomes possible once a public has formed and engaged in wide-ranging rational debate about matters of general interest. Contributions to this book suggest that the public may have just cause to be distrustful about such worthy aspirations.

A number of contributors point towards the absence, rather than presence, of a debating public, who appear to be marginalised, or excluded, in favour of 'experts' and spokespersons from government, industry or commerce, reminiscent of Keane's (1995, p. 263) observation that both commercial and public service media 'distribute entitlements to speak and to be heard and seen unevenly'. An over-reliance on established and often elite voices where the agenda is preset and carefully controlled resonates with the idea of representative publicity, interpreted as appearance before the people, a context quite different from that where status is set aside and a range of contributors can set the agenda and canvass a plurality of opinions. There are, however, examples where producers/editors do seek out the voices of 'ordinary' people in an attempt to provide a more authentic representation of everyday life (for example, Wilson, Chapter 14; Jones, Chapter 15). However, the predominant tendency is to construct and represent these participants as consumers, rather than citizens, and suggest individual solutions – rather than political action – as a way of resolving what are, essentially, public problems. Another contributor (Redley, Chapter 3) focuses on an earlier era to illuminate events during a period of war, where there was no interest in forming a public, but every intention to inform and indoctrinate one. This required the harnessing of elite and 'ordinary' voices – along with the media – to convey to the general populace the impression of a debating public and the creation of legitimate public opinion. This particular contribution demonstrates that even in the early years of the 20th century, 'manufactured' public opinion was a tool that could be used for political and economic ends both within and beyond the boundaries of the nation-state.

Informing, rather than forming, publics is obviously far less time consuming and costly. Hence, the increasing reliance on soundbites, phone-ins, surveys and public opinion polling which may be seen as a substitute for deliberative debate and later paraded as public opinion. A lack of public participation in the media prompts questions about the depth, appropriateness, quality and accuracy of information that enters the public domain, and a number of contributors (for example, Archer, Chapter 4; Collins, Chapter 7; Critcher, Chapter 8; Tampere, Chapter 12) point to the power of the media to accentuate, dismiss or reframe concerns about issues, institutions or individuals in the public eye. While the mass media may act as 'guardians of trust', as one contributor argues (Mehta, Chapter 13), the ongoing consolidation of ownership, locally and globally through processes of vertical and horizontal acquisitions, undermines rather than aids transparency about business interests and political connections, and commercial imperatives ensure that media-led campaigns tend to have a limited life span.

Such concerns lend weight to the view that the opinion conveyed in media representations must be treated with caution and not simply assumed to constitute *public* opinion, more a version of such that is being manipulated for political or commercial gain. In terms of trust, as well as having implications for citizenship more generally, it prompts questions about the validity of the public opinion that governments and business may speak of when major decisions are being taken on, for example, health, education, environment, transport, public order and, of course, going to war. It also foregrounds questions about citizen involvement in policy development, the independence of the mass media, and the potential of community and alternative media (see, for example, Jankowski, 2002).

Illusory nature of new media

Consumption of newspapers, magazines and analogue radio and TV services does not leave a traceable 'footprint' in the same way that use of digital audio services, computer networks and the Internet does. Nevertheless, there is an insidious continuity at play here. As with commercial media where audiences, listeners or readers were regarded as commodities to be sold on to advertisers in order to ensure that a network or newspaper remained viable, the symbiotic relationship enabled by interactivity in the course of, for instance, responding to reality TV, or purchasing online, enables a similar process of commodification.[5] However, in the latter case, while information is given freely in such transactions, the user may be unaware about the scope and ease involved in aggregating data to produce – and sell on – highly developed personal profiles and that this process may be assisted by way of secreted software about which they are unaware. This enables a more precise and customised targeting of individuals by advertisers, unlike the mass advertising approach of traditional broadcast media. Contributions to this book (for example, McStay, Chapter 10; Jones, Chapter 15; Gumpert and Drucker, Chapter 16) highlight the increasing reality of surveillance and dataveillance processes that result in a 'creative knowing' about which users may not always be cognisant, and which may be conducted under the guise of public good but actually driven by the ambition of private and/or political gain.

Digitalisation also introduces a deceptive and illusory characteristic to new media. This becomes evident in a number of ways. In the case of analogue recordings, it is difficult to completely eliminate extraneous noise and disguise the editorial process of, for instance, cutting and splicing tape, whereas digital media enables an apparently seamless production. As a result, the absence of such clues ensures that audiences are unaware that some form of intervention may have occurred. This can involve the insertion of advertisements or images for the purpose of 'product placement', and the alteration – or enhancement – of words, images or sounds to 'fit' a particular viewer/listener demographic, or social, political and economic context. The same technology has been used by radio companies to disguise the source of programming. Here, the syndication, or networking, of programmes to large numbers of stations can be 'localised' by occasionally 'dropping in' local jingles, time and weather checks by pre-recorded local voices, and advertisements for local businesses. Similarly, in reality TV shows such as *Big Brother*, a delay of 15 minutes or so between the live event and the represented version provides ample opportunity for producer/editorial intervention, somewhat undermining the argument that such genres can be trusted because – what appears to be – an immediate and live continuous feed removes or reduces suspicion about mediation.

The opportunities afforded by email, Internet 'gateways' such as *Google* and *Yahoo*, government portals, streamed reality TV and sites such as *Indymedia* lend weight to the arguments of protagonists and detractors, due to the almost limitless possibilities available for consumers and citizens to access a wide range of information, entertainment and educative resources. However, there is here a presumption of universal provision, and an assumption about the material resources and cultural competencies that are required to both access and use the facilities enabled by the Internet. While the continuing requirements to upgrade hardware and software will always put pressure on those with low incomes, one of our contributors (Allard, Chapter 9) illustrates that an inability to fully comprehend – and trust – the now increasingly mediated business environment facilitated by the Internet has implications for commercial success and personal satisfaction. This latter example also draws attention to the illusory nature of access. Ease of access – one click away – does not automatically make the workings of governments or business transparent, even though such an impression may be encouraged.

Ways forward

Implications for media communication in this Age of Suspicion

Consideration of the three themes above shows that the public are right to withhold their trust from both the power holders and the media, and in fact, should perhaps distrust more. Indeed, to coin a phrase, we argue for *justified suspicion in the Age of Mediated Communication*.

Given that in the contemporary public sphere, there is minimal interest in forming a public (in the public sphere sense), but every intention to inform and indoctrinate one for political or economic gains; given that governments and business have professionalised their communications; and given that this strategic communication non-transparently subsidises and co-opts media, the public are right to withhold their trust from both the power holders and the media. The public have particular cause to be distrustful about the media's key roles of providing a forum for information and debate, and acting as a check on the state by representing the public's views back to power.

New media may more readily allow the formation of publics, facilitate the representation of their views back to power and provide a means of seeing through or even avoiding the professionalisation of communication. In such ways, new media may facilitate the rebuilding of trust. However, given that interactivity disguises the process of commodification; given that digitalisation conceals the presence of editorial intervention and given the as yet unfulfilled promises of access and transparency promised by the Internet, we argue that public should be *more* distrustful of new media – and, if they are not yet, it will not be long before new media are tainted with the same aura of distrust as old media.

In order to build trust in the media and beyond, a key issue appears to be that of transparency (also see Duffy, 2003; Duffy, Williams and Hall, 2004). Strategic communication needs to be made more transparent, as does subsidisation and cooptation of media. Here, there is a role for independent regulatory bodies to devise an auditing system whereby media succumbing to strategic communication can be identified, and perhaps ranked. Certainly, as far as images go, technology exists to make digital photography more trustworthy – with various image-authentication systems revealing if someone has tampered with a picture (The Economist, 2006).[6] While this may lead to less trust, as the public realises how manipulated their media are, it should, in time, also lead to more specific trust, as those media free of strategic communication become known and more widely branded as such.

Hand-in-hand with transparency rankings, independent regulatory bodies should encourage comprehensive media literacy programmes, designed to reach all age groups. The public should be made aware of the many ways in which strategic communication can manifest, across all genres and media – old and new. Only then can they realistically and critically allocate their trust. Only then will those media genres and forms that truly deserve trust shine through. Moreover, media literacy needs to encompass structural dimensions,[7] ensuring that the public are aware of how trust is manipulated by the local/global political and economic context in which the media operate.[8]

Another key issue in building trust is accountability (O'Neill, 2002; Duffy, 2003; Scott, 2006). When asked what two or three specific changes would have to take place in order to improve honesty and trust in America today, 8 per cent said hold people accountable (Scott, 2006). Can the media do a better job of holding those in power accountable? Arguably, if they could, this would increase trust in political and economic institutions. Yet, how this could be done, is unclear.[9] While critical media are needed, overly adversarial responses from the media have been condemned as damaging trust (Government Communication Review Group Interim Report, 2003). One way forward could be to conduct Citizens' Juries on media, trust and accountability.[10] The Citizens' Jury approach is based on the use of a jury in the court process – the notion that there are many issues that are best decided by a group of ordinary people, without vested interest, applying their common sense and experience, with access to the best possible evidence (Stewart, Kendall and Coote, 1996). A Citizens' Jury on media, trust and accountability would go some way to working out how the media could contribute to accountability without further damaging public trust.

The issue of public trust in regulatory bodies is also a key issue. Here, demonstrable transparency, independence and accountability are essential elements. For example, in the UK there are longstanding concerns that the gamut of governing bodies, broadcasting councils and advisory committees – essentially quangos – that make-up the regulatory infrastructure are neither sufficiently diverse to represent the wider community for whom they claim to speak, nor adequately accountable to that public (Tunstall, 1983; Garnham, 1993; Sargant, 1993). Progressive voices continue to call for greater public involvement in the selection and appointment of members to such bodies, including the possibility of Citizens' Juries replacing the use of advisory committees (Collins and Murroni, 1996). The independent and representative nature of Citizens' Juries would enable a more transparent and democratic decision-making process, and they also epitomise the idea of active citizenship (Stewart, Kendall and Coote, 1996).

Future research directions

While trust and media relationships are emerging as a focus of study across a range of disciplines (as indicated in Chapter 2), there is a need for wider and more sustained exploration of these relationships. This book has scratched the surface of the many genres available through each medium, each of which will have specific trust relationships with their audiences. While more research is needed across all of these genres and forms, there is a danger that media studies will replicate its standard fascination with the news and the press. Indeed, in this book, the press is over-represented as a media form and genre examined, and others merit closer attention – in particular other factual or informational genres across the full range of media available, such as documentary, reality TV, talk shows and blogs. In addition, the operation of trust across entertainment genres such as film, drama and soap opera is under-researched and could be important given that realistic fictional representations may feed trust or distrust in the institutions represented in ways that are particularly emotional, morally instructive or otherwise memorable.

Another issue that merits attention is audience's media literacy. To what extent and why do audiences trust or distrust the information they receive from a range of media genres and forms? How is this modulated through audience familiarity with the codes and conventions of those genres and forms, and their knowledge of wider discursive repertoires with which to judge the accuracy of the reality presented in the media?

Our final suggestion is that media research projects that engage with the idea of trust should do so with a clearly theorised conception of trust. As a recent conference noted, our current understanding of the media and the social is relatively under-theorised (Conference on *Media Change and Social Theory*, September, 2006). As this book has indicated, both the media and trust are complex and multi-faceted concepts, with trust, in particular, having various nuances. Given their conceptual complexity and inflections, and given that any analysis of mass mediated trust will be engaged (either implicitly or directly) in studying relationships with audiences – which are also inherently complex – maximum clarity here should be sought. Furthermore, the concept of trust in itself could be taken forward through the study of mass media, to explore, for instance, how mass mediated trust differs from other forms of trusting relationships.

Notes

1. The vast budgets available to governments and the strategies they use are discussed in great detail by Franklin (2004) and in a different context by Murdock and Golding (2005).
2. In the 1990s, Jeff Kennett's Liberal (but in this context conservative) government in Victoria, Australia threatened to withdraw all advertising from *The Age* newspaper unless coverage of the government's performance improved.
3. For example, Anji Hunter, a close confidante and personal adviser to British Prime Minister moved from Downing Street to a PR role at British Petroleum (J. Rayner, 'Anji Hunter and Adam Boulton – A very political engagement', *The Observer*, 16 July (2006) 37). For information on the recruitment and movement of special/political advisors between the private sector and government on both sides of the Atlantic, see Red Star Research (www.red-star-research.org.uk).
4. Max Clifford, Britain's most successful publicist, acknowledges that 'an important part of PR is lies and deceit' (C. Cadwalladr, 'Circus Maximus', *The Observer Magazine*, 23 July (2006) 13–20).
5. The use of premium rate telephone and text numbers (costing twenty times as much as standard rates) to Reality TV shows has proved to be extremely profitable for the producers. For instance, the first series of *Pop Idol* in the UK generated £2.5m just from the votes cast by phone (M. Brignall, 'Britain's Bill for Premium Rate Phone Calls Rises to £1.6bn a Year – Highest in the World', *The Guardian*, 11 July (2006) 5).
6. *The Economist*, 'Image Technology: Keeping it Real', 19 August (2006) p. 72.
7. John Lloyd (2004, p. 16) laments the fact that media studies courses tend not to lay sufficient stress on 'the media's power, and ability to interpret the world'.
8. The British communications regulator, Ofcom, has statutory responsibility for the promotion of media literacy, which is defined as 'the ability to access, understand and create communications in a variety of contexts' (http://www.ofcom.org.uk/).
9. Set up as a charity in 1993, The *MediaWise Trust* (formerly *Press Wise*) has launched a 'Journalism and Public Trust' initiative to strengthen the trust between journalism and the public (see http://www.presswise.org.uk/display_page.php?id=83).
10. The concept of a Citizens' Jury has its origins in the 1960s and 1970s in Germany and the USA, and many such Juries on various issues have been organised in the UK since the mid-1990s.

References

V. Abt and M. Seesholtz 'The Shameless World of Phil, Sally and Oprah: Television Talk Shows and the Deconstructing of Society', *Journal of Popular Culture*, 28(1) (1994) 171–91.

V. Abt and M. Seesholtz '"The Shameless World" Revisited', *Journal of Popular Film and Television*, 26 (1998) 42–8.

J. Adam Smith, *John Buchan*, (London: Rupert Hart-Davis, 1965).

A. Alaszewski, 'Risk Communication: Identifying the Importance of Social Context', *Health, Risk and Society*, 7(2) (2005) 101–5.

S. Alcock, 'How Parents Decide on MMR', *British Medical Journal*, 324 (2002) 492.

L.M. Alcott and L. Gray-Rosendale, 'Survivor Discourse: Transgression or Recuperation?', in S. Smith and J. Watson (eds), *Getting a Life: Everyday Uses of Autobiography*, (Minneapolis: University of Minnesota Press, 1996) 198–225.

H. Aldrich, *Organisations Evolving*, (London: Sage, 1999).

H. Aldrich and C. Zimmer, 'Entrepreneurship Through Social Networks', in D.L. Sexton and R.W. Smilor (eds), The Art and Science of Entrepreneurship, (Cambridge, MA: Ballinger, 1986) 3–23.

F. Alford, *What Evil Means To Us*, (Ithaca: Cornell University Press, 1997).

M. Allen and R. Caillouet, 'Legitimation Endeavors: Impression Management Strategies Used by an Organization in Crisis', *Communication Monographs*, 61 (1994) 44–62.

D. Altheide, 'Notes Towards a Politics of Fear', *Journal for Crime, Conflict and the Media*, 1(1) (2003) 37–54.

American Civil Liberties Union, 'How "Patriot Act 2" Would Further Erode the Basic Checks on Government Power That Keep America Safe and Free', ACLU website. Retrieved 20 March 2003 from the World Wide Web: http://www.cdt.org/security/patriot2/030320aclu.pdf

A. Anderson, *Media, Culture and the Environment*, (Plymouth: UCL Press, 1997).

I. Ang, *Watching Dallas: Soap Opera and the Melodramatic Imagination*, (London: Methuen, 1985).

M. Angelou, *I Know Why the Caged Bird Sings*, (New York: Random House, 1970).

M. Angelou, *Gather Together in My Name*, (New York: Random House, 1974).

M. Angelou, *The Heart of a Woman*, (New York: Random House, 1981).

J. Archer, 'The Theory of Responsible Government in Britain and Australia', *Politics*, XV(2) (1980) 23–31.

J. Archer, 'Hanson, Howard and the Importance of Symbolic Politics', in B. Grant (ed.), *Pauline Hanson, One Nation and Australian Politics*, (Armidale: UNE Press, 1997) 89–108.

J. Archer, 'Legitimation and Trust', in G. Maddox and G. Young (eds), *Legitimation and the State*, (Armidale: Kardoorair Press, 2005) 88–108.

Aristotle, *Nichomachean Ethics*, M. Oswald (trans.), (Indianapolis: Bobbs-Merrill, 1962).

Aristotle, 'The Rhetoric', in D. Bailey (ed.), *Essays on Rhetoric*, L. Cooper (trans.), (New York: Oxford University Press, 1965) 55–83.

M. Armstrong, T. Barr, P. Coutts, R. Coutts, A. Knowles and S. Moore, *Trust in the Internet: The Key Bottleneck*, University of Adelaide, (2003). Retrieved 12 January

2005 from the World Wide Web: http://www.smartinternet.com.au/publication/newsletters/18/PDF/TrustInTheInternet-TheKeyBottleneck.pdf

A. Arvidsson, 'On the 'Pre-History of the Panoptic Sort': Mobility in Market Research', *Surveillance and Society*, 1(4) (2004) 456–74.

C. Atton, *An Alternative Internet.* (Edinburgh: Edinburgh University Press, 2005).

A. Ayios, 'Competence and Trust Guardians as Key Elements of Building Trust in East-West Joint Ventures in Russia', *Business Ethics: A European Review*, 12(2) (2003) 190–201.

R. Bachmann, 'Conclusion: Trust – Conceptual Aspects of a Complex Phenomenon', in C. Lane and R. Bachmann (eds), *Trust Within and Between Organisations*, (New York: Oxford University Press, 1998) 298–322.

B.H. Bagdikian, *The New Media Monopoly*, (Boston, MA: Beacon Press, 2004).

V. Bakir, 'Greenpeace v. Shell: Media Exploitation and the Social Amplification of Risk Framework (SARF)', *Journal of Risk Research*, 8(7–8) (2005) 679–91.

V. Bakir, 'Policy Agenda-Setting and Risk Communication: Greenpeace, Shell and Issues of Trust', *Harvard International Journal of Press and Politics*, 11(3) (2006) 1–22.

Baldwin, *What Contract?*, Rostrum Library, (2003). Retrieved 12 January 2004 from the World Wide Web: http://debate.uvm.edu/NFL/rostrumlib/ldcontractbaldwin0395.pdf

D.M. Barlow, 'Radio in Wales Post-devolution', in *2001 Radiodyssey Conference*, July, (Brighton, UK: University of Sussex, 2001).

D.M. Barlow, 'Re-assessing Radio: Role, Scope and Accountability', *Contemporary Wales*, 18 (2006) 140–55.

D.M. Barlow, P. Mitchell and T. O'Malley, *The Media in Wales: Voices of a Small Nation*, (Cardiff: UWP, 2005).

S. Barnard, *On the Radio: Music Radio in Britain*, (Milton Keynes: Open University Press, 1989).

M. Baron, *Independent Radio: The Story of Independent Radio in the United Kingdom*, (Lavenham, Suffolk: Terence Dalton, 1975).

R. Barthes, *Image, Music, Text*, S. Heath (trans.), (New York: Hill and Wang, 1979).

N. Baym, 'Talking about Soaps: Communication practices in a computer mediated culture', in C. Harris and A. Alexander (eds), *Theorizing Fandom: Fans, Subculture and Identity*, (New York: Hampton Press, 1998).

K.M. Bayne, *The Internet Marketing Plan: A Practical Handbook for Creating, Implementing, and Assessing Your Online Presence*, (Chichester: John Wiley, 1997).

BBC One, *Panorama*, (London, BBC, 2001, VHS Video).

BBC/Reuters/Media Center Poll, *Trust in the Media*, 3 May 2006. Retrieved 2 July 2006 from the World Wide Web: http://www.globescan.com/news_archives/bbcreut.html Than Governments' — Poll

C. Bean, 'Party Politics, Political leaders and Trust in Government in Australia', *Political Science*, 53(1) (2001) 17–27.

A.D. Beardsworth, 'Trans-Science and Moral Panics: Understanding Food Scares', *British Food Journal*, 92(5) (1990) 11–16.

Beccerra and A.K. Gupta, 'Trust within the Organisation: Integrating the Trust Literature with Agency Theory and Transaction Cost Economics', *Public Administration Quarterly*, 23(2) (1999) 177–203.

U. Beck, 'From Industrial Society to the Risk Society: questions of survival, social structure and ecological enlightenment', in M. Featherstone (ed.), *Cultural Theory and Cultural Change*, (London: Sage, 1992a) 97–123.

U. Beck, *Risk Society: Towards a New Modernity*, (London: Sage, 1992b).

U. Beck, 'The Reinvention of Politics: Towards a Theory of Reflexive Modernization', in U. Beck, A. Giddens and S. Lash (eds), *Reflexive Modernization: Politics, Tradition and Aesthetics in the Modern Social Order*, (Cambridge: Polity Press, 1994) 1–55.

U. Beck, 'Risk Society and the Provident State', in S. Lash, B. Szerszynski and B. Wynne (eds), *Risk, Environment and Modernity: Towards a New Ecology*, M. Chalmers (trans.), (London: Sage, 1996a) 27–43.

U. Beck, 'Subpolitics, Ecology and the Disintegration of Institutional Power', *Organisation and Environment*, 10(1) (1996b) 52–65.

U. Beck, 'Foreword', in S. Allan, B. Adam and C. Carter (eds), *Environmental Risks and the Media*, K. Cross (trans.), (London, Routledge, 2000a) xii–xiv.

U. Beck, 'Risk Society Revisited: Theory, Politics and Research Programmes', in B. Adam, U. Beck and J. Van Loon (eds), *The Risk Society and Beyond: Critical Issues for Social Theory*, (London: Sage, 2000b) 211–29.

U. Beck, 'The Terrorist Threat: World Risk Society Revisited', *Theory, Culture and Society*, 19(4) (2002) 39–55.

U. Beck, A. Giddens and S. Lash (eds), *Reflexive Modernization: Politics, Tradition and Aesthetics in the Modern Social Order*, (Cambridge: Polity Press, 1994).

H. Bedford and D. Elliman, 'Concern about Immunisation', *British Medical Journal*, 320 (2000) 240–3.

J. Berland, 'Radio Space and Industrial Time: The Case of Music Formats', in T. Bennett, S. Frith, L. Grossberg, J. Shepherd and G. Turner (eds), *Rock and Popular Music: Politics, Policies, Institutions*, (New York: Routledge, 1993).

F. Bianchini, 'Remaking European Cities: The role of cultural policies', in F. Bianchini and M. Parkinson (eds), *Cultural Policy and Urban Regeneration*, (Manchester: Manchester University Press, 1993) 1–20.

F. Bianchini and H. Schwengel, 'Re-Imagining the City', in J. Corner and S. Harvey (eds), *Enterprise and Heritage: Crosscurrents of National Culture*, (London: Routledge, 1991) 212–34.

P. Bickerton, M. Bickerton and U. Pardesi, *Cybermarketing: How to Use the Superhighway to Market your Products and Services*, (Oxford: Butterworth-Heinemann, 1996).

W. Biernatzki, 'Terrorism and Mass Media', *Communication Research Trends*, 21(1) (2001) 1–23.

P. Blau, *Exchange and Power in Social Life*, (London: John Wiley, 1964).

J. Blumler and M. Gurevitch, 'Rethinking the Study of Political Communication', in J. Curran and M. Gurevitch (eds), *Mass Media and Society*, 3rd edn, (London: Arnold, 2000) 155–72.

C. Bob, *The Marketing of Rebellion: Insurgents, Media, and International Activism*, (New York: Cambridge University Press, 2005).

R. Boele, H. Fabig and D. Wheeler, 'Shell, Nigeria and the Ogoni: A Study in Unsustainable Development. I. The Story of Shell, Nigeria and the Ogoni People – Economy, Environment, Relationships: Conflict and Prospects for Resolution', *Sustainable Development*, 9(2) (2001) 74–86.

J. Boissevain, *Friends of Friends: Networks, Manipulators and Coalitions*, (Oxford: Blackwell, 1974).

C.H. Botan and M. Taylor, 'The Role of Trust in Channels of Strategic Communication for Building Civil Society', *Journal of Communication*, 55(4) (2005) 685–702.

O. Boyd-Barrett, 'The Public Sphere', in O. Boyd-Barrett and C. Newbold (eds), *Approaches to Media*, (London: Arnold, 1995).

L.I. Brezhnev, *Leninlikul Kursil. Kõnede ja Artiklite Kogumik*, 5th edn, (Tallinn: Eesti Raamat, 1977).

A. Briggs and P. Burke, *A Social History of the Media: From Gutenberg to the Internet*, (Cambridge: Polity, 2002).

L. Brock, 'Oil, the Ogoni and Nigeria: A Conversation with Barine Yorbe Teekate', *Radical History Review*, 74 (1999) 25–30.

P. Brown, 'Popular Epidemiology and Toxic Waste Contamination: Lay and Professional Ways of Knowing', *Journal of Health and Social Behavior*, 33 (1992) 267–81.

M. Brown and J. May, *The Greenpeace Story*, (London: Dorling Kindersley, 1991).

J. Buchan, *Memory Hold the Door*, (London: Hodder & Stoughton, 1940).

P. Buitenhuis, *The Great War of Words: Literature as Propaganda 1914–18 and After*, (London: Batsford, 1987).

R.S. Burt, 'The Social Structure of Competition', in N. Nohria and R.G. Eccles (eds), *Networks and Organisations: Structure, Form, and Action*, (Boston, MA: Harvard Business School Press, 1992) 57–91.

C. Calhoun, *Habermas and the Public Sphere*, (London: MIT Press, 1992).

J.W. Carey, 'In Defence of Public Journalism', in T.L. Glasser (ed.), *The Idea of Public Journalism*, (New York: The Guilford Press, 1999) 49–66.

J.W. Carey, 'Historical Pragmatism and the Internet', *New Media and Society*, 4(4) (2005) 443–55.

D.K. Carlson, *Trust in Media*, 17 September, (2002). Retrieved 1 August 2006 from the World Wide Web: http://poll.gallup.com/content/default.aspx?ci=6802&pg=1

M.S. Carolan and M.M. Bell, 'In Truth We Trust: Discourse, Phenomenology, and the Social Relations of Knowledge in an Environmental Dispute', *Environmental Values*, 12 (2003) 225–45.

P. Carpignano, R. Anderson, S. Aronowitz and W. Difazio, 'Chatter in the Age of Electronic Reproduction: Talk Television and the "Public Mind"', *Social Text*, 25(26) (1990) 33–55.

G. Carter, 'This Is Not Reality', Speech given by Gary Carter to the *European Media Forum*, (London, 2002).

M. Carter, *Independent Radio: The First 25 Years*, (London: Radio Authority, 1998).

E.S. Casey, *Imagining: A Phenomenological Study*, (Bloomington: Indiana Forward Press, 1976).

C. Castelfranchi and R. Falcone, 'Towards a Theory of Delegation for Agent-Based Systems', *Robotics and Autonomous Systems*, 24 (1998) 141–57.

M. Castells, *The Rise of the Network Society*, 2nd edn, (London: Blackwell, 2000).

E.M. Caudill and P.E. Murphy, 'Consumer Online Privacy: Legal and Ethical Issues', *Journal of Public Policy and Marketing*, 19 (1) (2000) 7–19.

S. Chase, 'Forward', in J.B. Carroll (ed.), *Benjamin Lee Whorf: Language, Thought and Reality*, (Cambridge, MA: The MIT Press, 1956) v–x.

Cheskin, *Research and Studio Archetype. E commerce Trust Study*, (Redwood Shores, CA: Cheskin Research, 1999).

A.C. Clarke (ed.), *M. Tullius Ciceronis, Pro T. Annio Milone*, (Oxford: Oxford University Press, 1895).

L. Clarke and J.F. Short Jr, 'Social Organisation and Risk: Some Current Controversies', *Annual Review of Sociology*, 19 (1993) 375–99.

R. Clarke, *Introduction to Dataveillance and Information Privacy, and Definition of Terms*, (Australian National University, 1999). Retrieved 12 February 2004 from the World Wide Web: http://www.anu.edu.au/people/Roger.Clarke/DV/Intro.html

R. Clarke, 'While You Were Sleeping ... Surveillance Technologies Arrived', *Australian Quarterly*, 73(1) (2001). Retrieved 16 February 2004 from the World Wide Web: http://www.anu.edu.au/people/Roger.Clarke/DV/AQ2001.html

R. Cockroft and S.M. Cockroft, *Persuading People: An Introduction to Rhetoric*, (London: Macmillan, 1992).

J.S. Coleman, *Foundations of Social Theory*, (Cambridge: Harvard University Press, 1990).

J. Collins, *Food Scares and News Media: A Case Study Approach to Science and Risk in the News*, Unpublished PhD thesis, (London Guildhall University, 1999).

P.H. Collins, *Black Feminist Thought: Knowledge, Consciousness and the Politics of Empowerment*, (New York: Routledge, 1991).

R. Collins and C. Murroni, *New Media, New Policies*, (Cambridge: Polity Press, 1996).

Conference on Restoring the Trust in Journalism, *Journalism and the Public: Restoring the Trust*, August, (San Antonio, USA: Department of Communication Kennesaw State University, 2005).

Conference on *Media Change and Social Theory*, September, (Oxford, UK: St Hugh's College, The University of Oxford, 2006).

T.E. Cook, 'Introduction', in C. Grimes (ed.), *Whither the Civic Journalism Bandwagon?*, Discussion Paper D-36, Joan Shorenstein Center on the Press, Politics and Public Policy, John F. Kennedy School of Government, Harvard University, (1999). Retrieved 20 October 2005 from the World Wide Web: http://www.ksg.harvard.edu/presspol/publications/pdfs/83387_d-36.pdf

P. Cooke and K. Morgan, *The Associational Economy: Firms, Regions and Innovation*, (Oxford: Oxford University Press, 1998).

L. Cooper, *The Rhetoric of Aristotle*, (New York: Appleton, 1932).

J. Corner, 'Performing the Real, Television in a Post Documentary Culture', *Television and New Media*, 3(3) (2002) 255–69.

M. Covell, *Indymedia UK*, Speech given by M. Covell, Senior Staff Journalist, Indymedia UK to University of Wales, Aberystwyth students, December (Aberystwyth, 2003).

G. Craig, *The Media, Politics and Public Life*, (Crow's Nest: Allen and Unwin, 2004).

W.E.D. Creed and R.E. Miles, 'Trust in Organisations: A Conceptual Framework Linking Organisational Forms, Managerial Philosophies, and the Opportunity Costs of Controls', in R.M. Kramer and T.R. Tyler (eds), *Trust in Organisations*, (Thousand Oaks, CA: Sage Publications, 1996) 16–38.

G. Creel, *How We Advertised America: The First Telling of the Amazing Story of the Committee on Public Information That Carried the Gospel of Americanism to Every Corner of the Globe*, (New York: Arno, 1920).

A. Crisell, *Understanding Radio*, (London: Methuen, 1986).

A. Crisell, *An Introductory History of British Broadcasting*, (London: Routledge, 1997).

C. Critcher, *Moral Panics and the Media*, (Milton Keynes: Open University Press, 2003).

M.J. Cronin, *Doing Business on the Internet: How the Electronic Highway is Transforming American Companies*, (London: Van Nostrand Reinhold, 1994).

M.J. Cronin, *Doing More Business on the Internet: How the Electronic Highway is Transforming American Companies*, 2nd edn, (London: Van Nostrand Reinhold, 1995).

G. Cronkhite, *Communication and Awareness*, (Menlo Park, CA: Cummings, 1976).

J. Curran, 'Re-thinking the Media as a Public Sphere', in P. Dahlgren and C. Sparks (eds), *Communication and Citizenship*, (London: Routledge, 1991) 27–57.

J. Curran, 'Re-Thinking Media and Democracy', in J. Curran and M. Gurevitch (eds), *Mass Media and Society*, 3rd edn, (London: Arnold, 2000) 120–54.

J. Curran, *Media and Power*, (New York: Routledge, 2002).

S.M. Cutlip, A.H. Center and G.M. Broom, *Effective Public Relations*, 9th edn, (Upper Saddle River, NJ: Prentice Hall, 2006).

G. Cvetkovich and R.E. Lofstedt, (eds), *Social Trust and the Management of Risk*, (London: Earthscan Publications, 1999).

P. Dahlgren, 'Introduction', in P. Dahlgren and C. Sparks (eds), *Communication and Citizenship*, (London: Routledge, 1991) 1–24.

P. Dahlgren, 'The Public Sphere as Historical Narrative', in D. McQuail (ed.), *McQuail's Reader in Mass Communication Theory*, (London: Sage, 2001) 194–200.

P. Dahlgren, 'Internet Public Spheres and Political Communication: Dispersion and Deliberation', *Political Communication*, 22(2) (2005) 147–62.

S. Dale, *McLuhan's Children: The Greenpeace Message and the Media*, (Toronto: Between the Lines, 1996).

P. Dasgupta, 'Trust as a Commodity', in D. Gambetta (ed.), *Trust: Making and Breaking Cooperative Relations*, (Oxford: Blackwell, 1988) 49–71.

G. Davies, 'Local Radio Comes to Rural Wales', *Planet*, 85 (1991) 109–111.

J. Davies, *Broadcasting and the BBC in Wales*, (Cardiff: University of Wales Press, 1994).

A. Davis, *Publics Relations Democracy: Public Relations, Politics and the Mass Media in Britain*, (Manchester: Manchester University Press, 2002).

G. Deleuze, 'Postscript on the Societies of Control', *October*, 59(4) (1992) 3–7.

G. Deleuze and C. Parnet, *Dialogues*, (Paris: Flammarion, 1997).

J. Delhey and K. Newton, 'Who Trusts? The Origins of Social Trust in Seven Societies', *European Societies*, 5(2) (2003) 93–137.

Department for Constitutional Affairs, 'Hutton Inquiry', (2004). Retrieved 26 May 2006 from the World Wide Web: http://www.the-hutton-inquiry.org.uk/ index.htm

S. Drucker, 'The Image of Japanese on American Television', *Research Report, Proceedings, International Television Flow Project*, (Tokyo: Japan, 1999).

B. Duffy, *Who Do We Trust?*, (London: Ipsos MORI, 16 April 2003).

B. Duffy, M. Williams and S. Hall, *Who Do You Believe? Trust in Government Information*, (London: Ipsos MORI Publication, 2004).

S. Dunwoody and H.P. Peters, 'Mass Media Coverage of Technological and Environmental Risks: A Survey of Research in the United States and Germany', *Public Understandings of Science*, 1 (1992) 199–230.

E. Durkheim, *The Division of Labour in Society*, G. Simpson (trans.), (New York: Free Press, 1964).

M. Durkin and M.A. Lawlor, 'The Implications of the Internet on the Advertising Agency-Client Relationship', *Service Industries Journal*, 21(2) (2001) 175–90.

S.N. Durlauf and M. Fafchamps, *Social Capital*, NBER Working Paper, 10485, (Cambridge, MA: National Bureau Of Economic Research, 2004). Retrieved 20 May 2004 from the World Wide Web: http://www.nber.org/papers/w10485

R. Dyer, *Stars*, (London: British Film Institute, 1979).

T. Eagleton, *Ideology: An Introduction*, (London: Verso, 1991).

T. Earle and G.T. Cvetkovich, *Social Trust: Towards a Cosmopolitan Society*, (New York: Praeger, 1995).

Edlund, 'The Hutchins Commission, 50 Years Later', *Forum: Press-Government Relations*, (2000). Retrieved 2 February 2002 from the World Wide Web: http://itc.utk.edu/cgi-bin/netforum/comm520/a/3–58

M. Eide and G. Knight, 'Public/Private Service: Service Journalism and the Problems of Everyday Life', *European Journal of Communication*, 14(4) (1999) 525–47.

J. Elkington and A. Trisoglio, 'Developing Realistic Scenarios for the Environment: Lessons from Brent Spar', *Long Range Planning*, 29(1996) 762–9.

G. Ellis, 'Stereophonic Nation: The Bi-lingual Sounds of Cool Cymru FM', *International Journal of Cultural Studies*, 3(2) (2000) 188–98.

G. Elmer, 'A Diagram of Panoptic Surveillance', *New Media and Society*, 5(2) (2003) 231–47.

D. Epstein and D.L. Steinberg, 'Twelve Steps to Heterosexuality? Common-Sensibilities on The Oprah Winfrey Show', *Feminism and Psychology*, 5(2) (1995) 275–80.

D. Epstein and D.L. Steinberg, 'All Het Up! Rescuing Heterosexuality on The Oprah Winfrey Show', *Feminist Review*, 54 (1996) 88–115.

Estonian Parliament, Research Report, *Eesti Ühiskond 2002*, Estonian Society, (Tallinn, Turu-uuringute AS, 2002).

S. Ewen, *PR! A Social History of Spin*, (New York: Harper Collins, 1996).

C. Fairchild, 'Deterritorializing Radio: Deregulation and the Continuing Triumph of the Corporatist Perspective in the USA', *Media, Culture and Society*, 21 (1999) 550–61.

K.S. Fam, T. Foscht and R.D. Collins, 'Trust and the Online Relationship – an Exploratory Study from New Zealand', *Tourism Management*, 25(2) (2004) 195–207.

K. Fearn-Banks, *Crisis Communications: A Casebook Approach*, (Mahwah, New Jersey: Lawrence Erlbaum Associates, 1996).

N. Ferguson, *The Pity of War*, (London: Faber, 1998).

R. Ferguson, *Representing 'Race': Ideology, Identity and the Media*, (London: Arnold, 1998).

J. Fiske and J. Hartley, *Reading Television*, (London: Methuen, 1978).

M. Fitzpatrick, *MMR and Autism: What Parents Need to Know*, (London: Routledge, 2004).

R. Florida, *The Rise of the Creative Class And How It's Transforming Work, Leisure, Community and Everyday Life*, (New York: Basic Books, 2002).

M. Foucault, *Discipline and Punish*, (London: Penguin, 1977).

M. Foucault, *The Will To Knowledge: The History of Sexuality Vol. 1*, R. Hurley (trans.), (London: Penguin Books, 1978).

R. Fowler, *Language in the News: Discourse and Ideology in the Press*, (London: Routledge, 1991).

S. Frankel, C. Davison and G.D. Smith, 'Lay Epidemiology and the Rationality of Responses to Health Education', *British Journal of General Practice*, 41 (1991) 428–30.

B. Franklin, *Packaging Politics: Political Communications in Britain's Media Democracy*, 2nd edn, (London: Arnold, 2004).

L.J. Frewer, 'Trust, Transparency, and Social Context: Implications for Social Amplification of Risk', in N. Pidgeon, R.E. Kasperson and P. Slovic (eds), *The Social Amplification of Risk*, (Cambridge: Cambridge University Press, 2003) 123–37.

L.J. Frewer and S. Miles, 'Temporal Stability of the Psychological Determinants of Trust: Implications for Communication about Food Risks', *Health, Risk and Society*, 5(1) (2003) 259–72.

D.L. Fry and V.H. Fry, 'A Semiotic Model for the Study of Mass Communication', in M. McLaughlin (ed.), *Communication Yearbook 9*, (Beverly Hills, CA: Sage, 1986).

J.G. Fryas, 'Political Instability and Business: A Focus on Shell in Nigeria', *Third World Quarterly*, 19(3) (1998) 447–57.

F. Fukuyama, *Trust: The Social Virtues and the Creation of Prosperity*, (New York: Simon and Schuster, 1995).

F. Fukuyama, *The Great Disruption. Human Nature and the Reconstitution of Social Order*, (London: Profile Books, 1999).

M. Fuller, *Essays on the Software Culture: Behind the Blip*, (New York: Autonomedia, 2003).

M. Fusaro, *Generating Trust in Online Business*, (Canada: IQ Collectif, 2002).

E.A.M. Gale, 'Between Two Cultures: The Expert Clinician and the Pharmaceutical Industry', *Clinical Medicine*, 3(6) (2003) 538–41.

J.K. Galbraith, *The Culture of Contentment*, (London: Sinclair-Stevenson, 1992).

Gallup Poll, *Most Important Problem*, (2006a). Retrieved 26 May 2006 from the World Wide Web: http://brain.gallup.com/content/default.aspx?ci=1675

Gallup Poll, *Terrorism in the United States*, (2006b). Retrieved 26 May 2006 from the World Wide Web: http://brain.gallup.com/content/?ci=4909

D. Gambetta, 'Foreword', in D. Gambetta (ed.), *Trust: Making and Breaking Cooperative Relations*, (Oxford: Blackwell, 1988a).

D. Gambetta, 'Can We Trust Trust?', in D. Gambetta (ed.), *Trust: Making and Breaking Cooperative Relations*, (Oxford: Blackwell, 1988b) 213–37.

J. Gamson, 'Do Ask, Do Tell: Frank Talk on TV', *The American Prospect*, 23(Fall) (1995) 44–50.

J. Gamson, *Freaks Talk Back: Tabloid Talk Shows and Sexual Nonconformity*, (Chicago: University of Chicago Press, 1998a).

J. Gamson, 'Publicity Traps: Television Talk Shows and Lesbian, Gay, Bisexual and Transgender Visibility', *Sexualities*, 1(1) (1998b) 11–41.

O. Gandy, 'Data Mining and Surveillance in the Post 9/11 Environment', in K. Ball and F. Webster (eds), *The Intensification of Surveillance*, (London: Pluto Books, 2003) 26–41.

E.J. Gangarosa, A.M. Galazka, C.R. Wolfe, L.M. Phillips, R.E. Gangarosa, E. Miller and R.T. Chen, 'Impact of Anti-vaccine Movements on Pertussis Control: The Untold Story', *The Lancet*, 351(9099) (1998) 356–61.

H. Garfinkel, 'A Conception of and Experiments with "Trust" as a Condition of Stable Concerted Actions', in O.J. Harvey (ed.), *Motivation and Social Interaction*, (New York: Ronald Press, 1963).

N. Garnham, 'The Media and the Public Sphere', *Intermedia*, 14(1) (1986) 28–33.

N. Garnham, 'The Media and the Public Sphere', in C. Calhoun (ed.), *Habermas and the Public Sphere*, (London: MIT Press, 1992) 359–76.

N. Garnham, 'Public Service Broadcasting and the Consumer', *Consumer Policy Review*, 3 (1993) 152–8.

N. Garnham, 'The Media and the Public Sphere', in O. Boyd-Barrett and C. Newbold (eds), *Approaches to Media: A Reader*, (London: Arnold, 1995) 245–51.

B. Gary, *The Nervous Liberals: Propaganda Anxieties from World War One to the Cold War*, (New York: Columbia University Press, 1999).

Gauthier, 'The Social Contract as Ideology', *Philosophy and Public Affairs*, 6 (1977) 130–64.

D. Gazis, 'PASHAs: Advanced intelligent agents in the service of electronic commerce', in D. Leebaert (ed.), *The Future of the Electronic Marketplace*, (Cambridge, MA: MIT Press, 1998) 145–73.

H. Gebele, *Die Probleme von Krieg und Frieden in Grossbritannien wahrend des Ersten Weltkriegs*, (Frankfurt: Verlag Peter Lang, 1987).

J. Germain, 'For Online Finance – Image is Everything', *E-Commerce Times*, (2004). Retrieved 4 January 2005 from the World Wide Web: http://www.macnewsworld.com/story/35222.html

A. Giddens, *The Constitution of Society: Outline of the Theory of Structuration*, (Cambridge: Polity Press, 1984).

A. Giddens, *The Consequences of Modernity*, (Cambridge: Polity Press, 1990).

A. Giddens, *Modernity and Self Identity: Self and Society in the Late Modern Age*, (Cambridge: Polity Press, 1991).

A. Giddens, *The Transformation of Intimacy*, (Oxford: Polity Press, 1992).

A. Giddens, 'Living in a Post-Traditional Society', in U. Beck, A. Giddens and S. Lash, *Reflexive Modernization: Politics, Tradition and Aesthetics in the Modern Social Order*, (Cambridge: Polity Press, 1994a) 56–109.

A. Giddens, 'Replies and Critiques. Risk, Trust, Reflexivity', in U. Beck, A. Giddens and S. Lash, *Reflexive Modernization: Politics, Tradition and Aesthetics in the Modern Social Order*, (Cambridge: Polity Press, 1994b) 184–97.

A. Giddens, *Runaway World: How Globalisation is Reshaping Our Lives*, (London: Profile Books, 1999).

Gifts From the Heart', *Oprah.com*. Retrieved 14 June 2004 from the World Wide Web: http://www.geocities.com/rainforest/1078/oprah/heartgifts.html

M. Gillespie, *Public Remains Skeptical of News Media*, (Gallup News Service, 30 May 2003).

L. Gofton, 'Food Fears and Time Famines', *British Nutrition Foundation Nutrition Bulletin*, 15(1) (1990) 80–95.

P. Golding and G. Murdock, 'Culture, Communications and Political Economy', in J. Curran and M. Gurevitch (eds), *Mass Media and Society*, 3rd edn, (London: Arnold, 2000) 70–92.

D. Good, 'Individuals, Interpersonal Relations, and Trust', in D. Gambetta (ed.), *Trust: Making, and Breaking Cooperative Relations*, (Oxford: Blackwell, 1988) 31–48.

P. Goodwin, *Television under the Tories: Broadcasting Policy 1979–1997*, (London: BFI, 1998).

J. Gorst, *Commercial Radio: The Beast of Burden*, (AIMS of Industry, 1971).

Government Communication Review Group Interim Report (GCRGIR), chaired by Bob Phillis. September 2003. Retrieved 2 July 2006 from the World Wide Web: http://www.gics.gov.uk/access/review/interimreport.htm

M. Granovetter, 'Economic Action and Social Structure', *American Journal of Sociology*, 91(3) (1985) 481–510.

A.H. Griffith, 'Medicine and the Media – Vaccination against Whooping Cough', *Journal of Biological Standardization*, 9 (1981) 475–82.

C. Grimes, *Whither the Civic Journalism Bandwagon?*, Discussion Paper D-36, Joan Shorenstein Center on the Press, Politics and Public Policy, John F. Kennedy School of Government, Harvard University, (1999). Retrieved 20 October 2005 from the World Wide Web: http://www.ksg.harvard.edu/presspol/publications/pdfs/83387_d-36.pdf

L. Grindstaff, 'Producing Trash, Class, and the Money Shot: A Behind the Scenes Account of Daytime TV Talk Shows', in J. Lull and S. Hinerman (eds), *Media Scandals: Morality and Desire in the Market Place*, (Oxford: Polity, 1997) 164–202.

J.E. Grunig and T. Hunt, *Managing Public Relations*, (New York: Holt, Rinehart and Winston, 1984).

G. Gumpert, *Talking Tombstones and Other Tales of the Media Age*, (New York: Oxford University Press, 1987).

G. Gumpert, 'Communications and Our Sense of Community: A Planning Agenda', *InterMedia*, 24(4) (1996) 41–4.

G. Gumpert and R. Cathcart, 'Report on Television Stereotypes of Three Nations: France, U.S. and Japan', *International Television Flow Project*, Japan, (Tokyo, Japan: NHK, 1989).

GWR, *The Marcher Radio Group*, (Promotional material), (GWR Group, 2002).

J. Habermas, *Towards a Rational Society: Student Protest, Science, and Politics*, J.J. Shapiro (trans.), (London: Heinemann, 1971).

J. Habermas, 'The Public Sphere: An Encyclopaedia Article', *New German Critique*, 3, (1974) [1964] 49–55.

J. Habermas, *The Theory of Communicative Action: The Critique of Functionalist Reason,* (Cambridge: Polity Press, 1987).

J. Habermas, *The Structural Transformation of the Public Sphere: An Inquiry into a Category of Bourgeois Society,* (Cambridge, MA: MIT Press, 1989 [1962]).

J. Habermas, 'Further Reflections on the Public Sphere', in C. Calhoun, *Habermas and the Public Sphere,* (London: MIT Press, 1992) 421–61.

J. Habermas, *Between Facts and Norms,* (London: Polity Press, 1996).

J. Haggerty and R. Ericson, 'The Surveillant Assemblage', *British Journal of Sociology,* 51(4) (2000) 605–22.

P.A. Hall, 'Social Capital in Britain', *British Journal of Political Science,* 29 (1999) 417–61.

S. Hall, C. Critcher, T. Jefferson, J. Clarke and B. Roberts, *Policing the Crisis: Mugging, the State and Law and Order,* (London: Macmillan, 1978).

S. Hall, D. Hobson, A. Lowe and P. Willis (eds), *Culture, Media, Language,* (London: Hutchinson, 1981).

K. Hallahan, 'Seven Models of Framing: Implications for Public Relations', *Journal Of Public Relations Research,* 11(3) (1999) 205–42.

J. Hamill and K. Gregory, 'Internet Marketing in the Internationalisation of UK SMEs', *Journal of Marketing Management,* 13(1–3) (1997) 9–28.

H. Hardt, 'Reinventing the Press in the Age of Commercial Appeals: Writings on and about Public Journalism', in T.L. Glasser (ed.), *The Idea of Public Journalism,* (New York: The Guilford Press, 1999) 197–209.

I. Hargreaves and J. Thomas, *New News, Old News,* (London: Independent Television Commission, 2002).

I. Hargreaves, J. Lewis and T. Speers, *Towards a Better Map: Science, the Public and the Media,* (Bristol: ESRC, 2003).

R. Harrabin, A. Coote and J. Allen, *Health in the News: Risk, Reporting and Media Influence,* (London: The King's Fund, 2003).

Harris Poll, *Fewer Americans Than Europeans Have Trust in the Media – Press, Radio and TV,* (New York: Harris Interactive, 13 January 2005). Retrieved 2 July 2006 from the World Wide Web: http://www.harrisinteractive.com/harris_poll/index.asp?PID=534

K. Hart, 'Kinship, Contract, and Trust: The economic organization of migrants in an African city slum', in D. Gambetta (ed.), *Trust: Making, and Breaking Cooperative Relations,* (Oxford: Blackwell, 1988) 176–94.

C. Haste, *Keep the Home Fires Burning,* (London: Allen Lane, 1977).

K. Hayles, *How We Became Posthuman,* (Chicago, USA: University of Chicago Press, 1999).

F. Heinderyckx, 'Television News Programmes in Western Europe: A Comparative Study', *European Journal of Communication,* 8 (1993) 425–50.

D. Hendy, *Radio in the Global Age,* (Cambridge: Polity Press, 2000).

S. Herbst, *Reading Public Opinion,* (Chicago: University of Chicago Press, 1998).

E.J. Herman, 'The Propaganda Model: A retrospective', in D. McQuail (ed.), *McQuail's Reader in Mass Communication Theory,* (London: Sage, 2001) 60–8.

E.J. Herman and N. Chomsky, *Manufacturing Consent,* (London: Vintage, 1994).

D. Hesmondhalgh, 'Flexibility, Post-Fordism and the Music Industries', *Media, Culture and Society,* 18 (1996) 469–88.

D. Hesmondhalgh, 'The British Dance Music Industry: A Case Study of Independent Cultural Production', *British Journal of Sociology,* 49(2) (1998) 234–51.

D. Hesmondhalgh, *The Cultural Industries,* (London: Sage, 2002).

D.W. Hey, 'Virtual Product Placement', *TV Quarterly,* XXXII(4) (2002) 24–2.

S. Hier, 'Probing the Surveillant Assemblage: On the Dialectics of Surveillance Practices as Processes of Social Control', *Surveillance and Society,* 1(3) (2003) 399–411.

H. Himmelstein, *Television Myth and the American Mind*, (New York: Praeger, 1984).

B. Hindess, *Corruption and Democracy in Australia*, Democratic Audit of Australia, (Canberra RSSS, ANU, 2004).

S. Hjarvard, 'Pan-European Television News: Towards A European Political Public Sphere', in P. Drummond, R. Paterson and J. Willis (eds), *National Identity and Europe*, (London: BFI, 1993) 71–94.

T. Hobbes, *Leviathan*, C.B. MacPherson (ed.), (London: Penguin Classics New edn, 1982 [1651]).

P. Hobson-West, *'Needle Politics': Risk, Trust and Anti-vaccinationism*, (Nottingham: Institute for the Study of Genetics, Biorisks and Society, University of Nottingham, 2003).

S. Holmes, '"Reality Goes Pop!" Reality TV, Popular Music and Narratives of Stardom in Pop Idol', *Television and New Media*, 5(2) (2004) 147–72.

H. Holtz, *Databased Marketing*, (New York: Wiley, 1992).

b. hooks, 'Marginality as Site of Resistance', in R. Ferguson, M. Gever, T.T. Minh-ha and C. West (eds), *Out There: Marginalisation and Contemporary Cultures*, (Cambridge, MA.: MIT Press, 1990a) 341–43.

b. hooks, 'Talking Back', in R. Ferguson, M. Gever, T.T. Minh-ha and C. West (eds), *Out There: Marginalisation and Contemporary Cultures*, (Cambridge, MA.: MIT Press, 1990b) 337–40.

R. Hooper, *Regulating Communications in the Age of Convergence*, (London: Radio Authority, 2001a).

R. Hooper, *Keynote Speech – Manchester Symposium* (1 May), (London: Radio Authority, 2001b).

R. Horton, *MMR: Science and Fiction*, (London: Granta Books, 2004).

S. Høyer, E. Lauk and P. Vihalemm, *Towards a Civil Society, The Baltic Media's Long Road to Freedom. Perspectives on History, Ethnicity and Journalism,* (Tartu: Baltic Association for Media Research/Nota Baltica Ltd., 1993).

P. Hughes, J. Bellamy and A. Black, 'Building Social Trust Through Education', in I. Winter (ed.), *Social Capital and Public Policy in Australia*, (Melbourne: Australian Institute of Family Studies, 2000).

P. Hughes, S. King and J. Bellamy, *Insecurity in Australia. Summary Paper: Well-being and Security Study*, September (2004). Retrieved 7 May 2006 from the World Wide Web: http://www.anglicare.org.au/live3/index.cgi?E=hcatfuncs&PT=SL&X=getdoc&Lev1=web_res&Lev2=0010

S. Hynes, *A War Imagined: the First World War and British Culture*, (London: Pimlico, 1992).

ICM, *ICM/News of the World Terrorism Poll*, 24–25 March (2004). Retrieved 26 May 2006 from the World Wide Web: http://www.icmresearch.co.uk/reviews/2004/notw-terrorism-poll-Mar04.asp

ICM, *Guardian Poll*, 12–14 August (2005). Retrieved 26 May 2006 from the World Wide Web: http://www.icmresearch.co.uk/reviews/2005/Guardian%20-%20Aug/The%20Guardian%20Poll%20-%20aug%2005.asp

A.A. Idowu, 'Human Rights, Environmental Degradation and Oil Multinational Companies', *Netherlands Quarterly of Human Rights*, 17(2) (1999) 161–84.

E. Illouz, 'That Shadowy Realm of the Interior: Oprah Winfrey and Hamlet's Glass', *International Journal of Cultural Studies*, 2(1) (1999) 109–31.

E. Illouz, *Oprah Winfrey and the Glamor of Misery: An Essay on Popular Culture*, (New York: Columbia University Press, 2003).

Independent Broadcasting Authority, *Annual Report and Accounts 1975–6*, (London: IBA, 1976).

Insight, *Translating Customer Feedback into Actionable Business Intelligence*, (2002). Retrieved 10 March 2003 from the World Wide Web: http://www.island-data.com

Internet Advertising Bureau, *Internet Users Consume 12% Of Their Media Online*, (2003). Retrieved 9 October 2004 from the World Wide Web: http://www.iabuk.net/index.php?class=news&view=670

ITC, *New News, Old News*. Retrieved 12 December 2002 from the World Wide Web: www.ITC.org.UK

J. Jacobs, 'Alltag oder Vergangenheit? Einstellung zur Herrschenden Politischen Ordnung in den neuen Bundesländer, Polen, Tschechien und Ungarn', *Politische Vierteljahresschrift*, 42(2) (2001) 223–46.

N.W. Jankowski (ed.), *Community Media in the Information Age: Perspectives and Practice*, (New Jersey: Hampton Press, 2002).

B. Johannisson, 'Paradigms and Entrepreneurial Networks – Some Methodological Challenges', *Entrepreneurship & Regional Development*, 7 (1995) 215–31.

L. Johnson, *The Unseen Voice: A Cultural Study of Early Australian Radio*, (New York: Routledge, 1988).

J. Jones, 'Show Your Real Face: Investigating the Boundaries between the Notions of Consumers and Producers of Factual Television', *New Media and Society*, 5(3) (2003) 401–22.

J. Jones, 'Emerging Platform Identities, Big Brother UK and Interactive Multi-Platform Usage', in J. Jones and E. Mathijs (eds), *Big Brother International, Format, Critics and Publics*, (London: Wallflower Press/Columbia Press, 2004).

Jupitermedia, *Jupitermedia Finds Online Consumers Spend as Much Time Online as in Front of the TV*, (2006). Retrieved 1 April 2006 from the World Wide Web: http://www.jupitermedia.com/corporate/releases/06.01.30-newjupresearch.html

J. Jupp, *White Australia to Woomera: The Story of Australian Immigration*, (Cambridge: Cambridge University Press, 2002).

V. Kalmus, M. Lauristin and P. Pruulmann-Vengerfeldt (eds), *Eesti Elavik 21. Sajandi Algul. Ülevaade Uurimuse Mina. Maailm. Meedia Tulemustest*, (Tartu: Tartu University Press, 2004).

J.X. Kasperson, R.E. Kasperson, N. Pidgeon and P. Slovic, 'The Social Amplification of Risk: Assessing Fifteen Years of Research and Theory', in N. Pidgeon, R.E. Kasperson and P. Slovic (eds), *The Social Amplification of Risk*, (Cambridge: Cambridge University Press, 2003) 13–46.

J. Keane, 'Democracy and Media: Without foundations', in O. Boyd-Barrett and C. Newbold (eds), *Approaches to Media*, (London: Arnold, 1995).

T. Keller, 'Trash TV', *Journal of Popular Culture*, 26(4) (1993) 195–206.

T. Ketola, 'The Seven Sisters: Snow Whites, Dwarfs or Evil Queens? A Comparison of the Official Environmental Policies of the Largest Oil Corporations in the World', *Business Strategy and the Environment*, 2(3) (1993) 22–33.

A. Kiam, *Making Money on the Internet: Complete Beginners Guide*, (Harrogate: Net Works, 1995).

R. Kilborn, *Staging the Real: Factual TV Programming in the Age of Big Brother*, (Manchester: Manchester University Press, 2003).

P. Kim and H. Sawhney, 'A Machine-like New Medium – a Theoretical Examination of Interactive TV', *Media, Culture and Society*, 24(2) (2002) 217–33.

P. Knight, *Profits and Principles: Does There Have to be a Choice?*, (Shell Report, 1998).

H. Koskela, '"Cam Era" – The Contemporary Urban Panoptican', *Surveillance and Society*, 1(3) (2003) 292–313.

S. Koss, *The Rise and Fall of the Political Press in Britain*, (London: Fontana, 1990).

M. Koufaris and W. Hampton-Sosa, 'The Development of Initial Trust in an Online Company by New Customers', *Information & Management*, 41(3) (2004) 377–97.

C. Lane, 'Introduction: Theories and issues in the study of trust', in C. Lane and R. Bachmann (eds), *Trust Within and Between Organisations*, (New York: Oxford University Press, 1998) 1–30.

S. Lash, *'Replies and Critiques. Expert-systems or Situated Interpretation? Culture and Institutions in Disorganized Capitalism'*, in U. Beck, A. Giddens and S. Lash, *Reflexive Modernization: Politics, Tradition and Aesthetics in the Modern Social Order*, (Cambridge: Polity Press, 1994) 198–215.

P. Laslett (ed.), *J. Locke: Two Treatises of Government*, 3rd edn, (Cambridge: Cambridge University Press, 1988).

H. Lasswell, *Propaganda Techniques in the World War*, (New York: Peter Smith, 1927).

G.T. Lau and H.L Sook, '"Consumers"' Trust in a Brand and the Link to Brand Loyalty', *Journal of Market-Focused Management*, 4(4) (1999) 341–70.

E. Lauk, *Historical and Sociological Perspectives on the Development of Estonian Journalism*, Dissertationes de Mediis et Communicationibus Universitatis Tartuensis 1, (Tartu: Tartu University Press, 1997).

M. Lauristin, P. Vihalemm, K.E. Rosengren and L. Weibull (eds), *Return to the Western World. Cultural and Political Perspectives on the Estonian Post-Communist Transition*, (Tartu: Tartu University Press, 1997) 134–42.

M. Lauristin and P. Vihalemm, 'The Transformation of Estonian Society and Media: 1987–2001', in P. Vihalemm (ed.), *Baltic Media in Transition*, (Tartu: Tartu University Press, 2002) 17–63.

M. Lauristin and P. Vihalemm, 'Sissejuhatus: Uurimuse Mina. Maailma. Meedia Metodoloogiast ja Tähendusest', in V. Kalmus, M. Lauristin and P. Pruulmann-Vengerfeldt (eds), *Eesti Elavik 21. Sajandi Algul. Ülevaade Uurimuse Mina. Maailm. Meedia Tulemustest*, (Tartu:Tartu University Press 2004) 23–7.

ctric Law Library, *Lectric Law Library's Legal Lexicon*, (2004). Retrieved 8 January 2004 from the World Wide Web: http://www.lectlaw.com/def/f026.htm

D.L. LeMahieu, *A Culture for Democracy*, (Oxford: Oxford University Press, 1988).

T.C. Leonard, 'Making Readers into Citizens – The Old-Fashioned Way', in T.L. Glasser (ed.), *The Idea of Public Journalism*, (New York: The Guilford Press, 1999) 85–98.

L. Lessig, *Code and Other Laws of Cyberspace* (New York: Basic Books, 1999).

M. Levine, *The Mind and Mood of Australia (Just a Little Unplugged)*, Paper No. 20030901, presented by M. Levine, Chief Executive of Roy Morgan Research, to the Australian Institute of Company Directors, September, (Tasmania: 2003). Retrieved 7 May 2006 from the World Wide Web: http://www.roymorgan.com/news/papers/2003/20030901/

J.C. Levinson and C. Rubin, *Guerrilla Marketing in the Internet: A Complete Guide to Making Money On-Line*, (London: Piatkus, 1995).

P.M. Lewis, *Whose Media? The Annan Report And After: A Citizen's Guide to Radio and Television*, (London: Consumers Association, 1978).

D.J. Lewis and A. Weigert, 'Trust as Social Reality', *Social Forces*, 63 (1985) 967–85.

P.M. Lewis and J. Booth, *The Invisible Medium: Public, Commercial and Community Radio*, (London: Macmillan, 1989).

J. Lichtman, 'Introduction', in K. Scott, *Honesty and Trust in America Survey*, (Lichtman/Zogby Interactive poll, 22 May 2006) 4.

M. Lindstrom, *Clicks, Bricks & Brands*, (London: Kogan Page, 2001).

S. Livingstone and P. Lunt, *Talk on Television: Audience Participation and Public Debate*, (London: Routledge, 1994).

J. Lloyd, *What the Media are Doing to our Politics*, (London: Constable, 2004).

Local Radio Workshop, *Capital: Local Radio and Private Profit*, (London: Comedia, 1983).

R.E. Löfstedt and O. Renn, 'The Brent Spar Controversy: An Example of Risk Communication Gone Wrong', *Risk Analysis*, 17(2) (1997) 131–5.

P. Ludlow, *Crypto Anarchy, Cyberstates and Pirate Utopias*, (Massachussetts, MA: MIT Press, 2001).

N. Luhmann, *Trust and Power: Two Works by Niklas Luhmann*, H. Davis, J. Raffan and K. Rooney (trans.), (Chichester: John Wiley and Sons, 1979).

N. Luhmann, 'Familiarity, Confidence, Trust: Problems and Alternatives', in D. Gambetta (ed.), *Trust: Making and Breaking Cooperative Relations*, (Oxford: Basil Blackwell, 1988) 94–107.

N. Luhmann, *Essays on Self-Reference*, (New York: Columbia University Press, 1990).

D. Lupton, *Risk*, (London: Routledge, 1999).

D. Lyon, *The Electronic Eye: The Rise of Surveillance Society*, (Cambridge: Polity, 1994).

G. Maddox, *Australian Democracy in Theory and Practice*, (Pearson Education: French Forest, 2005).

D. Marr and M. Wilkinson, *Dark Victory*, (Sydney: Allen and Unwin, 2003).

D.P. Marshall, *Celebrity and Power: Fame in Contemporary Culture*, (Minneapolis: University of Minnesota Press, 1997).

G.J. Masciarotte, 'C'mon Girl: Oprah Winfrey and the Discourse of Feminine Talk', *Genders*, 11 (1991) 81–110.

R.C. Mayer, J.H. Davis and F.D. Schoorman, 'An Integrative Model of Organisational Trust', *Academy of Management Review*, 20(3) (1995) 709–34.

R.W. McChesney, 'The Problem with US Media', in R.W. McChesney and J. Nichols (eds), *Our Media, Not Theirs*, (New York: Seven Stories Press, 2002).

R.W. McChesney, *The Problem of the Media: U.S. Communication Politics in the Twenty-First Century*, (New York: Review Press, 2004).

M. McCombs and D. Shaw, 'The Agenda-Setting Function of the Mass Media', *Public Opinion Quarterly*, 36 (1972) 176–87.

D. McCullagh and A. Broache, *Allies Defend NSA Surveillance*, CNET News.co, (2006). Retrieved 12 February 2006 from the World Wide Web:=http://news.com.com/ Bush+ allies+defend+NSA+surveillance/2100-1028_3-6030518.htmlBush

J. McGuigan, *Culture and the Public Sphere*, (London: Routledge, 1996).

L. McLaughlin, 'Chastity Criminals in the Age of Electronic Reproduction: Reviewing Talk Television and the Public Sphere', *Journal of Communication Enquiry*, 17(1) (1993) 4–55.

M. McLuhan, *The Gutenberg Galaxy: The Making of Typographic Man*, (Toronto: University of Toronto Press, 1962).

M. McLuhan, *Understanding Media*, (London: Routledge, 1964).

D. McQuail, *Language in the News: Discourse and Ideology in the Press*, (London: Routledge, 2000).

A. McStay and V. Bakir, 'Privacy, Online Advertising and Marketing Techniques: The Paradoxical Disappearance of the User', *Ethical Space: The International Journal of Communication Ethics*, (forthcoming, 2006).

Medical Research Council, *Review of Autism Research*, (London: Medical Research Council, 2001).

MEEMA, *Mina, Maailm ja Meedia (Me, The World and The Media)*, Research Project Report, (University of Tartu, Estonia: MEEMA, 2003, 2005).

M. Merleau-Ponty, *Phenomenology of Perception*, C. Smith (trans.), (London: Routledge & Kegan Paul, 1962).

D. Merritt, 'Public Journalism and Public Life: Why Telling the News is Not Enough', in H. Tumber (ed.), *News: A Reader*, (Oxford: OUP, 1999) 365–78.

G.S. Messinger, *British Propaganda and the State in the First World War*, (Manchester: Manchester University Press, 1992).

T. Meyer, *Media Democracy: How the Media Colonize Politics*, (Cambridge: Polity Press, 2002).

J. Meyrowitz, 'Medium Theory', in D. Crowley and D. Mitchell (eds), *Communication Theory Today*, (Stanford, California: Stanford University Press, 1994) 50–77.

K. Middlemas, *Politics in Industrial Society*, (London: Andre Deutsch, 1979).

P.R. Milgrom and J. Roberts, *Economics, Organization and Management*, (London: Prentice Hall, 1992).

T. Miller, 'A View from a Fossil. The New Economy, Creativity and Consumption – Two or Three Things I Don't Believe In', *International Journal of Cultural Studies*, 7(1) (2004) 55–65.

G.J. Miller and A.B. Whitford, 'Trust and Incentives in Principal–Agent Negotiations', *Journal of Theoretical Politics*, 14(2) (2002) 231–67.

D. Miller, J. Kitzinger, K. Williams and P. Beharrell, *The Circuit of Mass Communication: Media Strategies, Representation and Audience Reception in the AIDS Crisis*, (London: Sage, 1998).

D. Milne, 'Did Man Really Land on the Moon' (2000). Retrieved 21 January 2004 from the World Wide Web: http://www.think.cz/books/NASAMoonedAmericaEN.html

W. Mishler and R. Rose, *Trust, Distrust And Skepticism About Institutions Of Civil Society*, SPP 252, (Aberdeen, University of Aberdeen, Centre for the Study of Public Policy Publications, 1995). Retrieved 5 May 2006 from the World Wide Web: http://www.abdn.ac.uk/cspp/view_item.php?id=252

W. Mishler and R. Rose, *Trust in Untrustworthy Institutions: Culture and Institutional Performance In Post-Communist Societies*, SPP 310, (Aberdeen: Centre for the Study of Public Policy Publications, University of Aberdeen, 1998). Retrieved 5 May 2006 from the World Wide Web: http://www.abdn.ac.uk/cspp/view_item.php?id=310

W. Mishler and R. Rose, 'What Are the Origins of Political Trust?', *Comparative Political Studies*, 34(1) (2001) 30–62.

W. Mishler and R. Rose, *What are the Political Consequences of Trust? A Russian Structural Equation Model*, SPP 374, (Aberdeen, Centre for the Study of Public Policy Publications, University of Aberdeen, 2005). Retrieved 5 May 2006 from the World Wide Web: http://www.abdn.ac.uk/cspp/view_item.php?id=374

A.K. Mishra, 'Organisational Responses to Crisis: The Centrality of Trust', in R.M. Kramer and T.R. Tyler (eds), *Trust in Organisations*, (Thousand Oaks, CA: Sage Publications, 1996) 261–87.

B.A. Misztal, *Trust in Modern Societies*, (Cambridge: Polity Press, 1996).

A. Mitra and E. Watts, 'Theorising Cyberspace: The Idea of Voice Applied to the Internet Discourse', *New Media and Society*, 4(4) (2002) 489–98.

G. Möllering, 'The Nature of Trust: From Georg Simmel to a Theory of Expectation, Interpretation and Suspension', *Sociology*, 35(2) (2001) 403–20.

P. Monaghan, 'Watching the Watchers', *Chronicle of Higher Education*, 52, (17 March 2006) A18.

C.E. Montague, *Disenchantment*, (London: MacGibbon and Kee, 1968).

M. Moore, *Dude, Where's My Country?*, (London: Penguin, 2003).

J. Moran, 'Don Delillo and the Myth of the Author-Recluse', *Journal of American Studies*, 34(1) (2000) 137–52.

R.M. Morgan and S.D. Hunt, 'The Commitment–Trust Theory of Relationship Marketing', *Journal of Marketing*, 58 (1994) 20–38.

Morgan Poll, *Australians Sceptical of the Media*, Finding No. 3952, (The Bulletin, 14 December 2005). Retrieved 5 May 2006 from the World Wide Web: http://www.roymorgan.com/news/polls/2005/3952/

MORI, *E-Commerce: Lack Of Consumer Trust Holds It Back*, (London: Ipsos MORI, 2 August 2000a). Retrieved 5 May 2006 from the World Wide Web: http://www.mori.com/polls/2000/ncc2000.shtml

MORI, *The Role of Scientists in Public Debate*, (London: Ipsos MORI, 2 March 2000b). Retrieved 5 May 2006 from the World Wide Web: http://www.wellcome.ac.uk/assets/wtd003425.pdf

MORI, *Trust In Online Resources, Poll*, The MORI Social Research Institute, (London: Ipsos MORI, 10 February 2005). Retrieved 5 May 2006 from the World Wide Web: http://www.ipsos-mori.com/polls/2004/cie.shtml

MORI, *Doctors Top Public Opinion Poll On Trustworthy Professions*, MORI Social Research Unit, (London: Ipsos MORI, 10 March 2005). Retrieved 5 May 2006 from the World Wide Web: http://www.mori.com/polls/2005/bma.shtml

MORI, *London Bombings Survey*, (London: Ipsos MORI, 13 September 2005a). Retrieved 26 May 2006 from the World Wide Web: http://www.mori.com/polls/2005/kings-hpa.shtml

MORI, *Post London Bombings Survey*, (London: Ipsos MORI, 5 October 2005b). Retrieved 26 May 2006 from the World Wide Web: http://www.mori.com/polls/2005/bbc050928.shtml

MORI, *Londoners Support Police Terrorist Response*, (London: Ipsos MORI, 5 October 2005c). Retrieved 26 May 2006 from the World Wide Web: http://www.mori.com/polls/2005/gla.shtml

MORI, *Political Monitor: Long Term Trends. The Most Important Issues Facing Britain Today*, (London: Ipsos MORI, 2006). Retrieved 26 May 2006 from the World Wide Web: http://www.mori.com/polls/trends/issues12.shtml

J. Morris, 'Defining the Precautionary Principle', in J. Morris (ed.), *Rethinking Risk and the Precautionary Principle*, (Oxford: Elsevier, 2000) 1–21.

T. Morrison, *Beloved*, (New York: Knopf, 1987).

T. Morrison, *Paradise*, (New York: Knopf, 1999).

D.E. Morrison and J. Firmstone, 'The Social Function of Trust and Implications for E-Commerce', *International Journal of Advertising*, 15(5) (2000) 1–17.

N. Munro, *National Context or Individual Differences? Influences on Regime Support in Post-Communist Societies*, Studies in Public Policy No. 347, (Glasgow: University of Strathclyde, 2001).

G. Murdock and P. Golding, 'Culture, Communications and Political Economy', in J. Curran and M. Gurevitch (eds), *Mass Media and Society*, 4th edn, (London: Hodder Arnold, 2005).

S. Murray, 'Our Man Gidfrey: Arthur Godfrey and the Selling of Stardom in Early Television', *Television and New Media*, 2(3) (2001) 187–204.

G. Mythen, *Ulrich Beck: A Critical Introduction to the Risk Society*, (London: Pluto Press, 2004).

D. Narayan, *Bonds and Bridges: Social Capital and Poverty*, (Washington: World Bank, 1999).

National Assembly for Wales, *Creative Future/Cymru Greadigol: A Culture Strategy for Wales*, (Cardiff: National Assembly for Wales, 2002).

T.E. Nelson and D.R. Kinder, 'Issue Frames and Group-Centrism in American Public Opinion', *The Journal of Politics*, 58(4) (1996) 1055–78.

T.E. Nelson, R.A. Clawson and Z.M. Oxley, 'Media Framing of a Civil Liberties Conflict and its Effect On Tolerance', *The American Political Science Review*, 91(3) (1997) 567–83.

A. Nicoll, D. Ellman and E. Ross, 'MMR Vaccination and Autism', *British Medical Journal*, 316 (1998) 715–6.

H. Nissenbaum, *Can Trust Be Secured Online? A Theoretical Perspective*, Boston University, (2001). Retrieved 11 July 2004 from the World Wide Web: http://www.univ.trieste.it/%7Eetica/1999_2/nissenbaum.html

P. Norris (ed.), *Critical Citizens*, (Oxford: Oxford University Press, 1999).

P. Norris, M. Kern and M. Just (eds), *Framing Terrorism. The News Media, the Government and the Public*, (London: Routledge, 2003).

H. Nossek, 'The Impact of Mass Media on Terrorists, Supporters and the Public at Large', in A. Merari (ed.), *On Terrorism and Combatting Terrorism*, (Tel-Aviv: University Publications of America, 1985) 87–94.

K. Oakley, 'Not So Cool Britannia. The Role of the Creative Industries in Economic Development', *International Journal of Cultural Studies*, 7(1) (2004) 67–77.

C.I. Obi, 'Globalisation and Local Resistance: The Case of the Ogoni versus Shell', *New Political Economy: Globalisation and the Politics of Resistance*, 2(1) (1997) 137–48.

Ofcom, *Radio – Preparing for the Future*, (London: Ofcom, 2004).

Ofcom, *Ofcom Awards New FM Commercial Radio Licence for Swansea*, (London: Ofcom, 2005).

K. O'Hara, *Trust: From Socrates to Spin*, (UK: Icon, 2004).

D.E. Olson, 'Agency Theory in the Not-For-Profit Sector: Its Role at Independent Colleges', *Nonprofit and Voluntary Sector Quarterly*, 29(2) (2000) 280–96.

T. O'Malley, *Closedown? The BBC and Government Broadcasting Policy, 1979–92*, (London, Pluto Press, 1994).

O. O'Neill, *A Question of Trust: The BBC Reith Lectures 2002*, (Cambridge: Cambridge University Press, 2002).

K. Oser, 'Old-line Marketers Drive New Surge in Online Ad Spending', *Advertising Age*, (2004). Retrieved 12 December 2004 from the World Wide Web: http://www.AdAge.com.html

M. Palmer, *Inquiry into the Circumstances of the Immigration Detention of Cornelia Rau*, (Commonwealth of Australia: Canberra, 2005).

E. Papadakis, 'Confidence and Mistrust in Australian Institutions', *Journal of Political Science*, 34(1) (1999) 75–93.

T. Parsons, *The Social System*, (New York: Free Press, 1951).

H. Patapan, J. Wanna and P. Weller (eds), *Westminster Legacies: Democracy and Responsible Government in Asia and the Pacific*, (Sydney: UNSW Press, 2005).

J. Peck, 'Talk About Racism: Framing a Popular Discourse of "Race" on The Oprah Winfrey Show', *Cultural Critique*, 27 (1994) 89–126.

J.D. Peters, 'Distrust of Representation: Habermas on the Public Sphere', *Media, Culture and Society*, 15 (1993) 541–71.

M. Petrovic, R. Roberts and M. Ramsay, 'Second Dose of Measles, Mumps and Rubella Vaccine: Questionnaire Survey of Health Professionals', *British Medical Journal*, 322 (2001) 82–5.

J. Petts and S. Niemeyer, 'Health Risk Communication and Amplification: Learning from The MMR Vaccine Controversy', *Health, Risk and Society*, 6(1) (2004) 7–23.

J. Petts, T. Horlick-Jones and G. Murdock, *Social Amplification of Risk: The Media and the Public*, (Sudbury: HSE Books, 2001).

W. Philips, 'The Frozen Waves: Radio in 1982', *Admap* (1982) 380–8.

W. Philips, 'Radio'83: Out of Steam', *Admap* (1983) 348–52.

D. Pickton and A. Broderick, *Integrated Marketing Communications*, (London: Prentice Hall, 2001).

M. Piore and C. Sabel, *The Second Industrial Divide: Possibilities for Prosperity*, (New York: Basic Books, 1984).

S. Platon and M. Deuze, 'Indymedia Journalism: A Radical Way of Making, Selecting and Sharing news?', *Journalism*, 4(3) (2003) 336–55.

A. Ponsonby, *Falsehood in Wartime: Containing an Assortment of Lies Circulated through the Nations during the Great War*, (London: Allen and Unwin, 1928).

R. Poole, 'Public Spheres', in H. Wilson (ed.), *Australian Communications and the Public Sphere*, (South Melbourne: Macmillan, 1989) 16–26.

S. Poon and C. Jevons, 'Internet-Enabled International Marketing: A Small Business Network Perspective', *Journal of Marketing Management*, 13(1–3) (1997) 29–41.

Populus, *The Times Poll*, 8–10 July (2005). Retrieved 26 May 2006 from the World Wide Web: http://www.populuslimited.com/poll_summaries/2005_07_08_ times.htm

R. Pound and G. Harmsworth, *Northcliffe*, (London: Cassell, 1959).

W.W. Powell, 'Neither Market Nor Hierarchy: Network Forms of Organisation', *Research in Organisational Behaviour*, 12 (1990) 295–336. Adapted and reproduced in G. Thompson, J. Frances, R. Levacic and J. Mitchell (eds), *Markets, Hierarchies & Networks: The Co-ordination of Social Life*, (London: Sage, 1991) 265–76.

M. Pusey, *Jurgen Habermas*, (London: Routledge, 1987).

R.D. Putnam, *Making Democracy Work: Civic Traditions in Modern Italy*, (Princeton, NJ: Princeton University Press, 1993).

R.D. Putnam, 'Bowling Alone: America's Declining Social Capital', *Journal of Democracy*, 6(1) (1995) 65–78.

R.D. Putnam, *Bowling Alone: The Collapse and Revival of American Community*, (New York: Simon and Schuster, 2000).

Radio Authority, *Radio Authority Licence Award Procedures and Strategy for Independent Local Radio*, (London: Radio Authority, 1999a).

Radio Authority, *Formats to Replace Promises of Performance for Radio Authority Licensees*, (London: Radio Authority, 1999b).

Radio Authority, *Radio Regulation for the 21st Century*, (London: Radio Authority, 2000).

N. Radzhinski, *Stalin*, (Tallinn: Varrak, 2000).

J. Rawls, *A Theory of Justice*, (Cambridge, MA: Belknap Press, 1999 [1971]).

D. Read, *The Power of News: The History of Reuters*, (Oxford: Oxford University Press, 1992).

M.G. Redley, 'John Buchan at Milton Academy', *John Buchan Journal*, 22 (2000) 22–32.

M.G. Redley, 'Henry Newbolt and John Buchan: A Literary Friendship?', *John Buchan Journal*, 28 (2003) 25–42.

H. Rheingoldian, *The Virtual Community*, (London: Secker and Warburg, 1998).

B. Richards, 'The Real Meaning of Spin: Containment and Compression in Modern Politics', *Soundings*, 14 (2000) 161–70.

B. Richards, *Emotional Governance: New Ideas on Media and Democracy*, (Basingstoke: Palgrave, forthcoming 2007).

D.N. Rodowick, *Reading the Figural*, (NC: Duke University Press, 2001).

Roper Center for Public Opinion Research, *Los Angeles Times Poll*, 15–7 January (2005). Retrieved 19 February 2006 from the World Wide Web: http://www.roper-center.uconn.edu/cgi-bin/hsrun.exe/roperweb/pom/pom.htx;start=HS_special_topics? Topic=terrorism

Roper Center for Public Opinion Research, *NBC News/Wall St. Journal Poll*, 26–9 January (2006a). Retrieved 19 February 2006 from the World Wide Web: http://www.roper-center.uconn.edu/cgi-bin/hsrun.exe/roperweb/pom/pom.htx;start=HS_special_topics?Topic=terrorism

Roper Center for Public Opinion Research, *Fox News/Opinion Dynamics Poll*, 24–5 January (2006b). Retrieved 26 May 2006 from the World Wide Web: http://www.ropercenter.uconn.edu/cgi-bin/hsrun.exe/roperweb/pom/pom.htx;start=HS_special_topics?Topic=terrorism

C. Rose, 'Beyond the Struggle for Proof: Factors Changing the Environmental Movement', *Environmental Values*, 2 (1993) 285–98.

C. Rose, *The Turning of the 'Spar*, (London: Greenpeace, 1998).

R. Rose, *Getting Things Done With Social Capital: New Russia Barometer VII*, SPP 303, (Aberdeen: University of Aberdeen, Centre for the Study of Public Policy Publications, 1998). Retrieved 7 May 2006 from the World Wide Web: http://www.abdn.ac.uk/cspp/view_item.php?id=303

R. Rose, *New Baltic Barometer IV: A Survey Study*, Studies in Public Policy No. 338, (Glasgow: University of Strathclyde, 2000a).

R. Rose, *Russia Elects a President: New Russia Barometer IX*, Studies in Public Policy 330, (Glasgow: University of Strathclyde, Centre for the Study of Public Policy, 2000b).

R. Rose, W. Mishler and C. Haerpfer, *Democracy and its Alternatives: Understanding Post-Communist Societies*, (Oxford: Polity and Baltimore: Johns Hopkins University Press, 1998).

S. Rose-Ackerman, 'Trust, Honesty and Corruption: Reflection on the State-Building Process', Archives of European Sociology, XLII(3) (2001) 526–70.

J. Rosen, 'The Action of the Idea: Public Journalism in Built Form', in T.L. Glasser (ed.), *The Idea of Public Journalism*, (New York: The Guilford Press, 1999) 21–48.

D.M. Rosseau, S.B. Sitkin, R.S. Burt and C. Camerer, 'Not So Different After All: A Cross-Discipline View of Trust', *Academy of Management Review*, 23(3) (1998) 393–404.

B. Rothstein, 'Social Trust and Honesty in Government: A Causal Mechanisms Approach',, in J. Kornai, B. Rothstein and S. Rose-Ackerman (eds), *Creating Social Trust in Post-Socialist Transition: Political Evolution and Institutional Change*, (New York: Palgrave Macmillan, 2004).

J.J. Rousseau, *The Social Contract*, M. Cranston (trans.), (London: Penguin Classics, 1968).

Rudall Blanchard Associates, *Brent Spar Abandonment BPEO*, (Shell Exploration and Production, 1994).

M. Russo, *The Female Grotesque: Risk, Excess and Modernity*, (London: Routledge, 1995).

L. Saad, '*Military Still Tops in Public Confidence*', (The Gallup Poll, 7 June 2006). Retrieved 5 May 2006 from the World Wide Web: http://poll.gallup.com/content/?ci=23227

D.B. Sachsman, 'The Mass Media and Environmental Risk Communication', In J.G. Cantrill and M.J. Killingsworth (eds), *Proceedings of the Conference on Communication and Our Environment*, (Big Sky, Montana, 1993): 1–4.

L. Salter, 'Democracy, New Social Movements and The Internet', in M. McCaughey and M. Ayers (eds), *Cyberactivism: Online Activism in Theory and Practice*, (UK: Routledge, 2003) 117–44.

L. Salter, 'Colonisation Tendencies in the Development of the World Wide Web', *New Media and Society*, 7(2) (2005) 291–309.

K. Sanders, *Ethics and Journalism*, (London: Sage, 2003).

M. Sanders and P.M. Taylor, *British Propaganda during the First World War, 1914–18*, (London: Macmillan, 1981).

M.L. Sanders and P.M. Taylor, *British Propaganda during the First World War, 1914–18*, (London: Macmillan, 1982).

N. Sargant, 'Listening to the Consumer', *Consumer Policy Review*, 3 (1993) 159–66.

M.B. Sarkar, B. Butler and C. Steinfield, 'Intermediaries and Cybermediaries: A Continuing Role for Mediating Players in the Electronic Marketplace', *Journal of*

Computer-Mediated Communication, 1(3) (1995). Retrieved 2 September 1997 from the World Wide Web: http://jcmc.huji.ac.il/vol1/issue3/sarkar.html.

R. Schickel, *Intimate Strangers: The Culture of Celebrity in America*, (Chicago: Ivan R Dee, 2000).

L.G. Schiffman, E. Sherman and N. Kirpalani, 'Trusting Souls: A Segmentation of the Voting Public', *Psychology & Marketing*, 19(12) (2002) 993–1007.

P. Schlesinger, G. Murdock and P. Elliott, *Televising 'Terrorism': Political Violence in Popular Culture*, (London: Comedia, 1983).

T. Schultz, 'Mass Media and the Concept of Interactivity: An Exploratory Study of Online and Reader Email', *Media Culture and Society*, 22 (2000) 205–21.

W.S. Schulze, M.H. Lubatkin, R.N. Dino and A.K. Buchholtz, 'Agency Relationships in Family Firms: Theory and Evidence', *Organisation Science*, 12(2) (2001) 99–116.

K. Scott, *Honesty and Trust in America Survey*, (Lichtman/Zogby Interactive poll, 22 May 2006). Retrieved 5 May 2006 from the World Wide Web: http:// www.zogby.com/ Lichtman%20Final%20Report%205-22-06.pdf

A. Seligman, *The Idea of Civil Society*, (New York: Free Press, 1992).

A. Seligman, *The Problem of Trust*, (Princeton: Princeton University Press, 1997).

P.M. Senge, *The Fifth Discipline: The Art and Practice of the Learning Organization*, (London: Century Business, 1992).

R. Sennett, *The Corrosion of Character: The Personal Consequences of Work in the New Capitalism*, (London: W.W. Norton, 1998).

S.P. Shapiro, 'The Social Control of Impersonal Trust', *American Journal of Sociology*, 93(3) (1987) 623–58.

J. Shattuc, *The Talking Cure: TV Talk Shows and Women*, (New York: Routledge, 1997).

R. Shaw and M. Stone, *Database Marketing*, (New York, Wiley, 1990).

Shell-UK, 'Winning Hearts and Minds', *Brent Spar*, Shell-UK Ltd, (1995) 8.

F. Shen, 'Effects of News Frames and Schemas on Individuals' Issue Interpretations and Attitudes', *Journalism and Mass Communication Quarterly*, 81(2) (2004) 400–16.

A. Silver, 'Trust in Social and Political Theory', in G.D. Suttles and M.N. Zald (eds), *The Challenge of Social Control*, (Norwood, MA: Ablex Publishers, 1985).

G. Simmel, *The Sociology of Georg Simmel*, K.H. Wolff (trans., ed.), (New York: Free Press, 1950 [1908]).

G. Simmel, *The Philosophy of Money*, 2nd edn, (London: Routledge, 1990 [1900]).

A. Simon and M. Xenos, 'Media Framing and Effective Public Deliberation', *Political Communication*, 17 (2000) 363–76.

J. Singh and D. Sirdeshmukh, 'Agency and Trust Mechanisms in Consumer Satisfaction and Loyalty Judgments', *Journal of Academy of Marketing Sciences*, 28(1) (2000) 150–67.

A. Smith, 'Breaking the Old and Constructing the New: Geographies of Uneven Development in Central and Eastern Europe', in R. Lee and J. Wills (eds), *Geographies of Economies*, (London: Arnold, 1997).

R. Solnit, *River of Shadows: Eadweard Muybridge and the Technological Wild West*, (New York: Viking Press, 2003).

C. Sparks, 'Liberalism, Terrorism and the Politics of Fear', *Politics*, 23(3) (2003) 200–6.

C. Squire, '"Empowering Women?" The Oprah Winfrey Show', *Feminism and Psychology*, 4(1) (1994) 63–79.

D. Stark, 'Recombinant Property in East European Capitalism', *American Journal of Sociology*, 101(4) (1996) 993–1027.

B. Steinhard, 'Liberty in the Age of Technology', American Civil Liberties Union, Retrieved 6 December 2006 from the World Wide Web : http://www.aclu.org/ filesPDFs/global-agenda.pdf

N. Stevenson, *Understanding Media Cultures: Social Theory and Mass Communication*, (London: Sage, 1995).

N. Stevenson, *Understanding Media Cultures*, 2nd edn, (London: Sage, 2002).

J. Stewart, 'Public Sector Management', in J. Summers, D. Woodward and A. Parkin (eds), *Government Politics, Power and Policy in Australia*, 7th edn, (French Forest: Pearson Education, 2002) 67–87.

J. Stewart, E. Kendall and A. Coote, *Citizens' Juries*, (London: Institute for Public Policy Research, 1996).

T. Stoller, *Access Radio: The Next Steps*, (London: Radio Authority, 2001).

W. Stone, *Measuring Social Capital: Towards a Theoretically Informed Measurement Framework for Researching Social Capital in Family and Community Life*, Research Paper No. 24, (Melbourne: Australian Institute of Family Studies, 2001).

W. Stone and J. Hughes, *Social Capital: Empirical Meaning and Measurement Validity*, Research Paper No. 27, (Melbourne: Australian Institute of Family Studies, 2002). Retrieved 5 May 2006 from the World Wide Web: http://www.aifs.gov.au/institute/pubs/RP27.pdf

P. Sztompka, 'Looking Back: The Year 1989 as a Cultural and Civilizational Break', *Communist and Post-Communist Studies*, 29(2) (1996) 115–29.

P. Sztompka, *Trust: A Sociological Theory*, (Cambridge: Cambridge University Press, 1999).

P.M. Taylor, *The Projection of Britain: British Overseas Publicity and Propaganda, 1919–39*, (London: Cambridge, 1981).

S.J. Taylor, *The Great Outsiders: Northcliffe, Rothermere and the Daily Mail*, (London: Weidenfeld & Nicholson, 1996).

H. Taylor, *Americans Generally More Trusting than the British – Except for Newscasters*, (London: Ipsos Mori, 11 November 1998). Retrieved 5 May 2006 from the World Wide Web: http://www.mori.com/polls/1998/harris.htm

P.M. Taylor, *British Propaganda in the Twentieth Century*, (Edinburgh: Edinburgh University Press, 1999).

H. Taylor and R. Leitman (eds), 'Survey on Trust in Different Industries Finds Reasonably High Trust in Pharmaceuticals, Less Trust in Biotech and High Distrust of Health Insurance and Management Care', *Health Care News*, (1), (26) (2001). Retrieved 5 May 2006 from the World Wide Web: http://www.harrisinteractive.com/news/newsletters/healthnews/HI_HealthCareNews2001Vol1_iss26.pdf

The Oprah Winfrey Show: 'Oprah's Diets', (London, Channel 4, 28 November 1995, VHS video).

The Oprah Winfrey Show: 'Lose Weight, Lose Friends', (London, BBC2, 23 December 1995, VHS video).

C.W. Thomas, 'Maintaining and Restoring Public Trust in Government Agencies and Their Employees', *Administration and Society*, 30(2) (1998) 166–93.

J.B. Thompson, 'Social Theory and the Media', in D. Crowley and D. Mitchell (eds), *Communication Theory Today*, (Cambridge: Polity Press, 1994) 27–49.

N.P. Thompson, S.M. Montgomery, R.E. Pounder and A.J. Wakefield, 'Is Measles Vaccination a Risk Factor for IBD?', *Lancet*, 353 (1995) 2026–9.

T. Todorov, *The Fantastic: A Structural Approach to a Literary Form*, (Cleveland: The Press of Case Western Reserve University, 1973).

F. Tonkiss and A. Passey, 'Trust, Confidence and Voluntary Organisations: Between Values and Institutions', *Sociology*, 33(2) (1999) 257–74.

Transparency International, *The Transparency International Global Corruption Barometer: A 2002 Pilot Survey of International Attitudes, Expectations and Priorities on Corruption*, (Berlin, Germany: Transparency International, 3 July 2003).

Retrieved 1 May 2006 from the World Wide Web: http://ww1.transparency.org/pressreleases_archive/2003/2003.07.03.global_corr_barometer.en.html

C. Triandis, *Individualism and Collectivism*, (Boulder, CO: Westview Press, 1995).

H. Tsoukas, 'David and Goliath in the Risk Society: Making Sense of the Conflict between Shell and Greenpeace in the North Sea', *Organisation: Actor Network Theory and Managerialism*, 6(3) (1999) 499–528.

J. Tunstall, *The Media in Britain*, (London: Constable, 1983).

T.R. Tyler and P. Degoey, 'Trust in Organisational Attributes: The Influence of Motive Attributions on Willingness to Accept Decisions', in R.M. Kramer and T.R. Tyler (eds), *Trust in Organisations*, (Thousand Oaks, CA: Sage Publications, 1996) 331–56.

T.R. Tyler and R.M. Kramer, 'Whither Trust?', in R.M. Kramer and T.R. Tyler (eds), *Trust in Organisations*, (Thousand Oaks, CA: Sage Publications, 1996) 1–15.

J. Uhr, *Terms of Trust, Arguments Over Ethics in Australian Government*, (Sydney: UNSW Press, 2004).

UK Parliament, *British Petroleum Act*, (London, HMSO, 1987).

United Nations, *Trade Facilitation and E-commerce in the ESCWA Region*, Economic and Social Commission for Western Asia, E/ESCWA/ED/2001/2, (United Nations, 17 January 2001). Retrieved 10 April 2006 from the World Wide Web: http://www.escwa.org.lb/information/publications/division/docs/ed-01-2-e.pdf

USA Congress, *USA Patriot Act, Uniting and Strengthening America Act by Providing Appropriate Tools Required to Intercept and Obstruct Terrorism Act of 2001*, (Washington, 2001). Retrieved 11 November 2005 from the World Wide Web: http://www.whitehouse.gov/infocus/patriotact/

E.M. Uslaner, 'Producing and Consuming Trust', *Political Science Quarterly*, 115(4) (2000) 569–90.

S. Vaughn, *Holding Fast the Inner Lines: Democracy, Nationalism and the Committee on Public Information*, (Chapel Hill: University of North Carolina Press, 1980).

P. Vihalemm and M. Lauristin, 'Journalism and Public Relations in Different Normative Contexts', in S. Eskelineni, T. Saranen and T. Tuhkio (eds), *Spanning the Boundaries of Communication*, (Jyväskylä: University of Jyväskylä Press, 2001).

P. Virilio, *Open Sky*, (London: Verso, 1997).

P. Virilio, 'Indirect Light', in J. Armitage (ed.), *Paul Virilio from Modernism to Hypermodernism*, (London: Sage, 2000) 57–70.

N. Vulkan, 'Economic Implications of Agent Technology and E-Commerce', *The Economic Journal*, 109 (1999) F67–F90.

A.J. Wakefield and S.M. Montgomery, 'Measles, Mumps and Rubella Vaccine: Through a Glass Darkly', *Adverse Drug Reaction Toxicology Review*, 19 (2000) 265–83.

A.J. Wakefield, S.H. Murch, A. Anthony, J. Linnell, D.M. Casson, M. Malik, M. Berelowitz, A.P. Dhillon, M.A. Thomson, P. Harvey, A. Valentine, S.E. Davies and J.A. Walker-Smith, 'Ileal-lymphoid-nodular Hyperplasis, Non-specific Colitis, and Pervasive Developmental Disorder in Children', *The Lancet*, 351 (1998) 637–41.

A. Walker, *In Search of Our Mothers' Gardens: Womanist Prose*, (London: The Women's Press, 1983).

P. Watkin, 'Swansea Sound: The First Two Years of the First Commercial Radio Station on Wales', *Planet*, 31 (1976) 21–4.

M. Weber, *The Protestant Ethic and the Spirit of Capitalism*, (London: Routledge, 2001 [1904]).

D. Welsh, 'Mobilising the Masses: The Organisation of German Propaganda during World War One', in M. Connelly and D. Welsh (eds), *War and the Media*, (London: I.B. Taurus, 2005) 19–45.

West Legal Dictionary (2003). Retrieved 11 January 2004 from the World Wide Web: http://www.wld.com/conbus/weal/wcontral.htm

D. Wheeler, R. Rechtman, H. Fabig and R. Boele, 'Shell, Nigeria and the Ogoni. A Study in Unsustainable Development: III. Analysis and Implications of Royal-Dutch Shell Group Strategy', *Sustainable Development*, 9 (2001) 177–96.

J. Whitney, *What's the Matter with Indymedia?*, (July 2005). Retrieved 28 July 2005 from the World Wide Web: http://www.alternet.org/module

B. Whorf, *Language, Thought, and Reality*, (New York: John Wiley, 1956).

N. Wiener, *Cybernetics, or Control and Communication in the Animal and the Machine*, (Cambridge, MA: MIT, 1961 [1948]).

O.E. Williamson, *Markets and Hierarchies: Analysis and Antitrust Implications. A Study in the Economics of Internal Organization*, (New York: Free Press, 1975).

O.E. Williamson, *The Economic Institutions of Capitalism*, (New York: Free Press, 1985).

P. Williamson, *Stanley Baldwin*, (Cambridge: Cambridge University Press, 1999).

P. Wilson, 'Jamming Big Brother', in J. Jones and E. Mathijs (eds), *Big Brother International, Format, Critics and Publics*, (London: Wallflower Press/Columbia University Press, 2004).

B. Winston, *Lies Damn Lies and Documentaries*, (London: BFI, 2000).

M. Woolcock, 'Social Capital and Economic Development: Towards a Theoretical Synthesis and Policy Framework', *Theory and Society*, 27 (1998) 1–57.

D. Wood, 'Foucault and Panopticism Revisited', *Surveillance and Society*, 1(3) (2003) 234–9.

R. Worcester, 'The Public's View of Waste and Environmental Matters', *Waste Management*, December (1995) 35–8.

B. Worcester, *Business and the Environment: In the Aftermath of Brent Spar and BSE*, HRH The Prince of Wales' Business and the Environment Programme, University of Cambridge Programme for Industry, (Cambridge: University of Cambridge 1996).

B. Wynne, 'May the Sheep Safely Graze? A Reflexive View of the Expert-Lay Knowledge Divide', in S. Lash, B. Szerszynski and B. Wynne (eds), *Risk, Environment and Modernity: Towards a New Ecology*, (London: Sage, 1996) 44–83.

M. Yar, 'Panoptic Power and the Pathologisation of Vision: Critical Reflections on the Foucault Thesis', *Surveillance and Society*, 1(3) (2003) 254–71.

S. Young, *The Persuaders, Inside the Hidden Machine of Political Advertising*, (North Melbourne: Pluto Press, 2004).

C. Zech, 'An Agency Analysis of Church-Pastor Relations', *Managerial and Decision Economics*, 22 (2001) 327–32.

L.G. Zucker, 'Production of Trust: Institutional Sources of Economic Structure, 1840–1920', *Research in Organisational Behavior*, 8 (1986) 53–111.

Index